GOVERNING
DISORDER

Laura Zanotti

GOVERNING DISORDER

UN Peace Operations, International Security,
and Democratization in the Post–Cold War Era

The Pennsylvania State University Press
University Park, Pennsylvania

Library of Congress Cataloging-in-Publication Data

Zanotti, Laura.
    Governing disorder : UN peace operations, international
    security, and democratization in the post-Cold War era /
    Laura Zanotti.
        p.   cm.
Includes bibliographical references and index.
Summary: "Examines post-Cold War discourses about the
use of power to promote international security. Uses case
studies of United Nations interventions in Haiti and Croatia
to highlight the dynamics at play in encounters between
local societies and international peacekeepers"—Provided
by publisher.
ISBN 978-0-271-03761-5 (cloth : alk. paper)
1. United Nations—Peacekeeping forces—Case studies.
2. Peace-building—Croatia—International cooperation—
Case studies.
3. Peace-building—Haiti—International cooperation—Case
studies.
4. National security—Croatia—International cooperation—
Case studies.
5. National security—Haiti—International cooperation—
Case studies.
6. Power (Social sciences).
I. Title.

JZ5538.Z34 2011
341.5'84—dc22
2010048461

It is the policy of The Pennsylvania State University Press to
use acid-free paper. Publications on uncoated stock satisfy
the minimum requirements of American National Standard
for Information Sciences—Permanence of Paper for Printed
Library Material, ANSI z39.48–1992.

This book is printed on Natures Natural, which contains 50%
post-consumer waste.

A Giovanni.

Continua sempre a guardare con gli occhi nuovi di chi è da poco venuto al mondo.
E non smettere di chiedere perché.

CONTENTS

PREFACE

This book results from my need to make sense of a life experience. It is rooted in my malaise in the face of what I perceived as a rupture between the narrative I had internalized as a United Nations (UN) political officer and the dynamics and outcomes I saw unfolding in the peacekeeping operations I was involved with.

The journey that brought me to writing this book started in Haiti in 1995. Tired of a well-paying but to me meaningless job in an international business consulting company, I joined the UN—as did I believe many of my colleagues—to "make a difference." The operation "restore democracy" in Haiti was my first peacekeeping assignment. The UN was mandated to bring back the elected president Jean Bertrand Aristide, who had been ousted by a coup d'état. As often happens to newcomers, I was puzzled by many things that were taken for granted by people who had been on the job for years. In Port-au-Prince I saw scenes that I had previously witnessed only in war movies (business consulting is generally conducted in rather anodyne places). The UN offices were situated within a gated compound guarded by soldiers; military helicopters were frequently landing in the airstrip close by; Port-au-Prince was flooded with people in uniform and military armored vehicles. Children watched us jogging in the morning from the cardboard and wood shacks behind the fence separating the UN military-guarded facilities from the rest of town, partly amused and partly puzzled. When we left our hotels and offices in the UN white Toyotas, we went by street sellers of amazing scrap iron artifacts, tap-taps (the local buses) overloaded with people and materials dangling in mysterious ways, and children going to school in their uniforms or hanging by their mothers who sold produce along dusty roads. I saw incredible poverty, yet an incredibly rich culture, accompanied by a strong pride for having won the war against the French and slavery.

A few years later, in 1999, I was part of a UN delegation mandated to devise the merging of the peacekeeping and the civilian components of the Mission in Haiti. My colleagues and I spent some time in Port-au-Prince, in the beautiful Hotel Montana, consulting with the representatives of the Friends of Haiti (the states that were involved in lobbying the UN about the peace operation there) to devise the new mandate for the UN operation. After putting together the outline of the mandate, we called for a meeting with the Haitian president, René Préval. We traveled in a long motorcade of UN cars, windows closed, through downtown Port-au-Prince, where children were playing in what looked like open sewers. Someone in the car was complaining about the discomfort caused by the holes in the road. We arrived at the presidential palace, our delegation much bigger than the presidential entourage. There, we "discussed" the UN mandate with the president. He was asking for development money, but we were going to give him "institution building." President Préval could not change much of what had been written at the Hotel Montana. We were, indeed, restoring democracy. We knew how to do it, and the president had just to sell our project to his constituency.

During that visit to Haiti, I came across a booklet written by the UN, a collection of laws and programs regarding the restructuring of the Haitian police. A memory from my undergraduate studies in philosophy resurfaced. Michel Foucault, *Discipline and Punish*. The disciplinarization of penal institutions in classical Europe, their connection with discourses of human rights, and their relevance as new modalities of power. I began to toy with the idea that our human rights and democratization projects were conducted along the same lines prescribed by Enlightenment reformers for the transformation of institutions of punishment in Europe.

A few years later, I was deployed to Croatia to perform the duties of deputy to the head of the United Nations Liaison Office (UNLO) in Zagreb. It seemed to me that the tools for protecting minority rights deployed in Croatia were by and large analogous to the ones employed in Haiti to reform punishment institutions: a combination of institutional engineering, training, reward and punishment, knowledge and control. In Croatia there were abundant funds available from the European Union (EU). But different actors at the local level were more or less openly resisting and manipulating the UN program of reintegration of the Serb minority.

After my Croatian assignment came to an end, I decided not to go back to my job at the UN Department of Peacekeeping Operations (DPKO) in New York City. I had lost my innocence, as well as the capacity to take at face value discourses promising the betterment of humanity. Unable by then not to rip apart (or, in more academic terms, "deconstruct") everything I was doing in that job, I felt more and more pressured to interrogate my life experience. I joined academia and started analyzing the UN efforts to bring about peace and democracy through the lenses provided by Foucault.

Why Foucault? I am often asked. The short, nonacademic answer would be because his analytical tools help me build a bridge between theoretical distance and participant observation. The UN has been looked at as an "agent," a normative institution that can speak truth to power; or as an irrelevant bureaucracy that reflects the agendas of the powerful; or again, as a very useful scapegoat for all failures of international politics. Instead, as a political officer, I saw the UN as a field with many (often inconsistent) rules of functioning, where divergent forces interacted but very little could be considered to be the result of one's will. Who is the agent in a peacekeeping operation? The Security Council? The member states that endorse the mandate but often fall short of making available the resources necessary to carry it out? The bilateral embassies that lobby the secretariat, or the ambassadors who negotiate deals outside institutional settings, at dinner tables? The political officer who records and drafts the scripts of the UN Mission, or her boss who edits and vets it to make it palatable to the multiple constituencies it addresses? The military and police on the ground? The UN looked to me like Foucault's archive in *The Archeology of Knowledge:* a space for transmitting, reinforcing, contesting, and actualizing in practice discourses that are imagined as "norms"; a field of forces, a space of confrontation among different and uneven claims whose outcome is never determined in advance and is always played within relations of power and in the context of contingent interactions with local situations and actors; a place where different and competing political agendas are negotiated, silenced, or enacted, and yet a governmental institution that deploys isomorphic technologies for directing conduct across a variety of situations.

For Foucault, power is the structure of human interaction. As such, power is ambiguous, its effects uneven and not overdetermined by its own planning rationalities. A Foucauldian methodology fosters the questioning of the (indeed reassuring) idea that there are "good actors" out there (the internationals, the proletariat, the nongovernmental organizations [NGOs], or President George W. Bush in his own narrative, just to quote a few) who fight evil. It prevents one from dwelling in spaces of unquestioned truth through the construction of yet another narrative of good and bad. I have chosen Foucauldian theoretical tools to analyze my experience as a peacekeeper because they help me question effects of truth through the exploration of the modalities through which international regimes of order are deployed. I have chosen Foucault because his work provides me with the instruments for studying the *how* of power, without having the pretension of reconstructing another overarching truth or appeasing prescriptions for action. By adopting a Foucauldian methodology, one is forced to navigate without a chart. This does not mean anything goes, but it means that once innocence is lost, one must face the uncertainty of the entrenchment of power in a number of unsuspected places and the contingent and uneven effects it produces in its interaction with a bewildering variety of local realities.

ACKNOWLEDGMENTS

I have been working on this book for a long time, both as a UN official and more recently as an academic. I have therefore accumulated numerous debts. My most recent are to my colleagues and former colleagues at Virginia Tech, Ilja Luciak, Tim Luke, Scott Nelson, Antonio Vasquez Arroyo, and to the members of the ASPECT working group for their insightful suggestions and advice. I am especially grateful to Edward Weisband for his comments and his invaluable encouragement and support. This work would have been much lonelier without the European University Institute's generous hospitality to me as a Jean Monnet Fellow. I am particularly indebted to Friedrich Kratochwil for conversations and guidance and for warning me about the downsides of academia, and yet believing in my intellectual project and supporting it. Thank you also to Pascal Venesson for offering me the opportunity to present sections of this work to his students, and for his comments and suggestions. I am also indebted to Michael Pugh for his insightful comments on this manuscript, and to the anonymous reviewers who have commented on sections of this project. Thank you also to my editor, Sandy Thatcher, who patiently waited for this book to be finished, and to Sue Breckenridge for her valuable editorial suggestions. I am also grateful to those who have given me advice on this work since its early stages: Nicholas Onuf, Elizabeth Prugl, and François Debrix. My appreciation also goes to the Latin American and Caribbean Center at Florida International University and to the Mellon Foundation for financially supporting my doctoral studies. I owe a lot to my former colleagues at the United Nations, too many to mention each one by name. Without our conversations and debates I could not have grasped the understandings that made this book possible. I am also thankful to the United Nations for having granted me the time off from work necessary to carry out this project. My final decision to leave the organization to undertake an academic career does not take anything away from my gratitude. This book goes in print in the aftermath of a catastrophic earthquake in Haiti, where many of my former UN colleagues and friends lost their lives. I would like to remember them all here. A very special thought goes to Andrew Grene, who generously mentored and facilitated the continuation of my research in Haiti after the completion of this book, but is among those who perished in the earthquake. I will always remember you, Andrew, as a valued colleague, a friend, and a source of inspiration. Finally, I am deeply indebted to my family for bearing with me and supporting me throughout this project.

ABBREVIATIONS

CLNM	Constitutional Law on the Rights of National Minorities
DPKO	Department of Peacekeeping Operations (UN)
EU	European Union
HNP	Haitian National Police
ICFY	International Conference on the Former Yugoslavia
ICG	International Crisis Group
ICTY	International Criminal Tribunal for the Former Yugoslavia
IDPs	Internally Displaced Persons
JLWG	Joint Legal Working Group
LTTP	Law on Temporary Take-Over and Administration of Specified Property
MAP	Membership Action Plan (NATO)
MICAH	International Civilian Support Mission in Haiti
MICIVIH	International Civilian Mission in Haiti
MOU	Memorandum of Understanding
NATO	North Atlantic Treaty Organization
NGOs	Nongovernmental organizations
NUTS	Nomenclature Territory of Statistics (EU)
OAS	Organization of American States
ODPR	Office of Displaced Persons and Returnees
OSCE	Organization for Security and Cooperation in Europe
RSK	Republika Srbska Krajina
SAP	Stabilization and Association Process
UN	United Nations
UNDP	United Nations Development Program
UNHCR	United Nations High Commissioner for Refugees
UNLO	United Nations Liaison Office
UNMIH	United Nations Mission in Haiti
UNPROFOR	United Nations Protection Force
UNPSG	United Nations Police Support Group
UNTAES	United Nations Transitional Administration in Eastern Slavonia
USD	United States dollars

ONE

INTRODUCTION

In place of the generalities of much grand theory, . . . [we] allocate theorizing a more modest role; concepts are deployed to demonstrate the negotiations, tensions and accidents that have contributed to the fashioning of various aspects of our present.

—Barry, Osborne, and Rose 1996, 4

With the end of the Cold War and the bipolar world order it had supported, international organizations began to expand their discourses of security to encompass a number of issues that they had previously considered to exceed their mandate. The wave of enthusiasm following the fall of the Berlin Wall prompted these organizations to reorganize their projects for international peacekeeping and development around the central theme of democratization. Toward the end of the 1980s, the World Bank had portrayed underdevelopment as a problem of "governance," redirecting its attention from the economic to the political sphere.[1] The fulfillment of international criteria for democracy thereafter became a key element of conditionality for the allocation of international assistance and for inclusion in supranational political and military organizations, such as the European Union (EU) and the North Atlantic Treaty Organization (NATO). In the 1990s democracy and good governance were adopted as organizing concepts for UN doctrines and practices of peacekeeping. After the beginning of the new millennium, international security became even more comprehensive. Not only did the UN engage in helping disorderly states overcome their problems, but it also reclaimed for itself the responsibility to protect populations from an array of dangers affecting their lives, including poverty, disease, natural disasters, and abusive governments. Security was reimagined as part of a holistic project aimed at managing risk. Article 2.7 of the UN Charter, which bars international intervention in internal affairs, also came under question. The borders between international and national spaces of governance blurred, and sovereignty came to be considered less an entitlement than a privilege dependent on performance.

This book applies the theoretical tools elaborated by Michel Foucault to explore the formation of the political rationale[2] that supported the post–Cold War international security regime, the techniques of government deployed in specific UN peacekeeping operations, and the effects (always partially unintended) of the encounters between these governmental endeavors and local societies. It speaks to three ongoing debates. First, it provides an empirical contribution to governmentality studies of international regimes by exploring the UN political imaginary and the

---

1. "Governance" was adopted in the 1990s as an analytical category and organizing concept for World Bank programmatic endeavors. For a discussion of the meanings of governance, see Schmitter (1997).

2. Mitchell Dean (1999) uses the term "episteme," Nikolas Rose (1999) uses the term "political rationale," Foucault (1991a, 1995) uses the terms "discourse" and "*savoir*," and Ian Hacking (2002) uses the term "style of thinking" to designate the forms of knowledge that go together with specific modalities of power. A discussion of the meanings and different uses of these terms is beyond the scope of this study. For my purposes, I will mostly use "political rationale" or "political rationality," which are the designations that seem to have the most direct connection to policy making. Dean defined "political rationality" as follows: "Any form of calculation about political activity, i.e. about any activity which has as its objective the influence, appropriation, redistribution, allocation or maintenance of powers of the government of the state or other organizations. Political rationality is a species of governmental rationality in so far as it entails thinking about directing the conduct of others or ourselves. To the extent that its objective is to influence the way governmental organizations exercise their powers, its concerns are quite distinct" (Dean 1999, 211).

techniques of government it promoted in the context of peacekeeping. Second, it addresses the effects of exporting institutional models and administrative mechanisms. Finally, it engages with theoretical debates on power and resistance and with the critical possibilities offered by Foucauldian methodologies for the study of international politics.

Recent scholarship has underscored the need to link the exploration of peacekeeping to theories of knowledge and has undertaken insightful explorations of the contestations and conundrums embedded in the liberal peace project (Pugh 2003, 104; Richmond 2005, 2008). Postmodernist-inspired studies have tied the analysis of peacekeeping to a critical examination of liberalism and its modalities for maintaining order (Bigo 2000; Debrix 1999; Dillon and Reid 2009; Duffield 2002a, 2002b, 2007; Duffield and Waddell 2006; Huysmans 2004; Jabri 2007; Larner and Walters 2004a, 2004b; Lipschutz and Rowe 2005; Maurer and Perry 2003; Merlingen and Ostrauskaite 2006; Reid 2007; Walters and De Haar 2005a, 2005b). However, empirically grounded theoretical inquiries into the modalities of liberal political rationalities for making peace, into the practices they foster, and into the effects they produce have remained marginal in the study of international relations, international organizations, and peacekeeping.[3]

With the exception of recent scholarship that empirically addresses the unintended consequences of peacekeeping (Andersen, Møller, and Stepputat 2007; Aoi, de Coning, and Thakur 2007), most of the existing literature on international organizations has focused on questioning their legitimacy, effectiveness, organizational functioning, or normative role. Legal and normative studies have stressed the need for improving international institutions and the international rule of law (Archibugi 1993, 2004; Falk 1991; Griffin 2003; Held 1995); investigations of peacekeeping and multilateral intervention have concentrated by and large on the question of the proper degree or proper ways of exerting international power or on improving UN operational capacity (Barnett 1995; Bellamy 2004; Bellamy and Williams 2004, 2005; Bellamy, Williams, and Griffin 2004; Diehl 1993; Doyle and Sambanis 2006; Durch 1993; Mayall 1996; Weiss, Forsyte, and Coate 2001; Zielonka 2006). This body of literature, however, has mostly taken for granted the political rationale of intervention.

3. While not focusing on theory, Paul Higate and Marsha Henry (2009) offer an empirically grounded interdisciplinary inquiry into peacekeeping's production of space, peacekeepers' (gendered) bodily performances, and how these practices intersect with local populations' diverse perceptions of security.

On the other hand, realists (Chandler 2001, 2006; Gower 2001; Zolo 2001) and Marxists (Gorg and Hirsch 1998) maintain, for different reasons, that international institutions reproduce and reinforce relations of power, thus considering them irrelevant or "superstructural." Realists rely on "container" theories of society (Beck 2000) that consider social phenomena as enclosed within entities that precede them, such as the "state." While offering important insights into the relations between institutions and material conditions (Robinson 1996), Marxist conceptualizations of power in terms of "economy" and "ideology" tend to foreclose more specific investigations into the articulations of power technologies and the multifaceted dimensions of inequality. Hardt and Negri (2000) attempted to bridge Foucauldian and Marxist conceptual approaches with their analyses of empire. Their elaboration of international power and resistance, however, remained largely embedded in a structural/dialectical conceptualization of history. While shifting the actor of universal emancipation from the "proletariat" to the "multitude," Hardt and Negri ended up reconstructing grand narratives of oppression and liberation, the latter resulting from yet another crisis of capitalism combined with the activism of multitudes.

Constructivist studies of international politics and international security emphasize the importance of norms, knowledge, and institutional culture (Barnett 1995; Finnemore 1996, 2003; Finnemore and Sikkink 1998; Katzestein 1996). However, many constructivists still regard ideas as a "missing independent variable," overlooked by other approaches (Walters and Haahr 2005b). Kratochwil and Ruggie (1986) have highlighted the methodological problems of adopting a positivist understanding of causality when dealing with normative formations. In criticizing regime theory, they have argued that it did not satisfactorily deal with the tension between embracing a positivist epistemology and an intersubjective ontology. Remaining attached to a positivist ontology (Sterling-Folkner 2000), some constructivist scholars focus on researching the extent to which ideas can be regarded as causes of behavior, and on whether or not international organizations, as places where normative prescriptions are generated, are to be considered "agents" endowed with a degree of influence on others. In summary, as Jackson and Nexon aptly put it,

> The majority of IR theories are substantialist—they presume that entities precede interaction, or that entities are already entities before they enter into social relations with other entities. The most common of these presupposed entities is "the state," but it is not the only substantialist starting

point. Other scholars begin with "the individual" or the "ethnic group," but the basic ontological move is exactly the same—units come first, then, like billiard balls on a table, they are put into motion and their interactions are the patterns we observe in political life. This analytical or ontological commitment to substances cuts across conventional divisions in the field, including theories in all major "paradigms" of IR. (Jackson and Nexon 1999, 293)

Analogies, for Clifford Geertz, play an important role in structuring knowledge (Geertz 1983). While arriving at very different conclusions on the role of international organizations in international politics, realist, liberal, and many constructivist research agendas remain haunted by the image of the Leviathan. Even François Debrix's pioneering Foucauldian analysis of peacekeeping as a mediatic simulacrum of order is driven by an understanding of UN peacekeeping as a (simulated) projection of the might of the Leviathan (Debrix 1999). Power, whether it be identified with military might, economic exploitation, or the capacity of producing ideas or projecting images of order, is intended as a capacity to act and to modify the behavior of others, a capacity of "subjects" imagined as pre-existing social relations.[4] International organizations are conceived as "subjects," either driven by exogenous forces or self-directed by virtue of their capacity for normative production or mediatic performance.[5] Central research questions concern how much, and how legitimately and effectively, international organizations are able to modify the behavior of others.

This study moves away from conceptualizations of power patterned on the Leviathan and from substantialist ontologies and epistemologies. For Foucault, analytics of power must "abandon the model of the Leviathan. . . . We have to study power outside the field delineated by juridical sovereignty and the institutions of the State" (Foucault 1997, 34). Power, in Foucault's view, is not to be understood as the capacity to impose one's will on others,

---

4. For a more extensive discussion of conceptualizations of power in the Western political science tradition, see Hindess (1996) and chapter 6 in this book.

5. Chad Lavin (2008) has critically explored the relations among liberal conceptualizations of responsibility, agency, and causality and their hegemonic effects. A full-fledged discussion of subjectivity, causality, and responsibility as well as elaborations on epistemology and ontology in international relations is far too complex to be addressed here. These issues are introduced in this context only to support the choice of a Foucauldian theoretical framework for the analysis of international relations and to justify a methodology that attempts to stay away from substantialist ontologies.

but as "infinitesimal mechanisms, which have their own history, their own trajectory, their own techniques and tactics" (Foucault 1997, 30). The "archive" (Foucault 1972a) is the analogy that drives this book's conceptualization of international organizations. Foucault conceives of the archive as a place where connections between discourses are created or severed, and where "knowledges" are transmitted or left to die (Foucault 1972a). Rather than exploring the effects of "ideas" on behavior (be it that of individuals, organizations or states), this study maps the contingent processes through which international discursive formations are produced, legitimized, disputed, twisted, interpreted, and used. Normative prescriptions are not regarded as "sentences"—that is, as formulations whose "meaning" is coterminous with their logical formulations—but as "statements," as elements whose field of significations and political effects must be understood as part of the discursive practices in which they are situated (Foucault 1972a). Norms, in other words, are not considered elements of cause–effect paradigms that presuppose their stability and independence. Instead, this book explores the genealogical formations of discourses of international order in the post–Cold War era and their effects as elements of governmental rationalities.

My aim is not to debate the degree of capacity or legitimacy of international organizations or to establish to what extent normative formations are the driving forces for their actions. Instead, I address how the legitimization of discourses and practices of international order has come into being at a particular point in time (the post–Cold War period) and has been articulated, implemented, and contested in particular practices of intervention. Relying on Foucauldian conceptualizations of power as the structure of the relations brought to bear (Hindess 1996), I explore the formations and transformations of security discourses at the UN and the multiple articulations, the points of application, and the unintended consequences of these techniques. My work relies on Marxist assumptions regarding uneven distributions of power and the key role of material and economic conditions for political life, as well as on Marxist critiques of functionalist and liberal conceptualizations that conceive of institutions as a separate sphere of society (Robinson 1996). In contrast with Marxist analyses, however, this inquiry focuses on exploring specifically *how,* in the liberal project of making peace, these uneven relations of power are deployed and contested. It outlines *how* international organizations' political rationales regarding security, peace, democracy, and good governance came into being, *how* these political rationales constituted intervention, and *how* they articulated the economy and the politics of recipient societies.

Language is not secondary to government; it is constitutive to it (Rose 1999, 28). Practices of government involve the production of truths with regard to what is governed. Through the reading of strategic documents produced by the UN between 1990 and 2005, and through the analysis of the UN policies in Haiti from 1994 to 2000 and in Croatia from 1996 to 2003, this book outlines the genealogy of knowledges, prescriptions, and discourses of international security; it maps the changes in what constitutes the referent and the legitimizing principles for international intervention; it explores the specific techniques by which states are reformed and transformed and their conduct monitored and steered by international organizations; it tracks the kind of identities international "government" promotes, the form of visibility it creates, and the (often unintended) political effects it produces.

The work of Michel Foucault provides the analytical instruments, the genealogical background, and the methodology I employ for understanding the traits of international power in the post–Cold War era and for explaining its effects. Building on Foucault's governmentality theories, this book addresses peacekeeping as a practice of government. In doing so, it challenges traditional divides between the appropriate methods for addressing processes that happen within state borders (traditionally the domain of political science) and outside state borders (traditionally addressed by international relations). For Foucault, government is the "conduct of conduct." Defined this way, government refers to diverse modalities of influencing behavior, including—in addition to the "government of the state"—"government of the self," the "government of souls and lives" (Foucault 1991, 87). For the purposes of this analysis, government is not defined as the derivation of a set of normative principles or institutions, or as the emanation of a sovereign subject's endeavors of domination. Instead, government is understood as mechanisms, practices, *savoirs,* and institutional arrangements placed in the context of peacekeeping and peace building in order to transform disorderly states and steer their conduct.[6] This book traces four main trajectories of the post–Cold War practices of international security: governmentality, biopolitics,

6. See also Mitchell Dean's conceptualization of power as an "inventive strategic, technical and artful set of 'assemblages' fashioned from diverse elements, put together in novel and specific ways, and rationalized in relation to specific governmental objectives and goals" (Dean and Hindess 1998, 8).

disciplinarity, and carcuralization. International governmentality is detected in political programs (such as bringing about "good governance") that intensify the connection between international peace and the transformation of government, while fostering international surveillance as the strategy for achieving peace. Biopolitical trajectories are found in UN discourses, such as those on "human security" and the "responsibility to protect," that introduce the protection of the population as the legitimizing criterion for intervention. These discourses reinforce connections among the international government of disorder, processes of knowledge, and the governing of people's lives. Disciplinarity refers both to the blueprint for institution building adopted by the UN in the context of prodemocracy peacekeeping and to the techniques adopted by the UN to transform the behavior of states. In other words, this book argues that, in the post–Cold War period, international organizations, on the one hand, attempt to rebuild institutions along disciplinary lines and, on the other hand, deploy disciplinary techniques in order to transform state behavior. Carceralization describes the overall modality of international power in the post–Cold War era. While intensifying mechanisms for normalizing deviant actors, international government produces unintended consequences, is resisted through an array of localized and multifarious mechanisms, and is never completely successful in achieving its stated goal.

Furthermore, Foucault's analysis of Enlightenment elaborations of the reform of penal institutions in classical Europe constitutes the background against which I trace the genealogy of the UN's reorganization of its political rationale and the mechanisms of government it deploys. In this way this study contextualizes and historicizes discourses that, organized around the ideas of democratization or the protection of populations, are presented as normative models of right and justice.

Finally, Foucault's notion of "eventalization" provides the methodological instrument for this research. Eventalization focuses on historical singularities and on the analysis of contingent configurations to unsettle what we take for granted and to draw more general analytical insights. In Foucault's words, "eventalization" entails a "breach of self-evidence. It means making visible a singularity at places where there is temptation to invoke an historical constant, an immediate anthropological trait, or an obviousness that imposes itself uniformly on all. . . . A breach of self-evidence, of those self-evidences on which our knowledges, acquiescences and practices rest: this is the first theoretico-political function of eventalization" (Foucault 1991b, 76). Eventalization aims at rediscovering multiple and plural causes, the "connections, encounters, supports, blockages, plays of forces, strategies and so on, which at a given moment establish what subsequently counts as being self-evident, universal and necessary" (Foucault 1991b, 76).

The analysis of the cases of Haiti and Croatia conducted in this book does not aim to reconstruct an overarching theory of intervention, nor does it treat these cases comparatively. Each case constitutes an "event" that, on its own merits, helps cast light on some features of the international security regimes in the post–Cold War era, on the dynamics that are at play in specific encounters between local societies and international peacekeepers, and on more general debates on the critical potential of Foucauldian inquiries into international politics. I was a participant-observer of the processes described here, serving as the UN DPKO political officer for Haiti until the year 2000 and performing the functions of the deputy to the head of the UNLO in Zagreb, Croatia, between 2001 and 2003. The period under consideration in the analysis of the cases of Haiti and Croatia coincides with the period of my direct involvement with these processes as a participant-observer. The very particular insights on interaction between UN political agencies and local societies that can be garnered through the direct involvement in these practices are not easily matched by analyses conducted through secondhand sources.

In addition to exploring the "how" of discourses and governmental techniques deployed by international organizations in the post–Cold War era, this book addresses the modalities and outcomes of the encounter between international political rationales and local societies.[7] Critical analyses of intervention and development have pointed out the overarching imperial scope and ethnocentric character of international intervention, whether peacekeeping or development (Chandler 2006; Escobar 1988, 1995; Latouche 1996; Sachs 1992; Slater 2006). With the exception of a few recent scholarly works that have explored the economic effects of peacekeeping (Ammitzboell 2009; Cockayne 2009; Cooper 2005, 2006; Pugh and Cooper 2004; Pugh, Cooper, and Turner 2009), studies focusing on the specific modalities of the "encounter" between international peacekeepers, state builders, and the recipients of intervention, although

---

7. My inquiry focuses on international organizations and does not include an anthropological analysis of local societies; it reflects my "situated" knowledge, garnered as a UN official.

providing very important insights into the cultural interaction between local and international actors have largely overlooked the economic effects of these encounters (Badie 2000; Bayart 1996; Pouligny 2006). In line with critiques of international intervention, my analysis concludes that in Haiti the importation of Western political models has fostered disorder, eroded the capacity of the state to govern, and reinforced international regulatory power. However, instead of recurring to the main traits of "Western" and "non-Western cultures" (Bayart 1996) or the externalization of political claims (Badie 2000),[8] I ground my explanation of the effects of intervention on the analysis of a specific political imaginary, the techniques of government it implements, and the economic unsustainability of the type of institutionalization prescribed. In this way I bring into the analytical framework some of the Marxist insights regarding the indissociability of institutions and society (Robinson 1996) left aside by cultural and sociological analyses of institution building.

Furthermore, this book offers elements of reflection on conceptualizations of power and resistance. It questions overarching demonizations of the former as well as romanticized versions of the latter (Mac Ginty 2008). Scholars working from a variety of theoretical perspectives have tended to romanticize local resistance, solidarity, or local civil society as a benign alternative to international practices of security and development (Duffield 2007; Hardt and Negri 2000; Jabri 2007; Lipschutz and Rowe 2005; Richmond 2008). Scholarship inspired by Giorgio Agamben's reading of Foucault (Agamben 1998) emphasized the oppressive aspects of liberal power. This literature dwells on conceptualizations of power that, centered on the problematic of sovereignty, emphasize domination and violence, and conceives of resistance as refusal and "dispossession" (Edkins, Pin-Fat, and Shapiro 2004; Prozorov 2004, 2007). While not dismissing oppressive effects of power, this book relies on Foucault's elaboration of power as the "relations brought to bear" (Hindess 1996) and provides an empirically grounded exploration of specific configurations of human interactions. It looks at power in its contingent manifestations and conceptualizes resistance as strategic transformative action. An analysis of the process of the pacification and Europeanization of Croatia shows that international normalizing and disciplinary endeavors were hijacked or accommodated (but very rarely "rejected") by different

8. For an analysis of the "culturalist accent" of Bayart's theories, see Engelbert (1997).

Croatian governmental agencies. In addition, multifarious processes of resistance to international normalization do not necessarily favor oppressed minorities; in fact, contrary to romanticized images, they may very well be instruments of oppression in the hands of local constituencies.

This book shows that the effects of international intervention are uneven. No overarching malignant trait is associated with international normalizing "power" or liberatory quality with local "resistance." While the connections between international intervention and imperial enterprises are undeniable (Chandler 2004), using these connections as a basis for dismissing international intervention as an overarching project of domination oversimplifies the complexity of the political dynamics that the intervention bears and triggers. This book does not support theories that new globalized forces of resistance (the multitude) will lead to a dialectical transformation of the structure of power and to a better or more democratic political situation (Hardt and Negri 2000). The analysis conducted here is more modest. The political effects of the strategic interaction of international power and local resistance can only be appraised in the context of the empirical and case-specific analysis. This book does not condemn international intervention as such, nor does it glorify it as a means to "speak truth to power." Instead, it considers international organizations and their security practices as a field of strategic interactions among different constituencies in uneven power positions. While in Haiti the combination of an ethnocentric political rationale and local poverty led to the failure of the UN's stated goals, in Croatia the international peacekeeping operation, coupled with the continued attention of the EU, succeeded to an extent in passing legislation to protect minorities and in forcing the local government to restore some of the property taken away during the war. Finally, this book does not conclude with yet another prescription on how to conduct better international interventions or on how to reorganize political communities in an era of globalization. Some scholars who criticize liberal interventionism have argued that the failures of internal politics must be attributed to the depoliticizing and imperial effects that are linked with the erosion of state sovereignty (Bickerton, Cunliffe, and Gourevitch 2007); others have argued that the "pursuit of emancipation involves working beyond and outside the state, ignoring rather than confronting it, as part of the rediscovery of politics in the practical solidarity of the governed" (Duffield 2007, 232); some have restated the value of locally based practices of resistance (Lipschutz and

Rowe 2005; Richmond 2008). However, most scholarly prescriptions for better politics end up constructing yet another reassuring recipe for good and bad, whether it be based on preserving sovereignty, abating it, or taking local action as the new way for organizing political agency and achieving a better life. This book does not provide another suggestion on how to pursue emancipation. More modestly, it provides theoretically contingent interrogations of established practices. One of the most interesting elements of Foucauldian analytics of power is that it moves away from the aspiration of reconstructing overarching alternative sets of reassuring directives for bettering political life. Instead, the critical and liberatory potential of Foucauldian methodologies resides in the problematization of what is taken for granted, the empirical study of modalities of power and its contingent effects, and the spaces they open for agonic political activities whose effects are never determined in advance. Foucauldian studies bring to light both the normalizing effects that idioms produce as well as the contestation and possibilities for agonic politics they elicit. Because of the focus on the contingent, the questioning of accepted understanding of subjectivity, and the reflexive interest in how practices of power and discourses intersect, Foucauldian analyses of international power do not lead to deterministic visions of political life. On the contrary, actors (individual or collective) are the result of processes of subjectification whose effects are open ended, never overdetermined, and always negotiated in the continuous, uneven struggles between modalities of power and strategic acts of resistance. The effect of inquiries conducted in this framework is to invite "a modification of historians' and others' relationships to truth through the problematization of what is given to us as necessary to think and do" (Barry, Osborne, and Rose 1996, 32).

ORGANIZATION OF THIS BOOK

Chapter 2 describes how Foucauldian theoretical tools apply to the study of the international security regime. Chapters 3 and 4 explore the shifting idioms of international security in the post–Cold War era and illustrate the disciplinary, governmental, and biopolitical trajectories of the UN political rationale. Chapter 5 addresses the genealogy of the imaginary that guided the prodemocracy institutional reforms in Haiti and their consequences. The discussion highlights the linkages in the UN political rationale among designing penal institutions along disciplinary lines, building a democratic state, and restoring international peace, and it explores the effects of the combination of this political rationale with local poverty. Chapter 6 investigates the strategic games of interaction between international normalizing regimes and local politics in Croatia. It makes the argument for a conceptualization of international power as the structure of human interaction and for a nonromanticized understanding of resistance. It also questions representations of international power as domination and illustrates instead its effects of carceralization. The conclusions bring together the analytical elements emerging from the book and propose a few reflections on the role of the UN in the post–Cold War era and on the critical possibilities opened (as well as on the questions that remain unanswered) by Foucauldian studies of international power and resistance.

RETHEORIZING THE POST–COLD WAR INTERNATIONAL ORDER

Things happen through the lines of force that form when a multitude of small shifts, often contingent and independent from one another, get connected up: hence it is these configurations of the minor that seem to me to form the most appropriate object for the work of a historian of the present.

—Rose 1999, 11

TAMING RISK, NORMALIZING DISORDER

After the end of the Cold War, discourses of democracy converged with discourses of security. Peace was reimagined as strictly connected to processes of institutionalization and government (Richmond 2005, 14). Threats to democracy are considered threats to international peace, and

Sections of this and the following chapter have been republished with minor modifications from *Alternatives: Global, Local, Political* 30, no. 4. Copyright © 2005 by Lynne Rienner Publishers, Inc. Used with permission of the publisher.

democratization is touted as a means to create a more secure and just world. In the 1990s UN involvement in democratization activities increased drastically.[1] Peacekeeping mandates expanded to include establishing liberal or democratic governments, rebuilding state administrations and public services, and performing most state functions in "transitional administrations."

In response to the new challenges it had to face, the UN underwent an intense institutional debate about democracy, its connections with development and peacekeeping, and the organization's role in bringing it about. It also engaged in a series of internal reforms aimed to better equip itself to perform its new role. In the context of this debate, "good governance" emerged as the framework within which democratization was thought about and operationalized.

The making of peace and the problematic of international security were increasingly delinked from the problematic of state borders or geostrategic balance. Democracy, identified with normality and operationalized as "good governance," is the discursive formation of an international regime that endeavors to prevent danger through the normalization of international actors. A new way of maintaining international order, based on the homogenization of political systems along the pattern of Western models, was elaborated in academia by democratic peace scholars. Democratic peace theories bring democracy into the problematic of security and provide explanations of international conflict based on the quality of states' domestic political regimes.[2] In the 1990s, democracy, democratization, and "good governance" became the organizing concepts for an array of UN activities, including development, electoral assistance, and peacekeeping interventions (Zanotti 2005).

1. For an overview of the role of the United Nations in democracy assistance, see White (2000). For a recent overview of the sixty-nine UN peace missions in place since the end of the Cold War, see Franke and Warnecke (2009).

2. Linked in general terms to "idealistic" interpretations of international relations, democratic peace theories found their first formulation in Kant's "perpetual peace" (Kant 1949). The fulfillment of internationally established criteria for democracy has become a key element of conditionality for the allocation of international assistance and for inclusion in supranational political organizations. In their modern versions, democratic peace theories offer two explanations for the linkages between democracy and international peace. *Monadic propositions* maintain that democracies are less inclined toward violent behavior, regardless of the regime type of their potential opponents. *Dyadic propositions* maintain that democracies, while being as war prone as nondemocracies, do not go to war with other democracies due to cultural similarities and/or economic linkages. For a discussion of democratization theories, see Elman (1997, 1–57).

Discourses of security portray states that do not have transparent, codified, and comprehensive internal law and electoral systems, or do not abide by international benchmarks of "good government," as "rogues"[3]: outcasts of international society and unpredictable bundles of threats. Foucault explored the construction of the king as "moral monster" during the eighteenth century: "The despot is the permanent outlaw, the individual without social ties. The despot is the man alone" (Foucault 2003b, 94). Likewise, post–Cold War discourses of security construct authoritarian states as political monsters. Liberal democracy became a marker of identity, the distinctive trait of normality and abnormality, as well as the benchmark to be achieved in order to be included into supranational political and military organizations and to obtain international aid. As a benchmark of normality and a criterion for inclusion in or exclusion from international associations, liberal democracy became a technology of international government of insecurity. The EU explicitly emphasized democracy as a criterion for the admission of new members, and included democratization of bordering countries as a key element of its security strategy.[4] In the 1990s the World Bank and the UN Development Program (UNDP) introduced "good governance" as a requirement for international aid (World Bank 1992, 1994; UNDP 1994); the centrality of political criteria for international conditionality was also restated at the 2005 United Nations World Summit.[5] Democracy became a new "cartographic practice of naming political space" (Rosow 2000). New discourses of danger are formulated as oppositional identities, where areas of instability are remapped in the form of "borderlands," characterized by disorder, irrationality, and excessive violence (Duffield 2002b). What is to be protected is no longer

3. The *Compact Oxford English Dictionary* defines "rogue" as follows: "**1** a dishonest or unprincipled man. **2** a mischievous but likeable person. **3** an elephant or other large wild animal with destructive tendencies driven away or living apart from the herd. **4** a person or thing that is defective or unpredictable." "Rogue" states are represented as a combination of these traits: dishonest, unprincipled, unpredictable, wild, and endowed with destructive tendencies.

4. In 1993 the EU established the "Copenhagen criteria" as a benchmark to be achieved by Eastern European countries prior to admission, including democratic governance, minority and human rights guarantees, and the existence of a functioning market economy. See European Commission Enlargement, Accession Criteria, available at http://ec.europa.eu/enlargement/enlargement_process/accession_process/criteria/index_en.htm (accessed 27 March 2010). See also European Security Strategy, available at http://www.consilium.europa.eu/cms3_fo/showPage.ASP?id=266&lang=EN&mode=g (accessed 27 March 2010).

5. The subordination of international aid to the need for developing countries to "take responsibility" for their own development and promote good governance was restated in the UN's *Report of the International Conference on Financing Development* (UN 2002) and reemphasized during the 2005 UN World Summit by numerous speakers (http://www.un.org/summit2005). For a discussion of political conditionality in the 1990s, see Crawford (2001).

Inclusion of deviant individuals in virtuous communities is only possible through "ethical reconstruction" (Rose 1999, 267). Likewise, inclusion into supranational associations and international organizations marks the divide between civilized and abnormal states, and is contingent on "moral transformation." "International community" emerges as a mechanism of active government that enacts identity formation and moral reformation, as well as a tool for managing risk and improving international security through normalization. Inclusion or exclusion from international political associations as well as international assistance are conditional upon a state's willingness to undergo disciplinary processes and to achieve internationally established standards with regard to a vast array of issues, spanning from human rights, to political organization, to economic matters. The process of pacification and Europeanization of Croatia, discussed in chapter 6, illustrates the deployment of an assemblage of governmental practices aimed at transforming a "rogue" state into a suitable and "functional" member of the EU.

The international normalizing regime has two poles. On the one hand, it works by setting in place *savoirs* and regulations regarding the whole. On the other hand, it fosters techniques for the transformation of individual states in order to make them similar to the "model group." Case management risk, a liberal modality of state government, becomes a technology of international security. As Mitchell Dean has shown, case management risk relies on the assessment of individuals and on multifarious interventions to reduce the danger of abnormal behavior: "Those judged 'at risk' of being a danger to the wider community are subject to a range of therapeutic (e.g., counseling, self-help groups, support groups), sovereign (prison, detention centers), and disciplinary (training and retraining) practices in an effort either to eliminate them completely from communal spaces (e.g., by various forms of confinement) or to lower the dangers posed by their risk of . . . criminal behaviour, long-term unemployment and welfare dependency" (Dean 1999, 189). Internationally, the potential risk posed by each state is assessed case by case, and a mix of techniques of evaluation and transformation are put in place. In this context, the main goal of governments is no longer to manage national economies in the interest of national populations. Instead, it is to rank well in comparison to other countries with regard to the "competitiveness" of their institutions and the regulating mechanisms that they impose on the economy (Hindess 1998). International organizations set up an array of rules, regulations, and monitoring mechanisms that define the functioning of local administrations;

they redesign state administrations in such a way that they work in a disciplinary and disciplined manner; they establish mechanisms of reward/punishment and inclusion/exclusion (for example, admission into Euro-Atlantic structures or access to financial assistance); and they institute mechanisms for performance assessment with regard to a multitude of issue areas, which include the well-being of populations. The process by which the UN sought to establish democracy in Haiti through the reengineering of penal institutions along the lines of a governmental imaginary that took shape during the Enlightenment, and the process of pacification and Europeanization in Croatia, where an array of international organizations and bilateral actors established governmental mechanisms of reward and punishment aimed both at preventing war and at re-subjectifying the country as a functioning member of the European community, illustrate how, in practice, liberal political rationalities for taming disorder have been deployed (and resisted) in different ways in very diverse contexts.

The political rationale that inspired the prodemocracy peacekeeping of the 1990s prescribed institutional reforms as the means through which torn societies ought to be rebuilt, ordered, and democratized, and governments were to be made able and responsible for knowing, steering, and fostering an array of aspects of citizens' lives. Starting the new millennium, under the organizing concept of human security, a distinct but overlapping modality of international government of insecurity intensified. International organizations increasingly engaged in biopolitical activities of population management as a tool for making peace and fostering international security. In his 2005 proposals for UN reform, UN Secretary-General Kofi Annan advocated that the UN had to intervene in such issues as protecting people from gross violations of human rights that were previously considered to fall within a state's jurisdiction. "Human security" and "the responsibility to protect" signal the expansion of the understanding of international threats, which now include all factors that negatively affect human life and well-being, and shift the referent and source of legitimacy of international organizations from states to populations. By stipulating an international "responsibility to protect" populations, Annan made the subjectification of nondemocratic states as political monsters the new basis for legitimizing forcible intervention. Government performance is no longer only a benchmark of normalization but also a condition for exercising the right to full sovereignty. In the new millennium, abnormality (conceived as nondemocratic rule) explicitly opens the way to coercion. In classical Europe, the outlaw (subjectified as "monster") elicited extreme measures (Foucault 2003a, 81–107); similarly, in the post–Cold War period, "rogue" states, those who were not responsible toward their own citizens and other states, elicit forcible intervention.

In the post–Cold War era, normalization, democratization, security, and the use of force to govern "abnormality" converge in prodemocracy peacekeeping.

TRAJECTORIES OF INTERNATIONAL POWER: DISCIPLINARITY, GOVERNMENTALITY, BIOPOLITICS, AND CARCERALIZATION

The post–Cold War international normalizing regime operates along modalities that are isomorphic to the techniques of power that, according to Foucault, marked the great transformation of power in classical Europe. Disciplinarity, governmentalization, biopolitics, and carceralization are the trajectories of this regime. These trajectories refer both to techniques adopted by international organizations to provide security in the international arena and to the political imaginary along which international organizations promote reforms of states. These government techniques elicit the creation of specific types of institutions and societies, open the space for particular kinds of resistance, and foster particular mechanisms of security and forms of liberty.

In classical Europe, techniques for the social control of deviant elements (paupers, lepers, fools) shifted from confinement to disciplinarity. Similarly, international order in the post–Cold War era no longer relies mainly on containment and confinement of sources of danger, but on capillary and widespread techniques of transforming abnormal states into responsible, peace-loving, predictable, transparent, and well-functioning members of the international community. Disciplinarity illustrates a modality of normalizing deviant states through techniques that include training, counseling, codification of governmental procedures, surveillance, and periodical reporting, as well as a specific imaginary along the lines of which disorderly states are rebuilt and democratized by redesigning their institutions along disciplinary lines. In classical Europe, discipline manufactured individuals to make them suitable elements of society. In the post–Cold War era, discipline manufactures states to change them from "rogue sources of threat" into acceptable and productive members of the "international community."

With the advent in classical Europe of governmentality as a modality of rule distinct from sovereignty, local varieties were codified through an array of *savoirs* and administrative procedures (statistics, censuses, patronyms) designed to know and control what had to be governed. Rules, regulations, and monitoring mechanisms proliferated in order to punish tiny infractions, optimize behavior, and manage social processes (Foucault 1991a; Pasquino 1991; Scott 1998). Governmentality designates a modality of "conduct of conduct"[7] that relies on proliferating rules and regulations and performance assessment mechanisms, and that focuses on institutional reforms as the engine for social change (Dean 1999; Rose 1999). It designates both modalities of rule that international organizations, under the organizing concept of good governance, purport to promote within states, and the governmental modalities by which international organizations promote and steer the behavior of states considered sources of danger. While governmentalization refers to the intensification of the association between instruments of knowledge and instruments of rule and applies mainly to governments as the target of optimization, biopolitics applies to population and concerns itself with managing and fostering its health and wealth. For Foucault, governmentality in classical Europe overlapped with biopolitics (Foucault 2003a). At the UN, the beginning of the new millennium brought an increasing concern with knowing, managing, and protecting the wealth and health of populations, which converged with UN governmental and disciplinary techniques for monitoring, steering, and reforming the institutions of disorderly states. In conjunction with the conceptualization of international security as "human security" and the reorganization of the task of international organizations around the notion of a "responsibility to protect" populations, biopolitics became a prominent trajectory of international government of insecurity. Instruments for assessing people's security proliferated, and intervention was legitimized on the grounds of a state's failure to protect its own citizens from gross violations of human rights.

With the advent in classical Europe of governmental modalities of rule, force became only one of the components of a more complex modality of power, to be used as a transitional step to tame "social monsters," that is, those who would reject disciplinarization and subjection to the law. In the post–Cold War period, the coupling of the use of force with correctional strategies intensified. While in UN peacekeeping operations

7. Foucault defines government as the "conduct of conduct" (1981a, 97).

coercion through military force was coupled with programs of institutional reform aimed at redesigning institutions along disciplinary lines, the subjectification of nondemocratic states as political monsters and the refocusing of security discourses on the protection of populations entailed the expansion of the legitimacy of international intervention. In post–Cold War international peacekeeping, practices of correction and coercion are deployed jointly in order to normalize international "delinquent" states, and to transform them into well-functioning members of the "international community." Peacekeeping testifies to the carceralization of the international arena. Carceralization does not succeed in normalizing deviant figures; instead it creates a never-domesticated population of "delinquents" that elicits the continuous deployment and intensification of governmental strategies of disciplinarization, normalization, regulation, and control. In the pages that follow, I will explain how disciplinarity, governmentality, biopolitics, and carceralization apply to the study of international power.

Disciplining Obscure Borderlands: Legibility, Predictability, Simplification, and the Building of Pacified States

The post–Cold War international regime promotes state building through the standardization of a variety of local processes so as to make them legible to state administrations through codification, record keeping, and the unification of procedures; at the same time, this regime endeavors to make the administrations of problematic states accessible to international scrutiny. James Scott described the political rationale guiding the passage from a premodern to a modern type of statecraft in Europe (which he calls high modernism) as a project of "legibility and simplification," devoted to "rationalizing and standardizing what was a social hieroglyph into a legible and administratively more convenient format" (Scott 1998, 2–3). Local practices "exhibited a diversity and intricacy that reflected a great variety of purely local, not state, interests" (Scott 1998, 2–3). State formation required the translation of this diversity into common standards "necessary for a synoptic view of an array of discontinuous local practices, whose bewildering variety . . . made them an impediment to administrative uniformity" (Scott 1998, 25). Simplification efforts were carried out by spreading administrative control through an array of instruments for knowing and managing people's lives, such as the creation of permanent family names, the commencement of a census, the standardization of measures, the unification of legal systems, the establishment of cadastral surveys, and the design of roads and communication networks. The UN, in its democratization efforts, imagines building modern states out of disorderly ones by making institutions work in a comprehensive, regulated, disciplinary, and disciplined manner, thus making the obscure processes of dangerous borderlands visible and legible to both citizens and international organizations. The processes of reforming penal institutions in Haiti, and the mechanisms of scrutiny put in place in the process of pacifying and Europeanizing Croatia, testify to these trajectories.

Disciplinarity is one of the technologies of power through which international organizations make local varieties legible to outsiders. Disciplinarity was adopted both as a blueprint for building the institutions of disorderly states and a technique of international government aimed at normalizing states through monitoring, counseling, reward or punishment, and training. Discipline, in Foucault's view, is not only *repressive* but also *productive*. It articulates functions and creates effective processes of activity. It organizes "cells," "places," and "ranks." "It creates complex spaces, at once architectural, functional and hierarchical" (Foucault 1995, 148). By establishing partitions, functions, rules, and hierarchical architectures, discipline creates structures within which individuals are interchangeable and defined by their respective positions within the functional space. Indistinct "masses" are transformed in this way into "distributed units" and placed in codified relations to one another. Discipline creates *intelligibility* through *visibility*. By partitioning space and positioning individuals in it, discipline establishes forms of taxonomy that make possible the measurement of quantities and the analysis of movements (Foucault 1995). Discipline is a self-regulating, self-reinforcing machinery, "whose effect will be maximized by the concerted articulation of the elementary parts of which it is composed" (Foucault 1995, 164). Disciplinary methods originated as ways for increasing the usefulness of the human body in total institutions, especially the military, and became subsequently a more generalized technique of modern power. Its modalities are a mix of coercion and supervision of the process of activity (rather than on its results) exercised through partition of space, time, and movement. Disciplinarity is correctional. Disciplines are the techniques through which individuals are brought to behave according to norms, that is, are made normal. In classical Europe, when power, previously centered on the person of the king, was exercised through society by the means of disciplinary institutions (the hospital, the prison, the psychiatric asylum, and so forth), punishment techniques changed from spectacular violence exerted on the body of the condemned (through public torture and executions) into mechanisms of correction of the soul. Atrocity, based upon the haphazard and spectacular unleashing of violence on the body of the condemned, was the manifestation of a type of power that ultimately lacked continuity. In Foucault's words, disciplinarity is the result of a need "not to punish less but to punish better; to punish with attenuated severity perhaps, but in order to punish with more universality and necessity; to insert power to punish more deeply into the social body" (Foucault 1995, 82). Along with the reconceptualization of international security in terms of risk management and the problematization of international danger in terms of the proliferation of multifarious and dispersed threats, in the post–Cold War period there is a need for inserting mechanisms of control deeply into potentially disorderly states, so as to tame risk by reducing unpredictability. "Rogue" states' modalities of functioning must be transformed so that they develop the capacity and assume the responsibility for governing disorder within their borderlands and behave as productive and predictable actors of the international community.

Disciplinarity not only provides a blueprint for rebuilding states, but its methods are also a key tool for governing international disorder through inclusion or exclusion from international communities. Examinations, in the form of reports to international bodies, occupy a central role in this context. Such examination has three effects: it transforms the "economy of visibility into the exercise of power"; it introduces individuality into the field of documentation; and it makes each individual into "a case" (Foucault 1995, 189–91). The effectiveness of training as a technique for modifying behavior is based on the possibility of establishing standards and measuring performance. Performance is documented in "standardized" (often statistical) manners and included in a field of comparisons. Each case is pinned down in its individuality and at the same time made comparable with others through an ensemble of indicators, benchmarks, and measurements. Through the writing and record keeping linked to examination, assessment criteria, corrections, inclusions and exclusions, reward and punishment, and further training are put in place. To summarize, discipline works through constant and capillary surveillance, mechanisms of reward and punishment diffused throughout the social body, definition and partition of functions, measurement, codification, record keeping, training, and examination. It creates visibility and fosters normalization. In classical Europe, disciplines were instruments for creating productive individualities. In the late twentieth century, after the collapse of the bipolar order, disciplinarity migrated to the international arena as one of the modalities for governing international insecurity. Scrutiny, counseling, and examination through international reporting are key elements of international processes of aid delivery and admission into regional organizations. In addition, institutional design along disciplinary lines increasingly accompanies international interventions, peacekeeping operations in particular. In Haiti the UN political imaginary linked the democratization and pacification of the country to redesigning penal institutions along disciplinary lines. In Croatia two events—the Erdut Agreement, which established the integration of Eastern Slavonia into the Croatian territory,[8] and the Stabilization and Association Process, which led Croatia to the European candidacy—institutionalized examination mechanisms for assessing, monitoring, and controlling progress toward internationally established benchmarks for respect of human rights and good government.

Governmentalizing International and National Government, Fostering Standardized Knowledge

Disciplinarity for Foucault was a technique of transformation of individuals with a view to normalization. Governmentality refers to (often related) techniques for managing populations and their living together. For Foucault, governmentality refers to two domains. On the one hand, governmentality is a method for studying processes of conduct of behavior; on the other hand, it is a historically specific form of government and a technique of power that—resulting from a series of transformations that started at the end of the Middle Ages—took its present shape in nineteenth-century Europe. It has the population as its target, it has political economy as its form of knowledge, and it corresponds to a type of society governed by security apparatuses (Foucault 1991a). These security apparatuses are exerted through the dispersion of techniques for controlling and steering behavior in society.[9] For Pasquale Pasquino, the formation of a "science of

8. The Erdut Agreement was the peace treaty that integrated Eastern Slavonia into the Croatian territory in exchange for respect of human rights. For a detailed analysis of the functioning of Erdut as a disciplinary and governmental mechanism, see chapter 6.

9. Roughly speaking, Foucault argues, one can recognize three historical forms of state in Europe. First is the "state of justice," based on "laws"; second is the "administrative state," rooted in territory and based on discipline and regulation; last is the "governmental state," focusing on population and apparatuses of security (Foucault 1991a, 104). In *Discipline and*

police" testifies to the connection between modern government and a specific body of knowledge. The modern meaning of police as an organization whose purpose is securing order and preventing dangers is a relatively recent invention. To this "negative" definition, Pasquino opposes a "positive" formulation, still current in the nineteenth century, which speaks of police as "cura promovendi salutem," which he translates as "concern to develop or promote happiness or the public good" (Pasquino 1991, 109–10). In this sense, the science of police purported to control, order, and regulate domains of life that were not previously governed. These included religion, customs, health, foodstuff, highways, tranquility and public order, sciences and liberal arts, commerce, manufactures and mechanical arts, servants, the poor, and so forth. The science of police is the point of departure for a modern body of knowledge (statistics, demography, social sciences, and so forth) having as its object the population and as its goal the promotion of its health and wealth. In this context, the areas that in the feudal world were the subjects of traditional customs, various jurisdictions, and multiple relations of authority and alliance became the field of application for these new sciences, which purport to make visible, knowledgeable, regulated, and altogether predictable the medieval "no man's land" that we today call (civil) society.[10] For Georg Obrecht, writing in Strasbourg in 1608, policing has three tasks: garnering information about the resources of population and territory; augmenting the wealth, health, and happiness of populations; and enriching the coffers of the state.

Foucault explores the genealogy of the "art of government" through anti-Machiavellian literature produced from the sixteenth to the eighteenth centuries. One of the earliest examples of anti-Machiavellian literature, Guillaume de La Perrière's *Miroir politique,* testifies to a radical change with regard to the advisory treatises to the prince. These treatises, exemplified by

Punish, Foucault elaborates on the articulation between governmentality and biopolitics as two poles of a modality of government that relies on techniques that differ from sovereignty: "One of these poles—the first to be formed, it seems—centered on the body as a machine: its disciplining, the optimization of its capabilities, the extortion of its forces, the parallel increase of its usefulness and its docility, its integration into systems of efficient and economic control, all this was ensured by the procedures of power that characterized the *disciplines: an anatomo-politics of the human body.* The second, formed somewhat later, focused on the species body, the body imbued with the mechanics of life and serving as the basis of the biological processes. . . . Their supervision was effected through an entire series of interventions and *regulatory controls: a biopolitics of the population*" (Foucault 1990, 139). A hermeneutics of Foucault's position in this regard is beyond the scope of this study. Disciplinarity, governmentality, and biopolitics are trajectories that constitute the assemblage of post–Cold War international security regimes.

10. Pasquino also notes that between 1600 and 1800 some 3,200 titles were published under the heading "science of police" (Pasquino 1991, 112–15).

Machiavelli's *The Prince,* focused on ways to maintain the sovereign's status. Instead, Foucault sees in La Perriere's text one of the earliest elaborations of "government" as a modality of power radically different from rule centered on the person of the king, or "sovereignty." The goal of government is not mainly the preservation of principality. Instead, government is the right disposition of things, arranged so as to lead to a convenient end (Foucault 1991a).[11] This sentence encapsulates the elements that make government different from sovereignty. First, government differs from sovereignty in its field of application. Sovereignty—as Foucault saw it manifested from the Middle Ages to Machiavelli—is exercised on territory. Territory constitutes the fundamental attribute of sovereignty, and the characteristics and life of population are "mere variables." Alternatively, government refers to a number of distinct fields within which the connections between people and things are to be disposed and organized. Second, government is plural. It relates to an array of issue areas, such as the government of a family, a convent, souls, children, and so on, and it concerns, besides the prince, a variety of individuals. In this context, the relation of the prince to his state becomes a special case among plural practices of government. Third, government differs from sovereignty both in its goals and in its tactics. In La Perriere's rendering, the goal of government is common good. For Foucault, within the tradition of sovereignty, common good is nothing but submission to the king. Instead, in the context of government, common good refers to the maximization of an array of desirable results within specific fields ("the right disposition of things"), such as the family's wealth and health and the provision of the means of subsistence for the population. In summary, to use a modern term, government is a "managerial activity," arranging things wisely in order to maximize outputs in specific fields of application. Government's ability to arrange things is connected to capillary control and supervision of individuals and wealth. In order to govern through control, it is necessary to develop instruments to know what has to be governed. For Foucault, the formation of the art of government was connected, beginning in the sixteenth century, to the development of the administrative apparatus of the territorial monarchies and to the

---

11. While an analysis of the origins of functionalism and its connections with governmentality is beyond the scope of this book, it is worthwhile to note that Foucault implicitly dates the origins of functionalism to anti-Machiavellian literature and links it to the genealogy of government. The functional division of space and tasks is also for Foucault one of the key features of disciplinarity. See Foucault (1995).

emergence, later in that century, of forms of knowledge that had to do with the "knowledge of the state, in all its different elements, dimensions, and factors of power, questions which were termed precisely 'statistics'" (Foucault 1991a, 96).

In the post–Cold War period, the problematic of international security is governmentalized both with regard to its techniques and to its referent. Fostering practices of "good government" within states is imagined to lead to international peace. As Luke and Ó Tuathail argue, failed states are portrayed as "those that . . . wrongly dispose of things by disrupting rational control over populations, territory and resources. As an agency of governmentality, the disciplinary articulations of successful state power center upon establishing and enforcing 'the right disposition of things' between human populations and their primary habitat—territorially defined statal space." In this perspective, failed states need to become the subject of administrative guidance (Debrix 1996; Luke and Ó Tuathail 1997, 714).[12] "Good governance" doctrines privilege institutional transformation as the engine for social change, and they prescribe that international organizations guide the conduct of governments through mechanisms of performance assessment and reward.[13] In the 1990s reform of government became, in the political rationale and programmatic actions of international organizations, a key instrument for achieving peace, security, and democracy all at once. In this context, reforming processes of government was considered the instrument through which social transformations ought to be brought about. Instead of applying directly to social spaces, good governance doctrines prescribed that governing was about reforming institutions of government. In this framework, reforms of rules and regulations and of mechanisms of government are considered the key to societal transformation; conversely, social spaces become increasingly institutionalized. Security, peace, and development, no longer considered the result of a balance of power or economic reforms, are expected to be the outcomes of the reformation of government processes (Dean 1999).

12. While Luke and Ó Tuathail (1997) and Debrix (1996, 1999) analyzed the role played by the media in the construction of global order, here I explore how processes of normalization of "rogue" states go beyond mediatic panopticism and operate through institutional and social engineering.

13. In this regard the "control" trajectory of government that is generally identified with the modalities of the science of police and the "liberal" trajectory of government that relies on incentives and "freedoms" in order to steer behavior overlap in the post–Cold War international security regime. For a discussion of these two trajectories of government, see Rose (1999 and 1996).

Withdrawal from direct intervention does not mean withdrawal from control. On the contrary, the range of social and economic processes subject to public power increased as a result of the proliferation of regulations (Moran 2003). Good governance fosters the extension of scrutiny, laws, and rules regarding an extensive array of aspects of life. It prescribes the standardization of techniques of assessment of performance, making processes "efficient," establishing calculated spaces, and forging calculating actors. International auditing procedures are the means through which states' behavior is monitored, assessed, ranked, and steered.

In the 1990s the United Nations' political rationale for dealing with international security was reorganized around the notion of good governance, and the problematic of international security became governmentalized. Good governance doctrines prescribe the universalization of governmentality both as a modality of state rule and one of international "conduct of conduct." These doctrines promote visibility, codification, and simplification at both the state and international level. They predicate institutional reforms that foster the reorganization of an array of local practices into administrable varieties in order to make them governable by modern state administrations. In addition, good governance doctrines promote modalities of rule based on the collection of capillary and standardized data pertaining to populations and governments. They prescribe the codification of a plurality of techniques aimed at knowing aspects of people's lives with a view to bettering and optimizing them. These doctrines advocate the proliferation of an array of regulations both within states and at the international level. They recommend that international organizations develop performance techniques to assess, reward, or punish the behavior of governments with regard to fields that were previously considered to fall within their sovereign jurisdiction. Through the creation of databases, standards, and indicators of performance, each government is placed within a mechanism of constant scrutiny, comparison, and discipline. In the post–Cold War period, each state is made the subject of "exams" and "clinical observation." Through the "exam" each trainee's performance is recorded and ranked, and through "clinical observation" each subject is included within a field of standardized statistical data and at the same time treated as an individual who must be accompanied through a unique path to sanity. These technologies of visibility, codification, and simplification play an increasingly central role in normalizing the international arena and maintaining order in the context of the proliferation of unpredictable threats.

Good governance doctrines predicate that reforming institutions is the key to bringing about social change, and they prescribe that processes of government apply to government itself instead of society. The process by which the objective of national government shifted from direct intervention in society (as in the welfare state) toward the reform of the performance of the existing governmental institutions has been called "reflexive government" (Dean 1999).[14] Once adopted as the political rationale for international action, good governance transposes at the international level the doctrinal shift that occurred with regard to domestic government in the last two decades of the twentieth century. When internationalized, this political rationale prescribes that peace, development, and democracy are brought about through the optimization of governmental processes. Thus, in the 1990s state institutions were the target of international government, and their reformation was the main instrument for achieving international security. The internationally sponsored reform of institutions of punishment in Haiti and the process of pacification and Europeanization of Croatia reflect this political rationale.

Toward the end of the twentieth century, government was increasingly exerted through the assessment of procedural compliance. Social engineering was sought less and less through direct intervention in societies, but rather pursued through third parties whose deeds were regulated, monitored, and steered through formal performance assessment instruments. This proliferation of assessments and regulations came to rely on the intensification of processes for collecting standardized information. Numbers became indispensable tools for linking the exercise of democratic government to the entities on which it depends (Rose 1999, 231). First, numbers, through electoral mechanisms, determine whose power is justified and confer legitimacy to political leaders (Porter 1995; Rose 1999, 197–232). Second, numbers operate as a diagnostic instrument for political life through opinion polls. Third, numbers make government both possible (as they map the characteristics of population, economy, and society) and subject to scrutiny (as numerical comparisons are essential for the scrutiny of authority in our modern societies). Finally, numbers are essential to the complex technologies through which governance is exercised

14. In Dean's words, "Reflexive government means that the central target and objective of national government becomes the reform of the performance of the existing governmental institutions and techniques. . . . The distinguishing feature of reflexive government is that the point of the reform of the institutions and mechanisms of government is to secure them in the face of processes that are deemed beyond governmental control" (Dean 1990, 179).

and to the formulation of government programs, such as in the form of population counts, tax collections, social indexes, economic indicators, and health indicators. As the analysis of the international intervention in Croatia will show, programs aimed at fostering internationally compatible methods of statistical collection are important for the UN-led democratization and pacification processes.[15] In the post–Cold War era, governments are scrutinized through the collection of an array of statistical data and indicators of performance, as well as an intensification of reporting to and by international organizations (the EU, the UN, the World Bank, the International Monetary Fund, the Organization for Security and Cooperation in Europe [OSCE], and many other multilateral and bilateral organizations). Reports function as a series of examinations to assess progress and determine inclusion or exclusion from international structures. These methods of government/knowledge constitute the international arena as an object to be known and transformed through political interventions. The international arena looks increasingly like a series of "centers for calculation" (the UN and its agencies, the EU, and NATO, just to name a few) where information and data are elaborated and adopted as the criteria for delivering rewards and punishment. The performance of government institutions is represented in standardized terms, measured, and included in a field of comparisons. Methods for assessing the performance of states are borrowed from financial management. They focus on formal aspects and numerical representation, and they encompass budgeting, auditing, establishment of benchmarks, and standardized indicators of performance. Numbers became a central means for "governing from a distance" in colonial times, when the need to govern an array of diverse phenomena in distant territories fostered the establishment of standardized ways of collecting information and assessing the performance of bureaucrats (Rose 1999, 197–232). In the post–Cold War era, numbers make available to international organizations information that is simultaneously capillary, individualized, and standardized. Statistics and performance indicators are central for international allocation of resources, programmatic actions, and project evaluations. Numbers enable the translation of heterogeneous elements into standardized forms, and therefore they enable collection and

---

15. Collecting data about the population can be very controversial in situations where a census is nonexistent or the composition of citizenship has been radically changed by war. In these situations numbers do not have a commonly accepted "matter of fact" to represent, and the collection of population data becomes a matter of political controversies (as in Croatia) or faces the obstacles of nonexistent technology (as in Haiti).

comparison. They are the instruments for creating "calculated spaces" on which governance programs are enacted. The standardization and association process, which regulated the accession of Croatia to the candidacy to the EU, testifies to this trajectory.

From Reforming Government to Governing Populations: Human Security as Biopolitics

In the 1990s, international government of insecurity was exerted through the intensification of mechanisms of knowledge and the transformation of government processes. However, after the problematic outcomes of prodemocracy peacekeeping and democratization processes in general, the certainty that government reforms alone could provide a viable path for international security and international peace faded. In the new millennium, international security was reconceptualized in terms of risk management. Risk is a trajectory of what Ulrich Beck called "second modernity," in which interconnections are extended and intensified, relations of causality do not follow linear paths, and the past is no longer a valid basis for predicting the future. Since risk is always situated in the future, its management is knowledge intensive, and it increasingly relies on the possibility of garnering accurate information on a plurality of potential sources of danger. Since relations of causality and the effects of the interaction of an increasing number of variables are increasingly difficult to predict, security is conceptualized in terms of prevention (Beck 1992). Vulnerability is a category directly linked to the notion of risk. While creating inequalities that cannot be conceptualized along the lines of traditional notions, such as class, risk also produces equalizing effects. While unequally distributed, vulnerability is shared by wealthy and poor alike and is not proportional to relative strength. For Beck (2000), risk calls for breaking the traditional categorizations for understanding societies. What he calls container theories of society consider territoriality a given basis for organization of political life. Once international danger is reconceptualized in terms of risk, states are no longer the only actors in international relations, and political communities can no longer be conceptualized in territorial terms. Identity and democracy define the new geography of security and risk. Risk circulates across borders. Dangerous elements are subjectified as "barbarian," a figure that, for Foucault, in classical Europe represented those who threatened civilization from within (Foucault 2003a). In this context, international security is pursued through the intensification of techniques of government aimed at knowing, monitoring, and taming a plurality of threats, which include those that affect, or are created by, populations.

Danger and vulnerability create new linkages, and political communities are reconceived in global terms.[16] Because interconnections between diverse variables are difficult to foresee, and risk societies cannot be conceptualized in terms of separate "containers," risk management demands holistic approaches. Biopolitics, or the science of living together (Foucault 2003a), emerged as a prominent trajectory of international rationalities of government. At the beginning of the new millennium, international instruments for knowledge and the government of insecurity expanded to encompass direct management of population life. With the adoption of human security as the organizing concept of the UN political rationale for intervention, biopolitics overlapped with governmental and disciplinary technologies of international order and became a prominent trajectory of international "conduct of conduct." Knowing and monitoring populations with a view toward promoting their health and wealth is now seen as a shared task between state administrations and international organizations, and protecting people has become the ultimate referent and legitimizing principle for international intervention.

Foucault calls bio-power the modality of rule that has its application in the life of the population and is connected to the formations of *savoirs* aimed at knowing processes of life (Foucault 1990).[17] The eighteenth-century demographic expansion and the emergence of the problem of population as a specific realm of knowledge and intervention led to the further disentanglement of the problem of government from the framework of sovereignty. Unlike the power of the sovereign, which according to Foucault was "deductive," bio-power is productive. Bio-power has as its goal to "reinforce, control, monitor, optimize, and organize the forces under it: a power bent on generating forces, making them grow, and ordering them, rather than one dedicated to impeding them, making them submit, or destroying them" (Foucault 1990, 136). Bio-power "exerts a positive influence on life, . . . endeavors to administer . . . it, subjecting

16. For Beck, ultimately, the United Nations, as the global collective security organization, is the most adequate institution for combating globalized risk (Beck 1992).

17. In some of his writings on the history of culture, Foucault emphasizes more than elsewhere that positivism constituted a rupture with regard to previous systems of knowledge (see, e.g., Foucault 1994). A discussion of Foucault's writings on epistemology and the connections between positivism and the rise of the governmentalized state are beyond the scope of this inquiry.

it to precise controls and comprehensive regulations" (Foucault 1990, 146).[18] Population became the subject of needs and aspirations, the fulfillment of which was identified with the goal of government and the "common good."

As the analysis conducted in chapter 4 will show, starting in the new millennium, populations became the subject of international organizations' scrutiny, monitoring, and regulation, and the promotion of their health and wealth came to be a central strategy of international security. As Michael Dillon and Julian Reid put it, "While international liberalism once aspired to some forms of world government, today's global liberal governance pursues the administration of life and the management of populations through the deployment of biopolitical techniques of power" (Dillon and Reid 2001, 46). International security organizations included the promotion of populations' wealth and health as an element of conditionality and a universal benchmark to be achieved by all states. Protecting populations from gross violations of human rights became a necessary condition for exerting full sovereignty and a key prerequisite for being admitted into supranational political organizations, such as the EU. In the plans for UN reforms proposed by Kofi Annan in 2005, protecting people and bettering their lives became the ultimate raison d'être of the UN. Conversely, states' failure to protect their own people from gross violations of human rights put in jeopardy the principle of noninterference stipulated in Article 2.7 of the UN Charter. While previously the care of people was considered part of a state's internal affairs, in the post–Cold War era the limit posed by state borders to international governmentality and forcible interventions faded. Disentangled from the centralization of fear, and increasingly connected with processes of knowledge, management, and regulation, the point of application of international power overlapped with traditional objects of sovereignty. When government of populations became a shared task between states and international organizations, government was to an extent deterritorialized. Simultaneously, the main attribute for sovereignty shifted from control over territory to the ability to govern, that is, the managerial ability to correctly arrange the disposition of people and material resources in order to optimize life performance.

18. This productive character of bio-power is central to the discussion of governmentality in the international arena. On the one hand, it delinks the discussion of power from the opposition of oppression vs. freedom. On the other hand, the productive character of bio-power establishes connections among regulations, disciplines, and contemporary notions of freedom and democracy. Freedom and resistance are not to be regarded as ideal types, but as specific forms of behavior constituted within historically determined power formations.

Correctional punishment, which emerged in classical Europe with the advent of disciplinarity, entailed a particular modality of social control, which Foucault called the carceralization of society. Carceralization subjectifies disorderly elements as *delinquents* and makes them the target of intensified strategies of knowledge, surveillance, and transformation (Foucault 1995, 257–92).[19] Disciplinary techniques created within total institutions in the second half of the nineteenth century in Europe expanded beyond the frontiers of criminal law to the entire social body, and they came to constitute what Foucault called a "carceral archipelago" (Foucault 1995, 297).[20] The techniques of punishment that apply to the delinquent differ from the ones that were imposed on the "offender" in the "juridical system." The latter was punished for his act, not corrected. Public executions were the ceremony through which wounded sovereignty was restored. In a carceral system, however, the entire life of the delinquent was to be known, examined, and taken charge of in order to transform the soul. The delinquent brings together two lines of subjectification: "The first was the series of 'monsters' moral or political, who had fallen outside the social pact; the second was that of the juridical subject rehabilitated by punishment. Now the delinquent makes it possible to join the two lines and to constitute under the authority of medicine, psychology or criminology, an individual in whom the offender of the law and the object of a scientific technique are superimposed" (Foucault 1995, 256). After the Cold War, "rogue" states are subjectified as delinquents. They are imagined as bearing a bundle of threats to other states and populations (be they citizens or foreigners) alike. The many representations of Haiti as a land of savages or a pariah state testify to this trajectory.[21] States that are unable to rule

19. "Arms trafficking, the illegal sale of alcohol in prohibition countries, or more recently drug trafficking show a similar functioning of this 'useful delinquency': the existence of a legal prohibition creates around it a field of illegal practices, which one manages to supervise. . . . Delinquency, with the secret agents that it procures, but also with the generalized policing that it authorizes, constitutes a means of perpetual surveillance. . . . Delinquency functions as a political observatory. In their turn, the statisticians and the sociologists have made use of it, long after the police" (Foucault 1995, 280–81).

20. "The frontiers between confinement, judicial punishment and institutions of discipline tended to disappear and to constitute a great carceral continuum that diffused penitentiary techniques into the most innocent disciplines, transmitting disciplinary norms into the very heart of the penal system and placing over the slightest illegality, the smallest irregularity, deviation or anomaly, the threat of delinquency" (Foucault 1995, 297).

21. For a discussion of representations of Haiti see Farmer (1994); McFayden et al. (1995).

according to law and therefore to protect their citizens fall within the category of political "monsters" and therefore elicit exceptional measures such as forcible international intervention. In 2004 the theme of states' "responsibility" and capacity to perform certain functions beneficial to their citizens was explicitly included in the UN debate on its role in international security. The report by the High-Level Panel on Change, Challenges, and Threat, nominated by Kofi Annan to devise new ways of bringing about international security, clearly links the notion of sovereignty to performance and responsibility (UN General Assembly 2004).

Prodemocracy peacekeeping is an instance of the carceralization of the international arena. Practices of correction and coercion operate in conjunction in order to normalize international delinquent states and transform them into well-functioning members of the "international community." Peacekeeping combines forcible interventions with expert counseling and assistance aimed at their rehabilitation.

The carceralization of international order, however, does not lead to normalization of the international space. While "delinquent" resistance elicits the intensification of mechanisms of disciplinarization and control, it also hampers their effectiveness. For Foucault, power is relational and every act of power entails acts of resistance (Foucault 1990, 143). Thus, while continuously intensified, normalizing power never achieves its goals. International mechanisms of control proliferate at different junctures of international and domestic processes of government, and these mechanisms are deployed by an array of actors, including international organizations, bilateral donors, and nongovernmental organizations that, while sharing political rationales, do not necessarily share specific goals and policy agendas. International carceral power is better understood as the proliferation of *dispositifs* of dispersed visibility than as the projection of the Leviathan.[22] Foucault moves away from the fixation with sovereignty and legitimacy and provides an elaboration of power as the ubiquitous feature of human interactions (Hindess 1996, 96–101). Resistance does not relate to power in an oppositional but rather in a transformative manner. For Foucault freedom is a practice in agonic relation with power, not a natural condition of human life. Liberty and power stand in a relation of "complicated interplay" (Foucault 1982b, 221). In Foucault's words, "At the

22. For a discussion of peacekeeping as a Panopticon-like mechanism and a simulation of the Leviathan, see Debrix (1999). For Debrix, peacekeeping maintains order by simulating the power of the Leviathan through representation of force and a Panopticon-like surveilling gaze broadcast and amplified through the media.

very heart of the power relationship, and constantly provoking it, are the recalcitrance of the will and the intransigence of freedom. Rather than speaking of an essential freedom it would be better to speak of an 'agonism' of a relationship which is at the same time reciprocal incitation and struggle; less of a face-to-face confrontation which paralyzes both sides than a permanent provocation" (Foucault 1982b, 221–22).

INTERNATIONAL NORMALIZATION'S EFFECTS

In this chapter I have argued that the post–Cold War international security regime works as a diffuse and comprehensive disciplinary governmental and biopolitical project aimed at increasing the security and predictability of the international arena through the normalization of delinquent states. Prodemocracy peacekeeping represents the most evident instance of the association between democratization and international security. However, notwithstanding the intensification of mechanisms of knowledge, transformation, control, and coercion in the post–Cold War era, the normalization of disorderly states is never completely successful. If indeed the domestication of delinquent states is never accomplished, why is that so?

The analysis of the cases of Haiti and Croatia, focusing on the encounter between the imaginary of international intervention and local societies, provides empirically based contributions to answering this question. While the outcomes of the UN peacekeeping operations explored here produced different and uneven outcomes with regard to bringing about transformations of "abnormal" states in the direction envisaged by peacekeepers and peace builders, they were effective in opening dispersed observation *dispositifs,* designed to last beyond the withdrawal of peacekeeping forces. These spaces of visibility facilitate multiple (though not necessarily coordinated) gazes and reforms by multilateral and bilateral technical experts alike. In Haiti and Croatia "democratization" and pacification may not be fully accomplished, but spaces of dispersed visibility are opened into "obscure" borderlands. However, in the encounter with local societies, international intervention also opened spaces for resistance and produced, for different reasons, unintended consequences. The exploration of the genealogy of the UN political rationale in Haiti and of its effects in a situation of extreme poverty conducted here adds an economic and material dimension to explanations of the interaction between intervention and local societies, dominated to this point by cultural analyses. Democratization through disciplinarization of penal institutions is a costly technique of government that cannot easily be exported in isolation from social and economic contexts. Instead of building the state and bringing about order, internationally driven and sponsored institutional reforms foster conditions of dependency and nurture disorder. The case of Croatia illustrates the complex modalities of interaction between international normalizing regimes and the resistance of local institutional actors. In Croatia, the UN intervention and the subsequent processes of Europeanization achieved, to a certain degree, their stated goals. However, as international institutions attempted to regulate in detail the conduct of state institutions and local administrations as well as the well-being of populations, local governmental agencies developed continuous and capillary resistance through the very instruments deployed by international bodies. The analysis of the process of pacification and Europeanization of Croatia opens the way for more general reflections on conceptualizations of international power and resistance. It questions both "a social ontology that converts boundaries and standards central to modern life into precepts of rationality, morality or self realization" (Connolly 1987, 9) and romanticized conceptualizations that unreflectively attach liberation or "emancipatory" qualities to resistance. It brings to light the normalizing effects that international political rationalities produce, the contestation they elicit, and the ambiguous outcomes of the interplay between power and resistance. One of the implications of conceptualizing resistance as an agonic activity imbricated with power is that no uncontested ethical value can be unreflectively attached to it. As opposed to romanticized images that portray resistance as an "ethically good" activity of the powerless against the powerful, the study of the process of pacification and Europeanization of Croatia shows that resistance to international power may very well entail a minority's oppression. If looked at from the standpoint of the Serbs, the Croatian administration's resistance to the inscriptions of international power was not particularly emancipatory or progressive.

The cases addressed in this book map the specificities of the encounters of international power with the realities of Haiti and Croatia. Each case in its own merit offers materials for drawing more general insights into the trajectories of post–Cold War international security regimes and their encounters with local societies. However, the cases explored do not constitute the ground for providing overarching praise or condemnation of international intervention. The relocation of politics beyond the state contains both dangers and opportunities (Jabri 2007, 170). As Foucault taught us, power must be studied in its contingent modalities and strategic interactions, and very little can be said about power in general (Foucault 2003a).

GOVERNMENTALIZING THE POST–COLD WAR INTERNATIONAL REGIME
The UN Debate on Democratization and
Good Governance

INTRODUCTION

This chapter and the next illustrate the governmental and biopolitical trajectories of the UN post–Cold War security discursive practices. As outlined in the previous section, governmentality is twofold. On the one hand, governmentality refers to a political rationale by which reforming processes of government is considered the instrument for reforming society (Dean 1999). On the other hand, it refers to modalities of rule that focus on ensuring the "right disposition of things" (Foucault 1991a, 93) and on fostering the "common good" by making a number of aspects of a population's life the subject of scrutiny and intervention. In the 1990s the language of governance colonized discourses of democracy, peace, and development. By focusing on institutional reforms as the key for social change, "good governance" doctrines internationalize reflexive and governmentalized modalities for governing disorder.[1] The trajectories along which "good governance" organizes and orients policy are three-fold: the focus on institutional reforms, based on the belief that they are

---

1. Philippe Schmitter has called governance a doctrine, as it does not constitute a structured philosophy (Schmitter 1997).

THREE

the engine for social change; the promotion of mechanisms of rule aimed at fostering predictable, efficient, and regulatory administrations within states; and the proliferation, at the national and international level, of regulatory mechanisms and monitoring instruments for steering performance. In times of proliferating threats, where total control of variables becomes impossible, international security is sought through techniques aimed at reducing risk and increasing predictability through the normalization of potentially dangerous actors. Governmentality is imagined as a multifaceted and universally valid technique of rule. However, despite its apparent anodyne neutrality and strict technicality, good governance fosters the formation of oppositional identities between the orderly space of the civilized and the unpredictable and obscure borderlands of the uncivilized. In order to maintain order and prevent the proliferation of international unrest, the perpetrators of the latter need to be tamed, made visible and regularized through processes aimed at reforming the way local governments govern their citizens.

CONCEPTUALIZING DEMOCRACY IN A GOVERNANCE FRAMEWORK: THE UN DEBATE IN THE 1990S

In the post–Cold War era, in response to increasing requests to intervene in democratization initiatives spanning from electoral assistance to peacekeeping operations with a strong component of institution building, the UN developed an intensive debate about its role in fostering democracy.[2] This debate included and translated, with various emphases, ideas

---

2. Beginning in 1988 an increasing number of UN member states showed interest in public discussions of democratization. In the 1990s UN involvement in prodemocracy activities drastically increased. While interventions in democratization had been carried out before, the number of requests for electoral assistance submitted to the UN climbed from seven between 1989 and 1992 to a total of eighty-nine by June 1995. By the year 2000, 50 percent of UNDP resources were allocated to governance programs, including public sector reforms, institutional strengthening, leadership development, and empowering the poor through strengthening civil society organizations (UN General Assembly 2001c). The number of peacekeeping operations mandated to the UN also increased after the end of the Cold War: two-thirds of the total of peacekeeping operations set up since 1948 were established after 1991 (UN General Assembly 2001a). Peacekeeping mandates reflected the general interest in democracy as a means for making and maintaining peace. They broadened to include democratization, rebuilding of state administrations, reestablishment of public services, and performance of state functions in the tasks of UN "complex" peacekeeping operations and "transitional administrations." In these "complex" peacekeeping operations, military forces are just one component of diverse international personnel mandated with creating new institutions.

of democracy and good governance elaborated in different schools of thought. Very broadly speaking, the Western debate about democracy developed along the lines of three traditions: liberal, republican, and socialist. While often merging and intermingling, these traditions privilege different views of what defines a just and democratic society and propose different ways for achieving it. The liberal tradition's main concern is with negative rights, such as the abstention of political authority from economic affairs and the protection of individual liberty from its interference. The republican and the socialist traditions, on the other hand, link democracy to a certain set of citizens' duties and to states' intervention to secure a certain degree of basic goods and services. However, the latter traditions differ in their understanding of how a just and democratic society can be achieved. The republican tradition concerns itself with issues of participation and consensus. The socialist tradition (in its various forms) shares with the republican one the idea that the common good is the result of social processes. However, it maintains that equality is central and privileges economic reforms over political deliberation as the means of achieving it.

"Good governance" doctrines originated within the Anglo-American neoliberal critique of the interventionist welfare state, but governance, like democracy, has acquired different meanings and has been discussed in different contexts. R. A. W. Rhodes identified at least six uses of "governance": the minimal state, corporate governance, the new public management, "good governance," socio-cybernetic systems, and self-organizing networks (Rhodes 1996). The World Bank in particular played a central role in elaborating the notion of "good governance" as the political rationale for international organizations in the 1990s. The World Bank defines governance as "the manner in which power is exercised in the management of a country's economic and social resources for development" (World Bank 1992, 92). Good governance for the bank refers to efficiency in public service, rule of law with regard to contracts, an effective judiciary sector, respect for human rights, a free press, and a pluralistic institutional structure. The means for achieving these goals are marketization of public services, reducing public sector overstaffing, budgetary discipline, administrative decentralization, and participation of nongovernmental organizations (NGOs) (Rhodes 1996, 656).

The themes elaborated in different schools of thought about democracy and governance were translated with uneven emphases in the 1990s UN debate about the organization's role in promoting democratization.

Between 1988 and 2003, five international conferences on democracy were organized with the support of the UN.[3] Starting in 1994, democracy was included in the agenda of the General Assembly under the item "Support by the United Nations System of the efforts of governments to promote and consolidate new or restored democracies."[4] However, it was only starting in 1997, with Secretary-General Kofi Annan,[5] that the debate on democratization became a debate on "good governance." Good governance also became the organizing concept for UN interventions in diverse fields, the key for achieving not only democracy but also development and peace. The attempt to reform the Haitian penal institutions according to the imaginary of the Enlightenment, and to make the Croatian government work according to the Copenhagen criteria, exemplifies the application of this political rationale.

The most comprehensive text produced by Secretary-General Boutros-Boutros Ghali on democracy, known as the Agenda for Democratization, includes ideas derived from the three Western traditions of democratic thought and exposes many conundrums regarding the definition and foundations of democracy, its relations to peace and development, and the role of the UN system in bringing it about.[6] The report reprises the

---

3. These conferences saw a growing participation of states, international organizations, and representatives of "civil society." Their final declarations became official documents of the United Nations and provided backgrounds and themes for the reports of the secretary-general to the General Assembly. The first conference was held in Manila, Philippines, in June 1988 and the second in Managua, Nicaragua, on 4–6 July 1994. The findings and recommendations were forwarded to the secretary-general of the United Nations via a letter from the permanent representative of Nicaragua to the United Nations (UN General Assembly 1994a). The third conference was held in Bucharest, Romania, on 2–4 September 1997. The findings and recommendations were forwarded to the secretary-general as a Note Verbale from the permanent representative of Romania to the United Nations, addressed to the secretary-general (UN General Assembly 1997b). The fourth conference was held in Cotonou, Benin, 4–6 December 2000, and its outcomes were forwarded to the secretary-general as a letter from the permanent representative of Benin to the United Nations addressed to the secretary-general (UN General Assembly 2001c). The fifth conference was held in Ulaanbatar, Mongolia, 18–20 June 2003, and its outcomes were forwarded to the secretary-general as a letter from the permanent representative of Mongolia to the United Nations addressed to the secretary-general (UN General Assembly 2003b).

4. In 1994, following the Plan of Action of the Second International Conference on New and Restored Democracies in Managua, the General Assembly requested that the secretary-general discuss how the UN system could support democratization. See UN General Assembly (1996b).

5. Secretary-General Kofi Annan presented the reports to the General Assembly under the agenda item "Support by the United Nations System of the Efforts of Governments to Promote and Consolidate New or Restored Democracies"; see UN General Assembly (1997c, 1998, 1999a, 2000a, and 2001b).

6. Former secretary-general Boutros Boutros-Ghali produced three reports and a letter to the General Assembly called "Support by the United Nations System of the Efforts of

liberal emphasis on electoral processes and institutions but also includes socialist and republican concerns about the relations between economic equality and participation. It identifies the "popular will" of specific societies as the terrain within which democracy must be rooted and yet considers democratization a universal goal and the task of international organizations. It indicates that development can be achieved without democracy, yet it considers democracy a fundamental component of sustainable development. It establishes a connection between democracy and international peace, but it also argues that democratization at the state level cannot be attained without the democratization of the international system. In summary, the Agenda for Democratization attempts to keep together and blend divergent traditions of thought and approaches to democracy. In doing so, it produces the effect of exposing the many aporias and difficulties connected with making democracy the task of international organizations.

The year 1997 marks a sea change in the way the UN elaborated its approach to democracy and its role in democratization. The newly elected secretary-general, Kofi Annan, in the first report on the issue of democracy he presented to the General Assembly, established a new starting point and clearly selected "governance" as the central organizing concept for all UN system activities regarding democracy (UN General Assembly 1997c). The conundrums embedded in debating the UN role in democratization along the lines of normative approaches were bypassed by elaborating the organizations' task as a series of techniques for optimizing institutional arrangements. This new thinking was widely accepted, according to the secretary-general, at the Third International Conference on New or Restored Democracies and Development, held in Bucharest in September 1997,[7] and the International Conference for Sustainable Growth and Equity organized by the UNDP in July of the same year. Furthermore, in the early 1990s the UNDP had already started a reflection on good governance and its role in fostering development.[8]

Governments to Promote and Consolidate New or Restored Democracies"; see UN General Assembly (1995b, 1996b, and 1996c).

7. At the Bucharest conference, in which eighty governmental delegations participated, "good governance" was accepted as "a major driving force of development" and as the organizing concept for international cooperation in peace-building and democratization.

8. "The year 1990 marked a milestone, with the presentation of the first UNDP annual report on the worldwide situation of human development in the world. . . . Since then, the relationships and dependencies between political systems and their capacities to establish consistent paths towards human development have become increasingly apparent. In this

Good governance emerged as the result of a critical revision of theories that considered economic factors as the main components of development. These include the "trickle down" theories of the 1960s, the "basic need" approaches of the 1970s, and the "structuralist" approaches of the 1980s. For the UNDP, the failure of all these approaches is due to the fact that they did not take into account the political dimension of development. Underdevelopment was now blamed on institutional malfunctioning, and the central concern of the UNDP to tackle the issue was the modernization of the institutions of the state.[9] In this framework the central assumption of "reflexive government," which sees in institutional reforms the main engine for social change, became not only a rationale guiding domestic governments' transformations but also the key tool for promoting economic development globally.

The 1997 UNDP-led conference on Sustainable Growth and Equity summarized key tenets of the governance framework (UNDP 1997). The emphases on institutions and on the regulatory character of government are central in this approach. A well-functioning state occupies a key role in development. Good governance—understood as "rule of law, predictable administrations, legitimate power and responsive regulation"—is vital in this endeavor. However, for the UNDP the task of the state is not to intervene directly in the provision of services, but to perform regulatory functions and develop instead an "enabling framework" for private investors and service providers. Downsizing the state and making it a regulatory and supervisory agency is considered the way to bring about development.[10] The theme of the regulatory function of the state is quite recurrent in the UN elaborations. It is reprised, for example, in the 1998 secretary-general's report on the role of the organization in supporting new or restored democracies (UN General Assembly 1998). In acknowledging the World Bank's contribution to strengthening democratic institutions in new and restored democracies through programs of public sector reform, the UN secretary-general indicates that the role of states must

---

way, governance became one of the most important tools for facilitating human development" (UNDP n.d., 5).

9. In the UNDP's words, "Latin American underdevelopment has characteristics of institutional atrophy and suborganization and institutional development can, therefore, give impetus to the closing of these gaps" (UNDP n.d., 10).

10. "Reviving growth entails downsizing the state and ensuring the independence of those institutions necessary to create the foundations for sustained economic growth. This includes institutions to ensure a sound monetary management and to secure property rights and contracts, as well as an effective judicial system" (UNDP 1997, 5).

change from providers of services into regulatory bodies, whose main function must be to enable the market and "civil society" to thrive.[11] The promotion of "regulatory states" becomes central in internationally led programs of democratization. Fostering these modalities of government constitutes, in the perspective of governance doctrines, the means for bettering disorderly states, facilitating development, and improving people's life conditions.

Good governance is a global project of state engineering that addresses—but does not limit itself to—state institutions. It also promotes programs of diffused institutionalization of social processes. The UN describes activities in this regard as "empowering civil society." These activities aim at facilitating the building of a number of institutions (NGOs, parties, interest groups, etc.) that are meant to collect citizens' demands and rechannel them to the center, as well as to provide social services. This process leads to a capillary diffusion into the social body of institutional mechanisms, a proliferation of codified processes, and a standardization of information so that social demands can be channeled, understood, and processed by governing centers.[12] Population, which in classical Europe became a central concern of government, becomes now a concern for international organizations. The engineering of a regulatory, governmentalized state is necessary in order to improve people's lives as well as the predictability of the international arena. This endeavor includes constructing what has to be governed (be they "rogue" states or populations within their borders) in such a way that it can be regulated and known by calculation centers (be they states or international organizations). Disseminating institutions able to channel social demands in such a way that they are at the same time orderly, readable, and manageable by the center is part of a project that aims at making obscure

11. "The effort here is to help countries to redefine the role of the State, moving from a heavily interventionist paradigm to one in which the State's main function is to provide an enabling environment in which both the market economy and civil society can flourish[;] . . . the challenge is to reform the core systems of government, such as budgeting and financial management, the civil service, procurement, records management and cabinet processes. A special thrust has been decentralization, helping countries to define the functions best carried out by subordinate tiers of government, and to create a clear framework of fiscal responsibilities and limits" (UN General Assembly 1998).

12. "A vibrant civil society is the key to a successful democratization process. Without the participation and active contribution of the citizens to social life, a true democracy cannot grow and prosper. Promotion of public participation and the formulation of well-informed public opinion are essential in the process of consolidation of democracy and the maintenance of democratic values" (UN General Assembly 1997c).

borderlands (be they "noncivilized" states or transborder areas that escape government) visible, transparent, and simplified. Good governance, like Foucault's governmentalized government, multiplies instruments for knowing populations and transforming indistinct masses into "civil societies." It promotes plural yet capillary and widespread mechanisms for knowing, ordering, and calculating unregulated and indistinct spaces.

The secretary-general underscored the comprehensive character of good governance endeavors:

> Good governance is effective, participatory, transparent, accountable and equitable and promotes the rule of law. Governance is led by the State, but transcends it by collaborating with the private sector and civil society. All three domains are critical for sustaining human development. The state creates a conducive political, economic and legal environment. The private sector generates jobs and income, and civil society facilitates political and social interaction and mobilizes groups to participate in economic, social and political activities. (UN General Assembly 1997c, para. 17)

Originated within a neoliberal school of thought, "good governance" prescribes much more than liberal political arrangements. As with La Perriere's government, good governance prescribes tools to achieve the "right disposition of things" with regard to an array of areas of social life. It is a plural and issue-oriented managerial activity expected to act at all levels (domestic and international) in order to bring about a smoothly functioning social machine and an orderly international arena.

In addition to being imagined as plural and comprehensive, good governance is thought to be universal. The methods of government it proposes are considered to be valid across borders and in all situations. Public management techniques can find useful application in all countries, regardless of local differences, and offer standardized solutions to an array of different problems. The UNDP indicates, "Although starting points of countries in terms of economic development are different, the same modern tools for public management are applicable in all countries."[13] A mix of consensus, coercion, and surveillance needs to be used to convince states to undertake prescribed reforms: "The context for implementation will be through policy dialogue with individual member States, effective systemic surveillance and international cooperation, and capacity building to

13. Statement attributed to Ruth Richardson, former minister of finance, New Zealand (UNDP 1997, 5).

enhance economic, financial and administrative institutions" (UN General Assembly 1997c, para. 57). In other words, good governance is to be imposed on reluctant followers through an array of disciplinary instruments.

Good governance does not only constitute the rationale for transforming troubled states into democracies and for engineering good societies. It also constitutes the driving concept for UN reforms. In addition to recommending reforms aimed at building predictable, regulated, and regulatory states and administrable societies, the UN had to equip itself with the instruments for knowing, assessing, and steering the behavior of states and become an effective "calculation center" and performance-monitoring agency.[14] Programs for reform were extensively discussed both in the 1997 and the 1998 secretary-general reports to the General Assembly (UN General Assembly 1997c, 1998). In January 1997 "four Executive Committees were created. . . . Peace and security, economic and social affairs, development cooperation, and humanitarian affairs, with . . . human rights, designated as cutting across the first four and thus participating in all of them." Furthermore, the Subgroup on Capacity Building for Governance of the UN Administrative Coordination Committee in which nineteen UN organizations participated was established under the chairmanship of the UNDP. As recommended in Bucharest, a mechanism was also created to follow up on the implementation of the conference's recommendations regarding UN democratization activities. Furthermore, the secretary-general emphasized the importance of organizing and disseminating information about "programs directed at consolidating democratic development," and he stressed sharing "the progress made by each participating country towards democratization" (UN General Assembly 1998, para. 7). Items of concern were the creation of tools for comparing and assessing states' behavior with regard to international prescriptions on governance and democratization. These include a Web site on democratization and governance managed by the UNDP and the Department of Social and Economic Affairs, the development of an inventory of databases pertaining to democratization, and the creation of a self-assessment system for governments in the process of democratization. The report also emphasized the need for databases and information systems on aggregate debts and loan services. In this regard, the United Nations Conference on Trade and Development put in place

14. Proposals in this regard were also outlined in UN General Assembly (1997a).

its "Debt Management and Financial Analysis System" covering forty countries and representing more than 25 percent of the outstanding debt of developing countries.

UN-sponsored projects of data collection and standardization do not only constitute the basis for external scrutiny and audit of performance. They also provide each government with the tools for self-assessment with regard to its achievement of internationally set benchmarks.[15] As with the patients of Foucauldian clinical institutions, disorderly states' individual performance (or path to sanity) is monitored and assessed in comparison to a given population, on a scale from normality to deviancy. Each "patient" or disorderly state is normalized in a process that is both standardizing and individualizing. It is standardizing because the final goal is the achievement of standards of behavior that are the same for all. It is individualizing because each state that does not conform to international criteria is given means and tools for self-improvement specifically designed to fit its case.

The Millennium Declaration, adopted by the General Assembly in the year 2000, constituted a new context for discussing democratization and governance. The declaration established values, goals, and commitments for member states in order to improve "the lot of humanity in the new century" (UN General Assembly 2000b). The fundamental values included in the declaration are freedom, equality, solidarity, tolerance, respect of nature, and shared responsibility. The Millennium Declaration's goals encompass a broad range of issue areas and cover a vast number of aspects of human life: peace, security, and disarmament; environmental protection; human rights, democracy, and good governance; protecting the vulnerable; meeting the special needs of Africa; and strengthening the UN. The adoption of the Millennium Declaration entailed three effects in the United Nations' discussion about democracy and good governance. First, it brought back into light issues and languages that had been set aside after the Agenda for Democratization. It also provided the background for broadening the fields and issue areas to which the governance approach applies. Finally, it introduced the focus on populations and the risk management idioms that became the key organizing guidelines for secretary-general Kofi Annan's proposals for reconceptualizing collective security.

15. The World Bank has established an online interactive database that makes it possible to compare states' performance with regard to a series of "good governance" indicators (see World Bank 2009).

The 2001 secretary-general report to the General Assembly (UN General Assembly 2001b) reprised a number of controversial matters and anticipated some of the themes that Kofi Annan further developed in his 2005 proposals for UN reform (UN General Assembly 2005a). The 2001 report extensively discussed the outcomes and final declaration of the Fourth Conference of New and Restored Democracies, known as the Cotonou Declaration (UN General Assembly 2001c). In Cotonou, many delegations focused more on the foundations of democracy and its connection to rights, participation, and economic factors than on institutional reforms and forms of government. Concerns proper to the republican and socialist traditions, such as the need for democracy to guarantee a set of positive rights, were brought back into the debate. Conference participants emphasized that democracy "requires the gradual expansion of political space in order to guarantee the full exercise of the political, economic, social and cultural rights" (UN General Assembly 2001b, para. 7). Poverty and its local and international causes, to include the inequity of markets and the burden of foreign debts, were listed among the main obstacles to the consolidation of democracy. Connections between democracy and the rights of the vulnerable, such as "women, children and minorities," were also addressed. Echoing republican ideas reflected in the Agenda for Democratization, the report indicates that there is no universally valid recipe for democracy; instead, democracy must reflect the "culture, history, and political experience of its citizens." The secretary-general also underscored that indicators of efficiency of state administrations are not sufficient criteria for assessing democracy. However, notwithstanding previous statements about the local roots of democratic consensus, the secretary-general, in line with a liberal framework, asserts that it is possible to identify universal benchmarks for democracy: "The benchmark for a sustainable democracy is the extent to which a State acts in accordance with universal and indivisible human rights: the civil and political rights as well as the economic, social and cultural rights defined in international humanitarian law" (UN General Assembly 2001b, para. 27).

Notwithstanding this reproblematization in normative terms of themes regarding democracy, governance remains the main framework for translating democratization in operational programs and the main tool for achieving the goals of the Millennium Declaration. The road map for the implementation of the UN Millennium Declaration restates the fundamental role of "democratic governance" in this regard (UN General

Assembly 2001a). The secretary-general's report to the Economic and Social Council in 2002 also emphasizes the centrality of reforming government institutions for the implementation of the Millennium Declaration:

> Because governments play such a central role in the realization of the goals contained in the Millennium Declaration, developing their capabilities and effectiveness can not be stressed enough. There are repeated references in the Declaration and road map report to good governance and democracy, including improved capacity for public service delivery of basic social services, public administration reform, integrated planning, increased citizen participation in decision making, decentralization, transparency, accountability and combating corruption. (UN General Assembly and Economic and Social Council 2002)

Indeed, "state capacity deficits, weak political democratic institutions and inefficient and badly run public administrations" are identified as the main causes for the problems of developing countries (UN General Assembly and Economic and Social Council 2002). Common good can be achieved through all-encompassing and plural projects aimed at reengineering state institutions, the private sector, and civil society:

> Governance refers to the exercise of not only political but also economic and administrative authority in the management of a country's affairs at all levels. It encompasses and transcends the state to include the private sector and civil society organizations. As such, governance refers to the ability to manage the economy, mobilize resources, ensure a degree of social justice, promote an enabling environment for individual pursuits, as well as ensuring peace and security. (UN General Assembly and Economic and Social Council 2002)

The linkages between governance, security, and development were widely addressed in the context of the discussions regarding the implementation of the Millennium Declaration's goals.[16] The areas of application of "reflexive government" as a modality for steering international processes and as the engine for guiding social change were extended and spelled out in detail in this context. The connection between promoting

16. For instance, they were discussed in the secretary-general's report to the Economic and Social Council of June 1999 (UN Economic and Social Council 1999) and in secretary-general reports to the General Assembly in 1999, 2000, and 2001 (UN General Assembly

institutional reforms and maintaining peace and security was reinforced, as well as the centrality of democratization in new types of peacekeeping operations. In his August 2002 report to the General Assembly and to the Economic and Social Council on the Role of Public Administration in Implementing the Millennium Declaration, the secretary-general identified social injustice and the failure of governance institutions and public administration systems as the major causes of violent conflict. While social injustice is not debated further, the report comments extensively on the role of institutional reforms in maintaining peace. "Reinforcing institutions that ensure the peaceful coexistence of all social forces within a given polity" is vital for conflict prevention. Governance has a key role to play in peace building as well. In the secretary-general's words, "In post-violence situations the re-establishment of public administration and governance systems is a sine qua non for the building of sustainable peace" (UN General Assembly and Economic and Social Council 2002, para. 8–9).

The role of institutional reforms in bringing about development and justice is also debated in the August 2002 report. Law making and well-functioning administrations are preconditions for the implementation of the goals regarding development and poverty eradication. In this context, "strengthening legislative bodies and ensuring that they are based on an efficient administration is of the utmost importance since they serve as the main forums for reaching agreements and formulating concrete solutions to compelling problems" (UN General Assembly and Economic and Social Council 2002, para. 10). Developing electoral management institutions and mechanisms is important for creating accountable legislative bodies. "Decentralization" is "crucial to reduction of poverty as it allows citizens to voice their demands in a more efficient way and to be active partners in all stages of policy decision, implementation and evaluation." Furthermore, an efficient public administration, able to ensure the provision of basic services such as water, health, and education, is central to alleviating poverty (para. 13). Reforming the administration of justice is equally crucial for protecting the human rights of the vulnerable and for avoiding the "insecurity" and "discouragement of long-term investments" caused by corruption (para. 12).

1999a, 2000a, and 2001b), and they also constituted the topic of the Fourth International Conference of New and Restored Democracies, held in Cotonou, Benin, in December 2000 (UN General Assembly 2001c).

After reemphasizing the connections between governance, peace, human rights, poverty alleviation, and economic development, the report suggests an array of areas for international assistance. The areas of intervention identified (human resources, financial capacity, information, innovation, and technology capacity) are mostly of a technical nature and aim at optimizing institutional performance. Efficiency is of central concern in this regard. In order to implement the goals of the Millennium Declaration, states need financial resources. The secretary-general notes, "The problem that many developing countries face is not only how to generate more resources, but how to ensure that resources are spent efficiently." The secretary-general concludes that "in times of scarcity of financial resources efficiency can hardly be overestimated as a modality for getting more done with fewer resources" (UN General Assembly and Economic and Social Council 2002, para. 18). International organizations must therefore assist in improving effective administrative arrangements, in particular with regard to tax collection.

Notwithstanding its focus on optimization of institutional functioning, the secretary-general's report hints once again at the irreducibility of politics to institutional optimization and indicates that there are elements of the political sphere that escape administrative reforms. The secretary-general underscores that the application of modern techniques of financial management cannot be effective unless the process is accompanied by political will. However, the report does not further problematize the connections between technical reforms and political will. Instead, it continues by commenting on the troubles caused by technical weakness: "Experience shows that most technical weaknesses of the public financial management relate to untimely and inaccurate government accounting; budget review processes hampered by the lack of information; lack of modern methods of data management; highly routine rules that stress control; and inadequate training" (UN General Assembly and Economic and Social Council 2002, para. 20).

Optimizing techniques of financial management is not only a way of improving government in disorderly states. Instead, it is necessary in order to foster recipient states' accountability to external lenders and to improve the international capability of assessing and monitoring the use of funds. In this regard, the secretary-general underscores the weaknesses of government administrations in managing projects funded from abroad and the need to develop "new partnership mechanisms and effective accountability systems to oversee those who participate in these new partnership arrangements" (UN General Assembly and Economic and Social Council 2002, para. 20).[17] Optimization of outcomes is the result of efficient and harmonized performance-monitoring techniques, such as budgeting, auditing, and accounting: "Public financial management relates to the process of planning, programming and budgeting; budget execution and accounting; as well as auditing and evaluation of public resources. These government functions are aimed at ensuring that, to the maximum practical extent, the public resources—whether generated internally or externally—are utilized in accordance to the law and yield optimum results" (para. 20). These techniques emphasize "explicit standards and measures of performance, stress . . . greater discipline and control over resources use and . . . private sector style of management practices" (para. 20).

The instruments of government prescribed in "good governance" frameworks endeavor to make territory and population visible to governments, and illuminate the deeds of governments to international organizations and financial institutions. Good governance doctrines prescribe the multiplication both at the domestic and at the international level of instruments for knowing, assessing, and steering what has to be governed (auditing techniques, standardized data collection, performance indicators, etc.), with a view to bringing about at once democratization, development, and international security as part of a comprehensive and global project of governmentalization.

GOVERNANCE EFFECTS

This analysis of the UN debate on democracy in the 1990s has shown that different Western traditions of thought coexisted at the UN.[18] Liberal orientations emphasizing electoral mechanisms accompany the emphasis on cultural or participatory aspects of a more republican flavor. In some

17. Issues of financial management for developing countries were also discussed at the International Conference on Financing for Development held in Monterrey in 2002 (see UN 2002).

18. Oliver Richmond's exploration of liberal peace has shown that it contains various epistemological and ontological strands of Western tradition, that is, "a normative understanding of how peace would probably be in terms of a universal moral order . . . a positivist strand that seeks to create a basic level order through scientific investigation. . . . It also claims to contain a post-positivist strand, focusing on emancipation from hegemony" (2005, 209).

cases even the socialist tradition's concern with economic equality is included in the organizational concerns. However, a dominant framework emerged at the end of the 1990s: governance became the organizing concept for a wide range of UN activities in the fields of democracy, development, peace, and security.

As a discursive practice, governance elicits specific problematizations and solutions. As the political rationale for international organization programs, governance entails political effects worth exploring. Governance doctrines are at the same time internationalist and statist. They are internationalist because they foster standardized systems of control, monitoring mechanisms, and governing from a distance by international organizations. They are statist because they maintain that governments are in control of most variables within their territory. In this framework, development can be framed as a mostly internal problem. Its causes are not to be researched in the international economic order, capital concentrations, or distribution of wealth but mainly in the inappropriate functioning of the institutions of less-developed states.[19] If development is a responsibility of states' governments, the path to it is not marked by structural reforms of the international economic order, but by the reformation of bad governments.

Furthermore, "good governance" brings to its ultimate consequences liberal approaches to democracy. Both the UN secretariat and the UNDP emphasized the centrality for "good governance" of civil society participation. Nevertheless, participation, in this view, does not pertain to the process by which institutions are created and from which they draw their legitimacy, as in Habermas's republican emphasis on political debate (Habermas 1996). On the contrary, participation is seen as the outcome of technical interventions, aimed at optimizing state institutions and promoting capillary institutionalization of social processes. Classical

---

19. The assumption by which a government is in control of most variables within its territorial state has been called by James Ferguson a principle of "governmentality." In his analysis of the "development discourse" in the 1970s, Ferguson argued that "governmentality" was one of the main tenets of development theories. By representing the economy of a country as self-contained and under the control of government planning, the principle of governmentality created representations that made it possible for international institutions to work toward the results they promised. For Ferguson, these approaches are blind to internal politics and therefore have the effect of depoliticizing the state. In Ferguson's words, "Because government is the tool for planning and implementing economic and social policy, representations which ignore the political character of the state and the bureaucracy and downplay political conflicts within the nation-state are the most powerful" (Ferguson 1994, 74). The use Ferguson makes of the term "governmentality" is different from the one I have proposed in this book.

liberalism tended to identify democracy with a number of institutional arrangements. Participation and the exercise of political rights are, from this perspective, understood as the automatic outcomes of such institutional arrangements. "Good governance" extends institutionalization to a broader range of applications. Effective institutions are understood as the key to the "common good" and are expected to bring about peace, political liberties, and substantive rights. This framework favors top-down approaches to democratization, where participation is seen as the outcome of universally valid institutional design and standardized techniques of government.

"Good governance" constructs both states and the international arena as governmentalized spaces. As it is testified in the UN debate, good governance doctrines promote institutional arrangements that foster the reorganization of an array of local practices into administrable varieties; they promote the collection of capillary and standardized data and the codification of a plurality of rules and regulations aimed at knowing and steering aspects of a population's life; and they promote instruments and techniques in the hands of international organizations to assess, reward, or punish the behaviors of governments with regard to fields that were previously considered to be within states' sovereign jurisdiction. Reengineering institutions, fostering productivity, improving the life of the population (the "common good"), developing numerical *savoirs* and standardized representations, and expanding regulations and instruments for monitoring and assessing performance both within states and at the international level are all modalities of conduct of conduct predicated in the "good governance" discourse and implemented in international organizations' policies.

By attempting to make the international arena a "calculated space," international organizations endeavor to assess the deeds of each government with regard to internationally set benchmarks, to compare its "performance" to that of others, and to make decisions about rewards and punishments (such as the inclusion or exclusion from international structures or the allocation of international funds) based upon "measurable" and "objective" criteria. The international arena, similarly to civil society through the "science of police," is constituted as a field of knowledge and political intervention. Its elements are expected to act as "good governments" or democracies. Democracies must foster the well-being of their populations and maximize their health and wealth, and their deeds in this regard are subject to the scrutiny and correctional initiatives of international organizations. States became the subject of international scrutiny and reformation efforts aimed at making them function as "governments" instead of as uncontrolled "sovereigns" (in the Foucauldian understanding) and at making them the visible and predictable actors of a normalized international space.

Governance translates the abstract and controversial notion of democracy into a plurality of technical problems and issue-specific programs of institutional reform. This is an operational virtue that makes this framework appealing for international organizations concerned about the political neutrality and soundness of their programs. Peace is imagined as governance (Richmond 2005, 184), and governance is presented as an apolitical, technically sound, and universally valid endeavor; democracy can be delinked from the political debate and associated with good management procedures. Good governance is a capacious concept that creates consensus around matters that would otherwise remain politically controversial.[20] It provides the UN with a framework and a neutral technical language for addressing a wide range of issues and operationalizing diverse interventions. Notwithstanding its apparent anodyne technical neutrality, governance discourse extensively uses value-loaded metaphors and dichotomies, and reinforces oppositional identities. It aims to create visibility out of obscurity, transparency out of opacity, accountability out of corruption, efficiency out of redundancy, effectiveness out of aimlessness, rights out of abuses, rule of law out of unpredictability. The international arena is thus divided between the orderly space of the civilized and the unpredictable, obscure borderlands of the uncivilized. Indeed, some of the current themes of democratization and good governance show many similarities with elaborations of the "civilizing mission" that, according to Michael Adas, was embedded in the European colonial enterprise (Adas 1989). This enterprise was expected to bring peace and order, overthrow despotism and corruption, bring about fair taxation, improve populations' income, and foster productivity. For Adas the underlying assumption was that Europeans were the best possible rulers and represented the most advanced civilization. However, while the nineteenth-century *idée coloniale* was based on the idea of technological superiority, twentieth-century "good governance" is

---

20. See Schmitter (1997). Scott has found a similar capaciousness in Taylorism, another early twentieth-century technocratic discourse: "The vision of society in which social conflict was eliminated in favor of technological and scientific imperatives could embrace liberal, socialist, authoritarian, and even communist and fascist solutions" (Scott 1998, 99).

based on the superiority of Western forms of government and their adaptability to all societies. As Oliver Richmond aptly put it, "The liberal peace is unable to communicate across cultures, rests upon a legalistic framework, disassociates law from norms, rests upon preserving the pre-existing liberal order, and claims a problematic universality" (Richmond 2008, 150).

Metaphors of civilization and techniques of government that emerged in the West long before the end of the twentieth century converge in the discourse of governance to bring about a project of international security based on the creation of democratic and well-functioning states. The international arena, which during the Cold War was divided along the lines of the East and West, is now divided along the lines of the metropolitan, civilized world and disorderly borderlands. Democratization in a good governance framework becomes the means for reducing the risk posed by "disorderly" states and the "rogue" actors they are believed to harbor by making their processes of government more readable and codified, and for making obscure borderlands visible and predictable. These discourses open the way for the subjectification of states that do not embrace Western forms of democracy not only as inefficient but also as morally abject (in a scale from "corrupt" to "moral monsters"). As the next chapter will show, in the new millennium, the convergence of discourses of security, democracy, and development produces new ways of legitimizing international intervention in the name of the moral duty of ensuring "human security."

FOUR

ESTABLISHING A GLOBAL BIOPOLITICAL ORDER
Managing Risk, Protecting Populations,
Blurring Spaces of Governance

INTRODUCTION

At the beginning of the new millennium, the organizing concept for collective security shifted from "good governance" to "human security" and the responsibility to protect populations. While in the 1990s the points of application for the international government of insecurity were mostly state institutions, after the beginning of the new millennium populations and their well-being became the direct referent of collective security. The post–Cold War international security regime became increasingly biopolitical. As we have seen previously, biopolitics for Foucault designates a development of the managerial inclination of government, which applies primarily to populations, focuses on maintaining the equilibrium of processes of living together, and intensifies the development of an array of *savoirs* and regulatory mechanisms targeting life. New millennium discourses of security made populations central, both as victims and as

Sections of this chapter have been republished with minor modifications from Laura Zanotti, "Managing Risk, Protecting Populations, Blurring Spaces of Governance: Kofi Annan's Vision for a UN-Led Collective Security System in the New Millennium," in *The United Nations: Past, Present, and Future,* ed. Scott Kaufman and Alissa Warters, 1–13 (New York: Nova Science, 2009), with permission from Nova Science Publishers, Inc.

perpetrators of menace. In the face of the failure of the democratization efforts of the 1990s to bring about peace and development, and after the 9/11 attacks refocused the attention on nonstate actors as sources of threat, risk management became the increasingly accepted framework for organizing collective security. As noted above, for Beck (1992), risk demands a knowledge-intensive, holistic, and preventative approach. A variety of issue areas that were previously considered distinct, and whose linkage to international security was not firmly established—such as poverty, disease, and environmental degradation—converged into collective security discourses to form the new millennium political rationality for the UN. Vulnerability became an important analytical category that straddled conflict and development; protecting people was adopted as the legitimizing principle for international intervention when other means of normalization through institutional reform failed or were considered impracticable.

Dillon and Reid (2009) have shown that the biopolitical trajectory of liberal security is linked to the reconfiguration of the epistemic space of interpretations of politics along the lines of paradigms developed in biological and information science. Since Darwin, living entities have been reconceived not as fixed and self-contained, but as mobile and mutable. Living entities are contingent, and the laws that govern their appearance are not "causal" but "probabilistic." In this paradigm, change cannot be extrapolated with certainty from previous patterns (Dillon and Reid 2009, 60). For Dillon and Reid the reconceptualization of the international arena along the lines of a biological system endowed with morphogenic capabilities leads to a "hyperbolicization of security" aimed at exterminating those deviant forms of life that might emerge as a result of contingent mutations (2009, 85). While Dillon and Reid provide extremely useful insights on the linkages between scientific epistemologies, the construction of discourses of danger, and the practices of liberal security, the representation of the liberal project as a "will to kill" oversimplifies its complexities. The theoretical and empirical analysis conducted here shows that the most distinctive trait of post–Cold War ways of governing international disorder is not its will to eliminate deviant forms of life in order to protect the survival of the species, but the taming of the emergence of risk through the normalization of abnormal elements. While the annihilation of the unruly and the untamed is always looming as a possibility (which is indeed reinforced by the conceptualization of security as prevention), the most distinctive trait of liberal international government of disorder is the carcerialization of international order through the coupling of correction and coercion. Ultimately, violence and the annihilation of the enemy are modalities that liberal orders share with illiberal ones. What is distinctive of the liberal political imaginary is that the use of force is considered an extreme (and, taken alone, not very effective) dimension of a broader project of normalization enacted through the assemblage of a variety of disciplinary, normalizing, and coercive tools aimed at resubjectifying the "rogues" into "civilized" members of (international) communities. In the liberal imaginary, the use of force is connected to the intensification of correctional projects. These considerations do not imply that the liberal peace project is benign. They do, however, show its complexities and different strands and do not oversimplify its forms of operation by representing it as a homogenous and oppressive project of annihilation and extermination.[1]

The pages that follow explore, through a selection of UN documents, the intensification of the biopolitical trajectory of international security, the manner in which matters that were previously treated as separate converge into discourses of security, and the effects of these convergences for the legitimization of the use of force and traditional understandings of sovereignty. This chapter does not aim to elaborate a position on the ongoing debate of whether human security fosters the protection of the weak, or whether it reproduces and strengthens the power of the strong (see Bickerton, Cunliffe, and Gourevitch 2007; Chandler 2008; Duffield 2007; MacLean, Black, and Shaw 2006; Owen 2008; Paris 2001; Tadjbakhsh and Chenoy 2007; Thomas 2001).[2] My goal here is different and more limited. On the one hand, as mentioned above, I intend to map the modalities through which, in the new millennium, idioms that were originally dealt with as separate converged into discourses of security. On the other hand, I want to explore some of the consequences for the morphology of international power and for traditional conceptualizations of sovereignty when one shifts the referent of international security from the state system to populations. While focusing on populations, human security still relies on states as the primary providers of security (Duffield 2007) and emphasizes the need for intensifying governmental and disciplinary mechanisms of normalization through institution

---

1. For a critique of these representations of the liberal project, see also chapter 6.

2. The literature on human security is huge, and its complete review is beyond the scope of this work. For a recent debate on human security, see the special issue of *Security Dialogue* 39, no. 4 (2008).

building (Commission on Human Security 2003, 3). However, in the new millennium, the role of "good governance" and democracy in discourses of international security has changed. While no longer credible as the universal solution for all of humanity's problems, these political qualities became powerful markers of identity and legitimacy. Ultimately, they become the condition for the exertion of full sovereignty and for inclusion in supranational organizations (such as the EU). Human security articulates discourses of democracy and security into a political rationale that subjectifies nondemocratic governments as (actual or potential) political monsters, a bundle of threats within and outside their borders. The convergence of the lack of democracy and good government, abnormality, and moral aberration fosters a regrounding of the legitimization of intervention on moral rather than legal terms (Pupavac 2005). Thus, the legitimacy of coercive intervention on those who reject normalization—the political or moral monster-states that abuse or fail to protect their citizens—expands.

Human security marks the intensification, in the new millennium, of the carceral trajectory of the post–Cold War security regime, that is, a modality of rule that intensifies the connections between correction and coercion. Abnormal states, the "enemies of civilization" that escape predictability and rational behavior, must be transformed into a population of "delinquents," that is, into sources of threat that are the subject of a measured mix of scrutiny, correction, and coercion. Furthermore, human security fosters the redefinition of sovereignty along the lines of performance and blurs spaces of state and international governance that previously were, at least in principle, kept separate. Abjection and moral aberration open the way for a retheorization of sovereignty in terms of performance, and for endless practices of international government exerted through mechanisms of correction, coercion, or, as in the case of peacekeeping, a coupling of the two.

MANAGING RISK, PROTECTING PEOPLE, REENVISIONING SOVEREIGNTY

In a report titled *In Larger Freedom,* presented for approval at the World Summit, Kofi Annan made "the people" of the UN Charter's preamble the central referent and organizing concept for his vision of the reform of the organization (UN General Assembly 2005b). The UN charter included *in nuce* an aporia between the concept that the organization derived its legitimacy from the will of "we, the people" and the idea that state sovereignty constituted the outer limit to its intervention. In addition, three out of the four fundamental goals established in the charter's preamble concern bettering the life of the populace: "save succeeding generations from the scourge of war"; "reaffirm faith in fundamental human rights"; and "promote social progress and better standards of life in larger freedom." Only one of the four goals established here involves reinforcing respect for the legal international system. However, in Article 1, the charter refocuses on governments as the means for achieving the broader goals set forth in the preamble. Article 1 states that the UN's main purpose is to maintain peace and security through collective measures, develop friendly relations among nations, and promote international cooperation to solve *international* problems regarding "economic, social, cultural, or humanitarian character." Article 2.7 strongly reasserts sovereignty as the outer limit for UN intervention: "Nothing contained in the present Charter shall authorize the UN to intervene in matters which are essentially within the domestic jurisdiction of any state." In summary, notwithstanding the preamble's focus on populations, in the body of the UN charter, internal and international spaces of governance are kept distinct and are subject to different jurisdictions.

Kofi Annan's vision for UN reform harks back to the opening sentences of the preamble, that people are the ultimate source of legitimacy and the promotion of their better life the raison d'être of the organization. For Annan, while the UN is made up of sovereign states, international security means populations' security, and states play an important but instrumental role in achieving this security (UN General Assembly 2005b, annex, para. 2). In the case of states' incapacity or unwillingness to fulfill these functions, collective security organizations share the responsibility to protect populations, which includes, in the extreme cases of genocide or gross violations of human rights, forcible intervention.

For the former UN secretary-general, "larger freedom," the organizing concept for UN reform and a holistic project for bettering populations' life, is threefold. It includes "freedom from want, freedom from fear, and freedom to live in dignity." These aspects are inseparably linked and must be addressed together: "Progress in the areas of development, security and human rights must go hand in hand. There will be no development without security and no security without development. . . . And both development and security also depend on respect for human rights and the rule of law" (UN General Assembly 2005b, annex, para. 2).

In the new millennium, the security of humans became the organizing concept for the UN role. By redefining the referent of security from states to populations and threats in terms of risk and resilience, "human security" challenges conceptualizations based on "container" theories of society (Beck 2000), to emphasize dynamic interconnections and vulnerabilities. International security refocused on knowing and regulating populations' processes of living together in order to prevent danger, and biopolitics became a key trajectory of the international security regime.[3]

While many of the ideas put forth by Kofi Annan in *In Larger Freedom* are not original, the novelty of his approach lies in the systematic reorganization, under the umbrella of security, of discursive practices that were previously considered separate. Idioms that emerged in the context of UN debates about a variety of matters, including peacekeeping, disaster management, sustainable development, and gender, are now reorganized as part of a political rationale that intensifies international interventionism and biopolitical management of populations.

The discursive connections between the reduction of natural disaster risk and biopolitical techniques for the correct management of equilibrium among populations, economic growth, and natural resources was emphasized in UN policy documents regarding sustainable development. Agenda 21, issued from the 1992 Earth Summit (UNCED 1992), prescribed sustainable development as a way of reducing risk. By promoting a vision of development that takes into consideration people's well-being and the balance between economic growth and the exploitation of resources, sustainable development testifies to the migration at the international level of governmental tactics that focus on the "right disposition of things," arranged so as to lead to a convenient end (Foucault 1991a, 93), and of biopolitical modalities for maintaining the equilibrium of processes of living together. Before they became the organizing concepts for the reconceptualization of international security, the connection between correct strategies of development and the prevention of threats was underscored in the "Rio de Janeiro Platform for Action on the Road to Johannesburg" (UN ECLAC 2001). At the 2002 Johannesburg World Summit, the UN requested action for integrating disaster prevention considerations into sustainable development (UN General Assembly 2002a). Since the 1995 Beijing declaration, the problematic of gender was also included as part

3. The conceptualization of the international arena in terms of chaos was emphasized in the 1990s by U.S. policy makers across the political spectrum (see Luke and Ó Tuathail 1997).

of a holistic program of risk management through the fostering of women's proper exploitation of natural resources. The Declaration reads as follows: "Economic development, social development and environmental protection are interdependent and mutually reinforcing components of sustainable development. . . . Equitable social development that recognized empowering the poor, particularly women living in poverty, to utilize environmental resources sustainably is a necessary foundation for sustainable development" (UN General Assembly 1995a, Art. 36).

The notion of human security was also not new to the UN. Introduced in 1994 by the UNDP, human security is the result of six components: economic security, food and health security, environmental security, personal security, community security, and political security (UNDP 1994, 24). The idea that the responsibility for protecting populations was shared between states and international organizations and that this responsibility should be carried out through the intensification of instruments for knowing, assessing, and monitoring a multitude of factors affecting people's lives was spelled out in 1994 at the Yokohama conference on the prevention and management of natural disasters (UN 1994). The conference outcome document underscored that international institutions should promote knowledge; mobilize financial, scientific, and technological resources; and expand surveillance, information gathering, and dissemination. In the meantime, local governments and communities should assume the task of devising and implementing prevention strategies. The Yokohama document formulated its disaster prevention strategy in terms of shared vulnerability, a notion that in 2004 was adopted by the High-Level Panel on Change, Challenges, and Threat, nominated by Kofi Annan to devise the way ahead for collective security in the new millennium. The Yokohama document highlighted that vulnerability is mutual, uneven, and man-made. While disasters are natural, the level of impact they have on a specific community is largely the result of human activity (UN 1994). Relying on these debates, the 2004 UNDP report entitled *Reducing Risk: A Challenge for Development* provided a systematic reconceptualization of the problematic of development in terms of risk (UNDP 2004). The UNDP stressed the "multifaceted nature of risk" and emphasized that populations that are vulnerable to natural hazards are also vulnerable to hazards from other sources, such as economic or political forces. Economic globalization contributes to creating new geographies of risk. Uncontrolled urbanization and rural livelihood in marginal lands are two main factors of vulnerability. Globalization also entails the

respect the dignity and basic rights of the people within the state" (ICISS 2001, para. 1.35). The international security regime, in line with liberal governance prescriptions, increasingly relies on "agency" and "responsibility" (Duffield 2002a, 2002b; Pender 2007) as ways of governing disorder.

The UN's Commission on Human Security testified in May 2003 to the institutionalization of a biopolitical political rationality where human security became the new organizing concept for collective security.[5] The commission's first report underscored the conceptualization of the problematic of security in terms of risk and vulnerability, noting that these are a shared condition intensified by globalization: "Today's global flows of goods, services, finance, people and images spotlight the many interlinkages in the security of all people. We share a planet, a biosphere, a technological arsenal, a social fabric. The security of one person, one community, one nation rests on the decisions of many others—sometimes fortuitously, sometimes precariously. . . . Thus people throughout the world, in developing and developed countries alike, live under varied conditions of insecurity" (Commission on Human Security 2003, 2). Holistic prevention is the name of the game. For the commission, security should address not only violent threats but also risks deriving from hunger, poverty, disease, and environmental degradation, which taken together cause many more deaths than direct violence.

In the context of the reconceptualization of security in terms of risk management, populations are made the subject of intensified processes of scrutiny and classification, through which they are categorized according to vulnerability and risk indicators that provide the basis for tailored international governmental intervention aimed at addressing their specific needs. For instance, Resolution 1325, on women, peace, and security, connected gender, age, and vulnerability in armed conflict (UN Security Council 2000). It recommended both the implementation of institutional arrangements to ensure the protection of women and children, and the promotion of women's active participation in peace processes. International modalities of "government by community," by which, as we have seen in chapter 1, marginal groups are governed by giving incentives to responsibility and participation (Rose 1999), in the new millennium are applied not only to states as techniques of normalization but also to populations as techniques of encouraging responsibility. Thus, in the UN vision, women

5. The Commission on Human Security was established by the Japanese government in response to the secretary-general's call at the Millennium Summit.

not only must be protected through specifically targeted initiatives because they constitute a vulnerable category of people. They also must be "responsibilized" and made part of the international community of peacemakers by fostering their active participation in conflict resolution. International security is as much the responsibility of states as of individuals' responsible action. Statistical knowledge, central in biopolitical processes of government, is the instrument through which initiatives of protection and responsibilization can be better targeted and is in need of intensification and refinement. The 2006 secretary-general report on the implementation of Resolution 1325 (UN Security Council 2006) prescribes that the collection of statistical data "disaggregated by sex" is a key tool for protecting women, bettering their participation in peace processes, and, in summary, "mainstreaming gender into peacekeeping."

The 2004 Report of the High-Level Panel on Change, Challenges, and Threat systematically organized the discourses outlined above and constructed a political rationality of intervention centered on risk management, populations, and prevention (UN General Assembly 2004). Shared vulnerability was, for the High-Level Panel, the main reason for reinforcing the UN-led collective security system. Echoing Ulrich Beck's (1992) analysis of the connection between globalization and the creation of new communities of danger, the panel indicates that in the current international configuration of threats everyone is at risk, regardless of relative capabilities, and nobody is secure alone. The panel redefined the notion of international threat in biopolitical terms as it broadened it to include "any event or process that leads to large-scale death or lessening of life chances and undermines States as the basic units of the international system" (UN General Assembly 2004, 12). More specifically, international threats, partially reprising the six components of human security outlined by the UNDP in 1994, include six types: economic and social threats (poverty, infectious disease, and environmental degradation); interstate conflict; internal conflict, including civil war, genocide, and other large-scale atrocities; nuclear, radiological, chemical, and biological weapons; terrorism; and transnational organized crime (12). While threats to state security do not disappear from the picture, they are treated as one among the many other menaces with which the UN has to concern itself.

The convergence of the conceptual frameworks for addressing natural and man-made disasters, coupled with the refocusing of the referent of security from states to populations, opens the way for the intensification of prevention through normalization. In a world where it is increasingly difficult to control multiple variables, security is seen as depending upon taming risk sources by making them domesticated, visible, and predictable. In this context, the panel prescribes an intensification of governmental, disciplinary, and biopolitical instruments as the means the UN can use to manage risk in the international arena. Knowledge-intensive and disciplinary modalities for the conducting of conduct applied to state institutions—and when these fail, various degrees of involvement in protecting and managing populations, in conjunction, if necessary, with the use of force—are the prescribed techniques for governing international insecurity.

The modalities of the "science of police," which relies on knowledge and control, and liberal techniques of governing through responsibilities converge in the new millennium discursive practices of security. For the High-Level Panel, the UN role is twofold. First, it has to develop a wide array of "norms to govern some of the sources and accelerators of conflict" (UN General Assembly 2004, 35). These range from the punishment of crimes against humanity, to the management of natural resources, to arms control and disarmament, to terrorism and transnational crime measures. Second, the UN must assist in creating within each state the capacity to fulfill its responsibilities. In order to make itself able to perform its new tasks, the UN must revise its institutional arrangements. Because threats to security are interconnected, the UN must reinforce its functions of international governance and become better equipped for long-term initiatives normalizing after forcible intervention, as well as for monitoring, knowing, and assessing economic and social issues and for protecting human rights. In this regard, the panel prescribed the creation of a new institutional body, the Peacebuilding Commission, with the function of assisting countries transitioning from war to peace and developing "their capacity to perform their sovereign functions effectively and responsibly" (70). In addition, the panel recommended that the Economic and Social Council, the Human Rights Commission, the Security Council, and the General Assembly be reformed to better meet the new challenges.

The reconceptualization of collective security along the lines of complex vulnerabilities, population protection, and risk management not only entails an intensification of the normalizing trajectory of international government and an expansion of the issue areas within which the UN is called to intervene. It also expands the legitimacy of forcible international intervention, should prevention through normalization fail. When biopolitical modalities of international government migrated from the context of disaster management and development and became the organizing concepts for collective security, they created important tensions with traditional understandings of international order and sovereignty. For the High-Level Panel, states no longer have the exclusive responsibility to protect populations, nor is sovereignty the outer, inviolable limit to international intervention. States are a means, not an end. They must be protected not because they are intrinsically good, but "because they are necessary to achieve the dignity, justice, worth and safety of their citizens" (UN General Assembly 2004, 22). When states are not able or willing to protect people, "some portion of those responsibilities should be taken by the international community" (22). Populations are the ultimate referent of UN security and accountability. Responsibility, a virtue that the UN political rationale links to democracy and good governance, is not only to be promoted in order to achieve international security and upheld as a criterion for the accession to international political associations. It is also a necessary condition for exerting full sovereignty. Sovereignty is not the unqualified, ultimate source of legitimacy accruing to states. When good government programs fail, when states are unable or unwilling to undertake a series of duties with regard to citizens and to other states, international organizations must intervene, including with the use of force. While the notion of shared international and national responsibility for protecting populations was rather uncontroversial when discussed in the context of natural disaster management or development, when it converged into the problematics of security the "responsibility to protect" challenged, at least in principle, the territorialized international order.

BIOPOLITICS EFFECTS

Kofi Annan's proposals were accepted only in bits and pieces by the states that participated in the 2005 World Summit. The implications of the notion of human security remain contested. The fiercest opposition to the generalization of the "responsibility to protect" as the organizing principle of UN security activities was voiced at the World Summit 2005 by developing countries. Some organizational changes were accepted, some rejected, some put in limbo for further discussions. What came under contestation at the World Summit 2005 is a vision of international security that, by conceptualizing international threats in terms of risk and by intensifying the biopolitical trajectory of international security regimes, blurs spaces of governance and threatens the exclusionary principles that separate (at least ideally) the world inside state borders from the world outside. The reconceptualization of international threats around the notion of shared vulnerability; the inclusion of nonstate actors as both the victims and the perpetrators of threats to security; a broadened understanding of international menaces that include poverty, diseases, and ecological degradation; and the connection of the notion of full sovereignty to the notion of performance challenge, at least in principle, traditional understandings of sovereignty based on recognition and legal entitlements. Coupled with strategies of responsibilization there is an intensified blurring of spaces of governance and the increasing involvement of international actors in policy-making processes that were previously considered to fall under states' jurisdiction. Mark Duffield defined this reorganization of international order as a "world of contingent sovereignty where the traditional national/international dichotomy has blurred, the future lies in the enmeshing of ineffective states within international public/private governmental assemblages having the developmental technologies and ability to work directly at the level of populations" (Duffield 2007, 126).

In the new millennium, the relevant divide for the organization of governmental actions is no longer between spaces inside or outside states, but between "effective" states, who enjoy full sovereignty, and ineffective states, whose sovereignty has faded (Duffield 2007). Security is imagined as part of a holistic project of international governance that aims at reducing chaos by making factors of risk domesticated and predictable. In this context, the subjectification of nondemocratic states as moral monsters acquires a new political potential as the ground for an expanded legitimization of international intervention. The political qualities and "institutional capacity" of states, which democratic peace theories and good governance doctrines had taken as indicators for the potential of international threats and as the benchmarks for normalization, have now become a moral qualifier and a condition for exerting sovereignty. Ethical aberrations, such as gross violations of human rights and the failure to protect citizens, elicit the international "moral" duty to use force. Similar to what happened within states, liberal governance relies less and less on "entitlements" and increasingly on benchmarks and transformations of behavior as instruments of governance.

Regardless of what was officially accepted at the World Summit, the reconceptualization of the task of the UN in terms of risk testifies to the reinforcement, in the new millennium, of an international regime based on knowledge, surveillance, regulations, and assessment mechanisms where populations and states alike become the target of international governance and transformative disciplinary processes, and where coercion is justified on the subjectification of states along the moral divide between normal players and moral monsters. Political identity takes the place of actual threat as the legitimizing principle for international intervention, thus justifying a status of "unending war" (Duffield 2007). Samuel Huntington's remapping of danger along the lines of Western-Christian-democratic identities versus the rest has become the subtext for international politics of security. Threat must be tamed by transforming the "barbarians," a qualifier that in classical Europe referred to those who were seen as the absolute "others," the menaces to civilization as such, into the "savages," a qualifier referring to those who, through a mix of coercion, training, and assistance, could be civilized (Foucault 2003b, 193–98). In the 1990s international normalization had been pursued mostly through governmental endeavors of the transformation of state institutions into "democracies" and "good governments." In the new millennium, the inclusion of populations as the ultimate target of international security and the reconceptualization of sovereignty in terms of performance make good governance and democracy into markers of normal versus aberrant identities. In the carceralized international space, obscure borderlands of ethical aberration have to be transformed into spaces of delinquency through a combination of coercion and correction.

While critiques of the international regime of intervention (Chandler 2004; Dillon and Reid 2009; Duffield 2007; Reid 2007) have overarchingly condemned liberal regimes of security as imperial and oppressive, the intensification of the morphological configuration of international security as a carceral regime does not say anything about the "effectiveness" of this regime in achieving its own goals or the political desirability of the outcomes of intervention.[6] Discursive practices do not overdetermine political action, and their results must be considered in the specific context of their interactions. As Taylor Owen aptly puts it, "the relevant question in this regard, is not whether issues have been

6. While I share the concern about emancipation and oppression with the critical literature, I question broad oversimplifications of complex and situated engagements, such as peace operations are, as well as the representation of liberal rationalities as omnipotent, and of recipients of intervention as powerless. Indeed, these representations reproduce yet another ethnocentric imaginary.

securitized, but what are the consequences of such an act" (Owen 2008).[7] While political rationales for international order organized around "human security" foster an interventionist agenda, the outcomes of such interventions must be assessed on a case-by-case basis. The next chapters will focus on exploring the effects of the political rationales adopted by the UN in Haiti and Croatia in the years that preceded Kofi Annan's proposals for the reform of the UN. In Haiti the UN intervention's blindness to poverty ended up aggravating the issues it purported to solve. In Croatia local resistance to the international agenda of promoting minority rights cannot easily be romanticized as a case of benign local opposition to international domination.[8]

7. An in-depth discussion of the effects of political rationales of international order organized around discourses of human security is beyond the scope of this study. For a debate on the controversial effects of integrating humanitarian intervention within peace-keeping missions, see Weir (2006). See also Zanotti (2010b).

8. In some cases, biopolitical political rationalities produce the unintended consequence of opening opportunities for political actors that were previously at the margins of security, such as NGOs and community-based foundations that may or may not be aligned with overarching governmental strategies. While an analysis of nonstate actors and nongovernmental organizations is beyond the scope of this study and needs further investigation, I tend to disagree with Mark Duffield's argument that, without distinction, considers all NGOs as new actors of petty sovereignty, basically instrumental to liberal modalities of rule based upon the self-reliance of the poor (Duffield 2007). Similarly, I differ with Hardt and Negri's sanctification of the "social worker" as the champion of the multitude's emancipation (Hardt and Negri 2001), which, however, falls short of providing a thorough analytics of the specific role played by "social workers" in political processes. While it is true that NGOs do not by and large question the political rationales that justify their existence, generalized condemnations that see them as instruments of liberal governance fall short of grasping the many differences among actors in the field. Duffield argues that the alternative to liberal state-centered strategies of security, biopolitics, and governmentality is solidarity. But he falls short of indicating how this "solidarity" could be pursued in practice, and who would be the agents involved in bringing it about. For further reflections on this topic, see Stephenson and Zanotti (2008).

IMAGINING DEMOCRACY, BUILDING UNSUSTAINABLE INSTITUTIONS
International Disciplinarity in the UN
Peacekeeping Operation in Haiti

> *We should reject the idea that professional knowledge can or should be politically dispassionate. And we should not ourselves remain outside the fray. International governance distributes, makes some outcomes more likely and some less. Where the results are progressive, we should applaud, and where they are not, we should contest them. Doing so places us in the policy process, governing, ruling, no longer standing outside.*
>
> —Kennedy 2001, 480

> *The possibilities for liberal forms of freedom may historically depend upon the exercise of discipline.*
>
> —Barry, Osborne, and Rose 1996, 8

Sections of this chapter have been republished with minor modifications from *Security Dialogue* 39, no. 5: 539–61, Sage Publications LYD/Sage Publications, Inc., all rights reserved,

INTRODUCTION

In the previous chapters I have explored the features of the political rationale of the UN in the post–Cold War era and some of its effects. Through the reading of UN policy documents I have shown that the UN political rationale fosters normalization by means of three trajectories: governmentality, through the emphasis on knowledge and regulations, and the emphasis on techniques for the reform of state institutions; disciplinarity, through programs for redesigning state institutions along disciplinary lines and disciplinary modalities for normalizing deviant states; and biopolitics, through the emphasis on monitoring and bettering populations' life. I have also argued that this political rationale supports technocratic approaches to democratization and modalities of subjectification of international actors along the lines of normal, civilized, and democratic worlds versus obscure, morally abject, and disorderly borderlands. This political rationality blurs the spaces of national and international governance and expands the basis for justifying international intervention when states fail to perform according to internationally established standards.

This chapter uses the theoretical tools elaborated by Foucault in his analysis of disciplinarity and the reform of penal institutions in classical Europe to contribute an empirical exploration of the methods and effects of international peacekeeping in the post–Cold War era. It explores the political imaginary, the techniques of government, and the unintended consequences of the UN intervention in Haiti. This chapter shows that the United Nations' political imaginary can be traced back to the texts that guided the reform of penal institutions in classical Europe. The UN believed its effort at peace building in Haiti would result from making local institutions disciplined, visible, and centralized. The UN failure to achieve its stated goals is appraised in the contingent modalities of the encounter between an ethnocentric political imaginary, which takes for granted that modalities of government can be transplanted with benign effects, and the local conditions of extreme poverty. This chapter concludes that while imported institutional and political models purport to build independent, democratic, and well-functioning states, if they are introduced unreflectively, they may end up fostering disorder and dependence.

http://intl-sdi.sagepub.com/. ©2008 PRIO. A shorter analysis of the cases of Haiti and Croatia has also appeared in *International Peacekeeping* 13, no. 2 (2006): 150–67.

International intervention, be it peacekeeping or development, has been understood as the reflection of imperial aspirations, Western hegemony, or the projection of a (real or simulated) centralized power (Chandler 2006; Debrix 1999; Escobar 1988, 1995; Latouche 1996; Sachs 1992; Slater 2006). However, both international relations and development scholars have recently voiced the need for moving the research agenda beyond analyses that pattern intervention along grand narratives of empire and domination and exploring instead the specific modalities of deployment of international power. Mac Ginty highlighted the need for going beyond the general assumptions of both the supporters and the critiques of liberal peace; he also cautioned against the romanticization of local and traditional conflict resolution techniques and suggested instead an exploration of the specific modalities of the interactions between international and local peacemaking techniques (Mac Ginty 2008). Inspired by Foucault, some governmentality scholars focused on the exploration of multifarious and contingent government and techniques, both within states and internationally (Burchell, Gordon, and Miller 1991; Dean 1999; Larner and Walters 2004a, 2004b; Lipschutz and Rowe 2005; Perry and Maurer 2003; Rose 1999; Rose and Miller 1992; Walters and Haar 2005a, 2005b). Developmentalism (both in its liberal and in its Marxist version) has come under criticism because of its homogenizing construction of the "Third World" as a unitary space, whose dynamics can be explained in terms of exogenous factors (Bayart 1996), or as a stage leading to membership in the Western world (Badie 2000), or because it offered standardized technical solutions to all societal problems (Easterly 2007). Post-development theorizations have also been criticized for their "deductive" and centralized understanding of power, patterned on the metaphor of colonization.[1] Morgan Brigg (2002) advocated the need to explore instead the modalities of operation of power through development, in its multidimensional, contingent, and productive aspects.

Scholars disagree not only about the methods for studying international intervention and development but also on the effects of such intervention (Badie 2000; Bayart 1996; Bayart, Ellis, and Hibou 1999; Dia 1996; Duffield 2002a, 2002b; Mamdani 1996; Pender 2007; Pouligny 2006; Reno 1995). The Bayart/Badie divergence of views on the effects of the importation of Western institutions is a case in point. For Bayart, the

1. For a review of postdevelopment literature, see Brigg (2002).

encounter between imported state institutions (linked to cultures of production) and local "cultures of consumption" is not one between complete strangers. It entails processes of hybridization and appropriation whose effects on local societies are diverse but not necessarily disruptive. Badie argues instead that imported state structures inevitably end up fostering disorder and the disaggregation of political communities. Badie analyzes the failure of imported institutions along two lines: cultural incomprehension and utilitarian rejection. The territorialization of identities and the universalization of a Western legislative body that individualizes political relations clash with nonterritorially organized local communitarian cultures and foster the creation of counter-legitimacies. In addition, by linking microcommunitarian issues with international constituencies, imported institutions externalize political claims and dynamics, thus eroding the allegiance to local governments (Badie 2000). Supporters of internationally led state building as an instrument of conflict resolution focused on providing suggestions for improving the process and emphasized the need for stronger international supervision and commitment to "capacity building" (Chesterman 2003; Paris 2004). Critical analyses of the convergences between state building and international security argued instead that the failure of these endeavors is not rooted in contingent shortcomings but in the very nature of the process. While formally promoting the reinforcement of sovereignty, internationally led state building de facto separates policy making from local constituencies and political debates, and reinforces external regulatory power and conditionality (Chandler 2006; Bickerton 2007). While in agreement on the consequences of internationally led state building in the context of peacekeeping, Chandler and Bickerton differ in their explanations of the reasons for the focus of international intervention on institutional reforms. While for Chandler international state building is the result of international elites' "denial" of their imperial agenda (Chandler 2004), Bickerton more convincingly explains this trend as the result of "failed state theories" (Jackson 1990) that portray local societies as "politically deficient" and focus on technical initiatives, such as on building "efficient" administrations (Bickerton 2007).

In summary, critical analyses of intervention and development have pointed out the overarching imperial scope and ethnocentric character of these undertakings or the shortcomings of the institutions carrying them out. However, while it is well known that Western institutional models constitute the blueprint for international intervention, this body of literature has left unexplored the genealogy and specific modalities of articulation of the political rationale of international organizations. Furthermore, analyses that focused on exploring the specific forms of the "encounter" between international peacekeepers, state builders, and the recipients of intervention focused on the cultural divides between local and international actors, while largely overlooking the economic dimension of these encounters.

The application of Foucauldian analytical tools to the exploration of international state building in the context of peacekeeping adds new dimensions to the understanding of its modalities and to the explanation of its outcomes. The genealogical analysis conducted in this chapter shows that the UN political rationale was centered on redesigning the penal system in disciplinary terms, along the lines of the blueprint traced by the Enlightenment reformers. This way the UN attempted to extend the state's administrative instruments for governing populations. It fostered the subjectification of citizens as disciplined actors and promoted institutional centralization, codification, regularization, visibility, and simplification of local processes as well as the territorialization of political life.[2] However, the UN intervention did not achieve its stated goals, but instead produced ironic effects. In line with critiques of international intervention, this analysis concludes that in Haiti the importation of Western political models fosters disorder, erodes the capacity of the state to govern, and reinforces international regulatory power.[3] However, instead of reverting to generalizations regarding the main traits of "Western" and "non-Western cultures" (Bayart 1996), to the externalization of political claims that while offering interesting insights regard politics as a separate sphere of society (Badie 2000), or to a psychological analysis of international elites' hypocritical processes of "denial" (Chandler 2004), I ground my explanation of the effects of intervention in the analysis of a specific political imaginary, the techniques of government it implements, and the economic insustainability of the type of institutionalization it

2. The project of social engineering connected with state formation and the expansion of administrative procedures aimed at "making visible," simplifying, and homogenizing a vast variety of local processes has been called "high modernism" by Scott (1998). On high modernism, see also Moran (2003). On the territorialization of political life as a result of imported institutions, see Badie (2000, 58–70). For a discussion of governmentality see Foucault (1991a, 87–104).

3. While I recognize the validity of Chandler's conclusions on the *effects* of international state building, I do not subscribe to his explanation of the *reasons for the shifts* to institution building as a modality of international intervention. Chandler oversimplifies complex dynamics of power by attributing them to the hypocrisy and psychological conundrums of Western elites "in denial" of their imperial agenda (Chandler 2004).

prescribes. For Foucault "the indissociability of the economy and politics is not a matter of functional subordination, or of formal isomorphism. It is of a different order, and it is precisely that order that we have to isolate" (Foucault 2003b, 14). Here I explore this order in the context of international institution building and explain the failure of the UN's intended goals as the outcome of the encounter between an unreflectively universalized political model and the Haitian economic situation and resources.

HAITI, 1804–2004: A HISTORICAL ANALYSIS FROM INDEPENDENCE TO ARISTIDE'S DOUBLE OUSTER

A brief outline of the process of state formation in Haiti and the role of international forces in determining its political and economic structure will clarify the context of the UN's activities in Haiti. While a thorough discussion of this process is beyond the scope of this work and has been performed by others (e.g., Cox 1997; Farmer 1994; Hallward 2007; McFayden et al. 1995; Mintz 1995; Ridgeway 1994; Schmidt 1995; Trouillot 1988, 1990, 1995), this excursus has the purpose of broadly defining the environment within which the UN intervened in the 1990s, and to show how the formation of the Haitian state has always been entangled with the intervention of foreign powers.

Haiti earned its independence from France in 1804 as a result of the only slave revolt in history that led to the creation of an independent state (Farmer 1994). After independence, Haiti remained politically isolated. The Haitian revolution, unlike the other two contemporary revolutions—the American and the French—did not garner much international appreciation. The claims of Haitian slaves regarding "freedom" were not of the same order as those of the bourgeois classes in France or the United States; the Haitian claims addressed a simpler set of rights, such as the right to be one's own person and to own land. Indeed, Haitian independence challenged the common racial ideology and international economic structures (Mintz 1995).

France was the first international power to recognize Haiti in 1825, in exchange for a payment of 150 million francs in compensation for damages caused by the revolution. This payment set the stage for Haitian dependence on crops export and international loans to repay foreign debts. As of today, Haiti's social structure is divided between a wealthy merchant class connected to international commerce, a disenfranchised peasantry, and an urban petty bourgeoisie of state employees and army officers. The military played an important role in the formation of the new republic: military organization brought the rebel slaves to victory and constituted a positive element of identity and pride; the military also provided a good source of employment in an environment that did not offer many alternatives. All Haitian presidents before 1915 were military officers (Trouillot 1990).

Toward the end of the nineteenth century, in conjunction with the opening of the Panama Canal, the strategic interest of the United States in controlling the Caribbean intensified, and so did the struggle with European powers for the establishment of "areas of influence" in the region. In Haiti this policy was translated into a progressive acquisition of American control over the Banque Nationale, previously managed by Franco-German interests (Schmidt 1995). With the outbreak of World War I, the United States feared a strong German influence in a nearby country and started to consider a military intervention in Haiti, which started in 1915.

Shortly after the occupation, the Banque Nationale supervised and controlled the customhouses, which imposed direct taxation on exported goods and basically controlled the state's only source of revenue. As a consequence, the bank completely managed the finances of the Haitian government, from the gathering of resources to the redistribution of revenues. By 1920 Haiti's foreign debt was consolidated in the hands of North American investors. The United States' policy in Haiti supported economic initiatives to repay such debt as quickly as possible. Agricultural reforms aimed at restoring plantations as an efficient system of agricultural production, technical agricultural training, and improvement of the communication infrastructure of the country through road construction encountered resistance in the population. On the one hand, the attempts to reestablish the plantation system and the employment of forced labor to build roads (the so-called *corvées*) were regarded by the Haitian populace as a sort of restoration of slavery.[4] On the other hand, the sophisticated French-educated elites resented the United States' programs of technical education, which were perceived as racially loaded

4. Before independence in Haiti, a system of small land ownership developed alongside the plantation system. Slaves working on plantations were given land that was unusable for large-scale production but that would support the subsistence of their families. Furthermore, in conjunction with the increase of coffee consumption in France, small coffee estates run by a petty bourgeoisie were established in the interior. After independence, liberated slaves regarded land ownership as a main element of freedom.

and looked too much like the manual training programs for black Americans in southern United States. A general Haitian uprising against the occupation broke out in 1929. The U.S. Marines left Haiti in 1934.

In assessing the political effects of the U.S. occupation, Rolf Trouillot comments that, on the positive side, the occupation temporarily ended the military coups, reduced administrative corruption, stabilized the currency, and reduced foreign debt. However, the absolute priority given to debt repayment left few resources for internal investments and increased dependency on export-oriented agriculture. Furthermore, the occupation "exacerbated the contradictions embedded in the socio-economic structure, reinforced traditional conflicts, and broadened the dimensions of the crisis by centralizing the system" (Trouillot 1990, 103). The U.S. administration reorganized the army under the national *gendarmerie* (whose members committed numerous human rights violations) and concentrated political power in Port-au-Prince. The control of commercial activities, which before the occupation was in the hands of regional merchants, came under the control of a much more homogeneous class. This centralization provided François Duvalier with the terrain to construct his absolute power.

François Duvalier was voted into power in 1957, through the first elections in which all Haitian citizens, including women, were allowed to cast a ballot. Duvalier created de facto "consent" by linking the possibility of earning income to connections with the state and by destroying all citizens' aggregations outside the state's structure. A precondition for Duvalier's success was the centralization of military and state structures promoted under the U.S. occupation. Duvalier instituted a militia, formed mostly by peasants, who achieved some social advancement in this way; he centralized the higher education system under the umbrella of the Université d'Etat d'Haiti; he created the consent of the urban classes by attaching the possibility of a job in the administration to political support for the government. "Duvalierist totalitarism did not involve simply a willingness to use force, but also a strategy of economic redistribution that permitted him to recruit at a low price the individuals who executed it" (Trouillot 1990, 156).

François Duvalier's son, Jean-Claude, took power after the death of his father in 1971. Following the advice of United States Agency for International Development, the World Bank, and the International Monetary Fund, Jean-Claude Duvalier promoted foreign capital investments in the assembly industry, undertook programs of reduction of social spending and privatization, and focused on export-oriented agricultural production. These initiatives, combined with the increasing taxation on consumer goods necessary to repay international debts and a swine fever outbreak in 1981, to which Duvalier responded by ordering the slaughter of all Haitian black pigs, reduced the income of small landowners and caused an increase in food prices, which created an economic crisis of dramatic proportions. Many peasants suffering from hunger migrated to towns, where the meager salaries offered in the assembly industry could not compensate for the increasing cost of living.[5] While local agriculture suffered from Duvalier's policy, industrialization did not bring to Haiti the development it promised.[6] In addition to starving the population, Duvalier's economic policy exacerbated tensions between traditional agricultural elites, who opposed modernization, and the new oligarchies linked to agricultural exports and imports of manufactured goods, who supported it.

Riots started in 1984. Jean-Claude Duvalier fled Haiti in 1986, with the assistance of the United States. After few interim governments, an alliance in 1990 of the traditional merchant bourgeoisie, grassroots workers, peasants, and student organizations, all sharing a nationalistic orientation, supported the former Catholic priest Jean Bertrand Aristide, who won the internationally monitored elections of 16 December 1990.[7]

Aristide took office on 7 February 1991. His political project was rather at odds with the political agenda of the national oligarchies and international powers:

> The essence of Aristide's promise was democracy and nationalism. He was the living embodiment of anti-Duvalierism. . . . He was a staunch opponent of the U.S. neoliberal prescriptions for Haiti, which sought to 1) privatize State-run enterprises . . . 2) reduce taxes, duties and wages to suit foreign investors, 3) cut social spending and ensure regular debt payments

5. The population of Port-au-Prince grew from 144,000 inhabitants in 1950 to 2,499,000 in 2010 (figures from Mongabay.com, "Population Estimates for Port-au-Prince, Haiti, 1950–2015," available at http://books.mongabay.com/population_estimates/full/Port-au-Prince-Haiti.html; accessed 13 June 2010).

6. The assembly industry was not contributing to the local economy through taxation. Starting in 1972, foreign assembly firms paid no income taxes for the first five years, nor did they pay taxes on materials or equipment imports or the purchase of local raw materials. The value added for the country amounted to the laborers' salaries, which amounted to about 14 cents an hour (Ridgeway 1994, 134–35).

7. Elections were monitored by the United Nations and the Organization of American States (OAS).

to foreign banks and 4) foster an export-oriented economy, thereby increasing Haiti's already great dependence on foreign food and capital.

Aristide's program called for supporting Haiti's faltering national industries, revitalizing Haitian agriculture and increasing self-sufficiency through land reform, stanching the hemorrhage of contraband imports through regional ports. (McFayden et al. 1995, 7)

Once in power, Aristide attempted to implement some of the promises of his electoral campaign: subordinate the military to civilian control and reduce prices of staples and fuel. A military coalition led by General Raoul Cédras overthrew Aristide after fewer than eight months in office. The planners of the coup were Haiti's old-guard elite: the oligarchic families and their allies. The violence that ensued under the Cédras government triggered a refugee crisis on the coasts of Florida.[8] Between 1991 and 1993 the George H. W. Bush administration took diplomatic initiatives to quell the Haitian crisis. However, the Republican administration did not appreciate Aristide's politics and did not support his return (Ives 1994; Lawless 1992; Orenstein 1995). While the main preoccupation of President Bill Clinton's Democratic administration that followed remained to prevent a massive refugee exodus to the United States, under increasing pressures from Haitian American citizens and the Black Caucus of the U.S. Congress, Clinton began to work toward Aristide's return in the framework of an international intervention to "restore democracy." In quite a long process that will be outlined below, Aristide was brought back to power by the UN in 1994. Part of the conditions set by the United States for Aristide's reinstatement to power was that he would not run in the next presidential election, nor would extend his term to make up for the time spent in exile.

Aristide was reelected president and took office for the second time in February 2001, immediately after the withdrawal of the UN from Haiti. Aristide was again forced out of Haiti in February 2004, in the aftermath of a coup supported by the United States and France. Shortly thereafter, the UN returned to the country, where it is still confronted

---

8. In February 1991 a Florida federal district court issued a temporary restraining order to halt the forced expatriation of refugees. The Haitian refugees picked up at the sea would be taken to the U.S. base at Guantánamo Bay in Cuba. However, in May 1992 President George H. W. Bush signed the "Kennebunkport Order" under which all Haitian refugee boats would be interdicted and their passengers returned to Port-au-Prince with no prior screening for asylum seekers. In August 1992 a U.S. court declared this measure illegal under international and national law (McFayden et al. 1995, 4).

with issues that have worsened since the first peacekeeping operation was mandated in 1994. This book goes to press after a catastrophic earthquake struck Haiti in January 2010. The quake destroyed not only 75 percent of the buildings in Port-au-Prince but also the thin layer of state administrative structures that were in place. While the quake brought the extreme weakness of the Haitian state to the attention of world, it did not create it. As I argue elsewhere, international organizations' neoliberal political rationale that international assistance should focus on making institutions formally "democratic" and economically "cost effective" instead of fostering states' capacity to provide services to populations, coupled with the rechanneling of international funds from the state to NGOs as a tool for exerting conditionality, set the stage for disaster in Haiti (Zanotti 2010a).

THE UNITED NATIONS IN HAITI: A CHRONOLOGY

UN involvement in Haiti dates back to 1991, shortly after the coup that ousted Aristide, when the Security Council, together with the Organization of American States (OAS), voted for a trade embargo to put pressure on the military government. In April 1993 the first International Civilian Mission in Haiti (MICIVIH) was deployed by the General Assembly in conjunction with the Organization of American States in response to the worsening human rights situation (UN General Assembly 1993c). MICIVIH's human rights observers were present in Haiti from February 1993 until mid-October 1993, when they were evacuated on security grounds, and from the end of January 1994 to mid-July 1994, when they were again evacuated after the de facto authorities had declared their presence undesirable.[9] MICIVIH's activities resumed on 26 October 1994 with the reopening of the Port-au-Prince office. Before being evacuated in October 1993, MICIVIH's staff had grown to 230 people of forty-five nationalities, and its observers operated from thirteen offices spread throughout Haiti's nine geographic departments (MICIVIH 1995).

9. After the ousting of the MICIVIH, the tone of the United Nations toward the de facto government became stronger. In his report to the Security Council of 15 July 1994, Secretary-General Boutros Boutros-Ghali emphasized human rights violations and the intolerable deterioration of the situation in Haiti: "The situation in Haiti has deteriorated to an intolerable extent. The senior leadership of the Armed Forces of Haiti continues to defy the will of the international community and to inflict murder, rape and torture on the unfortunate people of Haiti" (UN Security Council 1994a).

The UN peacekeeping operation mandate was negotiated at Governors Island, New York, where, under pressure by the United States, Aristide's and Cédras's delegations met for negotiations on 27 June 1993. The ten-point agreement that resulted from this process, in which Aristide participated rather reluctantly, provided for a series of parliamentary, police, and army reforms under supervision from the United Nations and United States, a blanket amnesty for those involved in the coup, and the lifting of the UN sanctions. The agreement also outlined the terms of an international military intervention in Haiti under the UN flag and provided that Cédras would retire at some point before Aristide's return, scheduled for 30 October 1993.

In September 1993, the Security Council voted a resolution establishing the United Nations Mission in Haiti (UNMIH) with the mandate to assist in modernizing the armed forces and in creating a new police force (UN Security Council 1993b). However, when the USS *Harlan County,* carrying Canadian and United States military instructors, arrived in Port-au-Prince on 11 October, supporters of the de facto government protested at the port, and the ship was ordered back to Guantánamo. This incident led to the first withdrawal of the MICIVIH observers and to the reimposition of the embargo.[10]

On 31 July 1994, the Security Council, acting under chapter 7 of the UN Charter, authorized member states to constitute a multinational force and to use "all necessary means" to facilitate the departure of the military leaders and the return to democratic rule (UN Security Council 1996b). President Aristide was brought back to power on 15 October 1994 by a multinational force under U.S. command, one year later than agreed in the Governors Island accord. On 31 March 1995, the leadership of the multinational force was transferred to UNMIH. Elections were held on 17 December 1995, and president Andre Préval took office on 7 February 1996.

When its mandate came to an end, UNMIH was replaced by the United Nations Support Mission in Haiti (UNSMIH), which was followed by the Transition Mission in Haiti (UNTMIH) and the Civilian Police Mission in Haiti (MIPONUH). After the mandates of the MICIVIH and MIPONUH came to an end, the General Assembly deployed the International Civilian Support Mission in Haiti (MICAH) (UN General

---

10. See UN Security Council (1993a). This resolution for the first time explicitly established a connection between the situation in Haiti and international security. In supporting its decision the Security Council emphasized the following aspects of the Haitian crisis: failure of

Assembly 1999e). Its goal was to consolidate the results of both the civilian and military operations and provide advice and assistance to the Haitian government on human rights and reforming the judiciary and the police. In addition, the mission was tasked with facilitating international dialogue with political and social actors in Haiti. MICAH was withdrawn one year later because of a lack of international funding and support. The UN returned to Haiti in 2004 with the Stabilization Mission in Haiti (MINUSTAH) after the second ousting of Aristide.

FROM HAPHAZARD EXCESS TO LAWFUL REGULARITY: THE MAKING OF THE STATE THROUGH THE REFORM OF THE JUDICIAL SYSTEM

Considered at the time of its authorization by the Security Council an exceptional case, the deployment of peacekeepers to restore democracy in Haiti under chapter 7 of the UN Charter translated into policy the link, promoted by democratic peace theories, between democracy, institutional reforms, and international security and legitimized a military intervention aimed at quelling an internal conflict through democratization.[11]

For the UN, state building, democratization, and pacification were to be carried out through the reform of the judiciary, the prison system, and the police. Foucault has shown that the transformation of punishment from the modality of confinement to the modality of correction was central in the formation of new modalities of state power in classical Europe (Foucault 1995). Here I start from Foucault's analysis of the reform of penal institutions in classical Europe to show that the political imaginary elaborated by the Enlightenment reformers constitutes the subtext for the UN programs in Haiti. When punishment was delinked from the sovereign's revenge and became a means for preventing crime and creating domesticated subjects, its certainty and logical evidence replaced its theatrical display.[12] The Enlightenment reformers prescribed

the diplomatic attempts to "establish a dialogue with the Haitian parties," concern for humanitarian crises including *mass displacement of population,* and concern for "the number of Haitians seeking refuge in neighboring member states." The Security Council concluded that "the continuation of this situation threatens international peace and security in the region."

11. Secretary-General Boutros Boutros-Ghali highlighted the novelty of this kind of operation (UN 1996).

12. For ease of argument, sovereignty and government are treated here as distinct modalities of power. However, in line with Foucault, I do not see them as mutually exclusive.

the reorganization of institutions of punishment in order to ensure continuity, consistency, and proportionality between offense and penalty. Haphazard and excessive punishment was replaced by mechanisms relying on laws and rules that made it the logical consequence of the crime committed. Multiple and overlapping jurisdictions, which allowed both for excess and for tolerance, were simplified and their functions codified (Foucault 1995, 73–103). In his later work, Foucault moved from the analysis of disciplinarity to the study of modalities of government that applied to populations and their living together, such as the science of police and biopolitics. The "science of police"—a project of the "urbanization of territory" through the construction of roads, hubs of communication, and instruments for monitoring and knowing populations—is central in the genealogy of the governmental reason that accompanied the formation of the "modern state and its apparatuses" (Foucault 2007, 336, 354).

The UN problematized the situation in Haiti and understood the corrective actions it was mandated to put in place along the lines of the blueprint traced by the Enlightenment reformers. Accounts of the institutions of punishment by MICIVIH (1996a) and the UNDP (1999) echo Enlightenment narratives regarding punishment as Foucault (1995) reports them. UN texts record that penal institutions in Haiti lacked certainty and regularity; they were held hostage by the head of state's personal decisions; plural and overlapping jurisdictions had authority over the same issue while leaving a variety of matters ungoverned; modalities of punishment lacked legal codification; and proportionality between offense and penalty was haphazard. Haitian institutions allowed both for excess and impunity and were not equipped for punishing illegalities in a consistent and differentiated manner. Therefore, they were to be transformed from the strong arm of the dictator into a disciplinary and regulated system that governed in a consistent manner throughout the territory. The Haitian penal system had to be made comprehensive (that is, no overlap or gap must exist in its jurisdiction), continuous (no disruption between justice, police, and prison administration), predictable (it must function in a consistent manner), and functionally distinct (it must be free from outside influence). This way the UN programs of reform attempted to establish techniques of government that extended

---

Instead, these modalities often do overlap and coexist. The type of punishment apparatus envisaged by the Enlightenment reformers is an "ideal type" that even in modern states has not been fully implemented.

and homogenized administrative instruments for fostering, knowing, and controlling people's lives.

The UN programs of institutional reform in Haiti were constructed around the six rules that, according to Foucault (1995, 93–99) inspired the Enlightenment reformers' reorganization of the modalities of punishment from atrocity to correction. While these rules are never explicitly spelled out in UN documents, in the pages that follow I will show that they constitute the subtext for the UN political imaginary. The *rule of minimum quantity* establishes that the expected disadvantage from committing a crime must slightly outweigh the advantage. In order to be effective, punishment must be carefully measured. The *rule of sufficient ideality* stipulates that the idea of pain, not actual pain, deters crime. Punishment's point of application is not the body but the soul, and rules that govern it must be logical and self-evident. The *rule of lateral effects* makes prevention the central concern of penal systems. The *rule of perfect certainty* establishes that the linkage between crime and punishment be absolutely certain. The law must be clear and public, the gaze of its enforcers continuous, and its execution inflexible. The *rule of common truth* states that the verification of crime should be delinked from the traditional forms of torture and confession and be put under the domain of the common instruments of reason. The *rule of optimal specification* requires a comprehensive codification of illegalities, crimes, and related penalties.

The penal system in Haiti violated the Enlightenment's six rules in many ways. According to the MICIVIH and UNDP, the justice system was characterized by overall opacity, rooted in the lack of instruments for recording, mapping, and controlling population by a central state. About 40 percent of the Haitian population was not included in the civil register and therefore could not enjoy any rights as citizens (UNDP 1999, 18). The hubs of communication were scarce; roads were often in bad repair or nonexistent. A geographical and language divide separated the urban center from rural periphery. Urban elites expressed themselves in French, a language that was only spoken by 10 percent of the population, while the remainder spoke Creole. French was also the written language of formal justice, in a country where 60 percent of the population was illiterate. Codified law was outdated, and the Napoleonic Code was still the text of reference for formal justice. As a result of the divide between written and oral culture, the countryside had been traditionally out of the reach of formal justice. This violates the rule of optimal specification, which requires a comprehensive and detailed definition of illegalities.

UNDP and the MICIVIH reports describe the situation of the judiciary as disorderly, noncomprehensive, disconnected from the law, and characterized by overlapping systems, unclear rules, and private interests. Traditionally, the state had been present at the local level in Haiti only through its military apparatus. Before Aristide dismantled the army in 1995, justice was administered in the countryside by the *chefs de section,* the Duvaliers' police. After the army was dissolved, the countryside was left out of all state-administered forms of justice. Customary laws rooted in the Voudou religion were the main ways for maintaining order and resolving conflicts both in rural areas and among the poorest strata of urban populations, for whom formal justice was not available, too costly, or incomprehensible. In summary, in vast areas of the country, crime and its punishment escaped the Haitian state's gaze and administration. This violates the principle of perfect certainty. Overlapping systems do not guarantee continuity and consistency of punishment, nor do they allow for capillary surveillance with a view of prevention.[13] In addition to not being accessible to the majority of the population, and therefore non-comprehensive and inconsistent, the judicial system in Haiti was neither functionally distinct nor independent from political power and popular influence (MICIVIH 1996a). UN peacekeepers, in line with the rule of sufficient ideality, prescribed that the judiciary be transformed from having the power to judge based upon the "innumerable, discontinuous privileges of sovereignty" to having a public power that distributed its effects continuously and consistently (Foucault 1995, 81). In Haiti, the *rule of minimum quantity* was also violated. Punishment was administered in an anti-economic manner. For the UN reformers, a clear proportionality between the nature of the offense and the means of punishment was to be established by law, thus preventing excess or leniency.

While the *rule of lateral effects* prescribes that the penal system focus on prevention, Haitian justice mostly either dealt with offenders caught at the scene of the crime or reacted to complaints, the foundations of which were seldom verified. There was no capability to prevent crime through surveillance, investigation procedures were not codified, and technical knowledge and forensic expertise were virtually nonexistent (MICIVIH 1996a). Foucault describes the incorporation of penal procedures within the realm of "common reason," or what he calls the shift

---

13. The words used by Foucault to describe classical European systems would equally apply to Haiti: "Penal justice was irregular first of all by virtue of the multiplicity of courts responsible for assuring it, without ever forming a single continuous pyramid" (Foucault 1995, 80).

from an "inquisitorial model" linked to the ritual of torture and confession to "investigation techniques" linked to expert *savoir,* as one of the key features of classical European transformation of modalities of punishment (Foucault 1995, 73–131). In the view of the UN reformers, similar transformations had to be brought about in Haiti, in compliance with the rule of common truth.

For the UNDP, the administrative disorder of the Haitian judicial system aggravated the procedural uncertainty of determination of guilt and allocation of penalty: roles and competencies of various judicial figures were not clearly defined, the separation between prosecutor and judge was not warranted, and cooperation between the judiciary and the police was scant (MICIVIH 1996a). The MICIVIH and UNDP's plans for reform established as a first priority an act of codification: the creation of a comprehensive civil registry. Population recording was the first step for the construction of a liberal-type state ("un état de droit," in the UNDP's words) and the necessary precondition for citizens' rights. Furthermore, the UNDP recommended improvements in the "technical qualities" of laws. Predictability and certainty of the judicial process should be implemented by separating the judiciary from the powers of the state through the creation of Conseil Superieur de la Magistrature (Superior Council of Judges), an independent body in charge of selecting, training, and disciplining magistrates. In addition, the MICIVIH and the UNDP advised improving tribunal administrations and aligning judicial and prosecutorial professional codes to international standards, creating a public legal system for the poor, granting defense lawyers a more relevant role in the penal procedure, and regulating preventive detention through the Ministry of Justice. They advocated the creation of a separate justice system and conditions of detention for minors; they called for the improvement of the material working conditions of judiciary officials, to include amelioration of equipment, supplies, communication infrastructure, and salaries, in addition to underscoring the need for technical training. In order to avoid overlaps and gaps, the UNDP advised that traditional methods of conflict resolution be included in the codified official system, so as to make the reformed justice institutions a completely comprehensive system. The UN reformers saw the building of a democratic judicial system as coterminous with the establishment of a rationality of government similar to classical Europe's science of police, that is, the intensification of the state's capacity to know and regulate what has to be governed. And they promoted the transformations of overlapping discontinuous and unregulated technologies of punishment into comprehensive, continuous and regulated, codified, visible, and transparent ones. The construction of the state in Haiti is imagined as the outcome of processes of homogenization of technologies of government throughout the territory, their centralization in the hand of the state, and the homogenization of local diversity.

From Confinement to Correction:
A Proportionate Measure of Penalty

For Foucault, the transformation of the disorderly and badly organized classical confinement institutions into institutions of correction and surveillance (the prison) can be analyzed along two trajectories: the connection of detention with law and the development of disciplinary mechanisms. In the ideals of the Enlightenment reformers, classical European arbitrary confinement was to be abolished in favor of detention, the duration of which had to be determined by judicial institutions according to codified laws and rules of objectivity. Structures designed to exclude and isolate those who were seen as bearers of danger of contagion or disorder (the lepers, the paupers, the fools) were to be reorganized along disciplinary lines. Confinement institutions were to be transformed from spaces whose inhabitants constituted an indistinct disorderly mass, separated from society and invisible to it, into partitioned architectures of visibility and surveillance (the Panopticon), observatories of behavior and laboratories of rehabilitation where the deviant citizens of the reformed, democratic state were to be constructed as disciplined subjects.[14]

UN descriptions of the Haitian prisons echo the Enlightenment reformers' descriptions of spaces of confinement in classical Europe. Before the return of Aristide, prisons in Haiti were managed directly by the military (the Forces Armées d'Haiti—FAd'H). There was no separate institution or organization specifically in charge of prison administration, no judicial body determining penalty independently from the military, and no external control of the military's methods of detention. Torture and ill-treatment were enduring practices; many detainees never had a trial or even a lawyer; records of prisoners and the length of their detention were haphazard; physical and hygienic conditions were abominable.

---

14. For an analysis of the reform of the prison system in England, see Ignatieff (1978).

In 1995 the UNDP and the MICIVIH prepared an extensive prison reform project envisioning the transformation of prisons from disorderly places of confinement into "rehabilitation institutions." The project included the establishment of a national prison administration, training programs for prison personnel, the preparation of prisoner registers and personal files, and the preparation of a manual of prison rules and regulations.[15] Most of the principles identified by Foucault as governing the Enlightenment's ideal type of "good penitential condition" (Foucault 1995, 270) are embedded in the United Nations' plans for reform: the principle of correction, the principle of technical supervision of detention, the principle of classification, the principle of modulation of penalties, the principle of penitentiary education, and the principle of auxiliary institutions.

For the UN, in order to democratize Haiti, punishment had to shift from the modality of revenge to the modality of correction. On the one hand, prisons were to be reorganized so that they functioned in a disciplined manner and dealt with prisoners according to disciplinary rules; on the other hand, prisons were to become part of a functionally distinct but legally integrated, centralized system of punishment together with the police and the judiciary. Echoing the Enlightenment reformers' vision, MICIVIH indicated that the ultimate goal of prison was to transform the soul of the delinquent into that of a responsible, law-abiding individual. Thus, punishment had to be regulated and predictable, as well as administered proportionally to the offense. The preparation of such a body of regulations was considered a first priority, and avoiding arbitrary detention the first step for promoting human rights (MICIVH 1997). In line with the principle of technical supervision of detention, prison reform programs included personnel training and technical assistance to prison administration officers, with a view toward developing the human and technical qualities necessary to perform their duties.

UN reformers put a special emphasis on record keeping and the creation of detainees' files. At a minimal level, these files had to include information such as identity, age, sex, and reason and duration of detention, as well as a record of the judicial status. In line with the principle of classification, the indistinct mass of detainees was to be organized and

---

15. The National Penal Administration (Administration Pénitentiaire Nationale—APENA) was created as a legal institution by decree on 29 June 1995. The decree sets forth the organizational chart of the penal administration in such a way as to create a disciplinary mechanism with well-defined internal rules and functions from a nonregulated environment. See Ministry of Justice, Republic of Haiti (1995).

made visible according to these categories. Conditions of detention were to be differentiated accordingly, especially with regard to minors. The principle of modulation of penalties, which prescribes standardization and individualization of punishment, can only be met through rigorous record keeping. UN reformers made it a priority to establish a system for collecting individual life histories—or criminal records. A broad amount of information about the prisoners had to be recorded and made available for scrutiny: the type of offense and amount of time spent in prison, the date of arrest, the meetings with judicial authorities, the status of trial, and more. In order to ensure proportionality, preventive detention was to be shortened to a minimum.

The principle of auxiliary institutions prescribes that crime prevention be diffused into the social body, and a variety of social actors and institutions contribute to achieving this goal. Accordingly, MICIVIH situates prison reform in the context of crime prevention and treatment of delinquents. Coordination must be enhanced and institutionalized both within and among various elements of penal institutions—that is, the judiciary, police, and penal administration—so that it is not dependent on informal networks and changing personal relations (MICIVIH 1997). The reformed Haitian penal systems must be comprehensive and continuous. The cogs of the disciplinary machinery cannot function in isolation, and each functionally distinct part must work according to specified rules in harmony with the whole. For the UN peacekeepers and human rights workers, the prisons, once transformed from institutions of confinement into institutions of correction, were to become a key instrument for managing social risk through the normalization of abnormal elements. The state to be built through the reform of these institutions was a state that exerted power in a disciplinary, disciplined, regulated, and continuous manner throughout its territory, a state equipped to know and normalize its population with no overlaps and gaps.

FROM RULER'S MILITIA TO POPULATION PROTECTION FORCE: DESIGNING THE NEW HAITIAN POLICE AS A DISCIPLINARY MACHINE

Traditionally, penal institutions in Haiti were structured to be the strong arm of the ruler. Under the Duvaliers, the *chefs de section* had the prerogative of administering civil and penal affairs in the countryside. After Aristide dismantled the army and the *chefs de section,* about ten security organizations were created to fill the void, some with the assistance of the multilateral forces, some at the initiative of local authorities, some organized spontaneously (MICIVIH 1996b). These forces, which employed many of the seven thousand former members of the Forces Armées d'Haiti, were not centrally organized or subject to government scrutiny.

The UN police reformers focused on centralizing the task of providing security in the hands of the government by substituting the Duvaliers' militias and the multiple security organizations with an organized, disciplined, and disciplinary civilian police. The UN extensive effort at disciplinary institutionalization is thoroughly documented in a booklet published in 1997 by the Haitian Ministry of Justice and the General Director of the Haitian National Police (HNP) in collaboration with the MICIVIH. The booklet, entitled *Protéger et servir: Recueil de textes et des réglementations applicables à la police nationale* (Protect and Serve: Collection of Documents and Regulations Applicable to the Haitian Police), prepared by the MICIVIH in order to make known the ways of functioning of the new police force, attests to a comprehensive codification effort (Ministry of Justice, Republic of Haiti 1997). It includes the text of the law by which the Haitian police was established, the rules and regulations for the employment of the HNP, and its code of conduct, in addition to a number of issue-specific instructions.

A police force that exerted authority through a display of power in order to protect the ruler was to be transformed into a disciplined and disciplinary institution devoted to the protection of the well-being and security of the population. This new role was underscored on the cover of the booklet, displaying the motto "protéger et servir" (protect and serve) and was reemphasized in article 3 of the foundational law that established the Haitian police.[16] Discipline is both regulatory and corrective (it entails both the rigorous application of rules and improvement of performance based on the critical consideration of the results of their execution); it enables surveillance through mechanisms of continuous and meticulous control; and it sets up mechanisms of reward and punishment aimed at reinforcing its effects. The central role of discipline in the newborn institution is spelled out in minute detail in the "Réglements

16. See *Loi portant à la Création, Organisation et Fonctionnement de la Police Nationale* [Law Pertaining to the Creation, Organization, and Functioning of the National Police], part 1, chap. 1, "Création et définition des institutions de la Police Nationale" [Creation and Definition of the Institutions of the National Police], reprinted in Ministry of Justice, Republic of Haiti (1997, 3–36).

intérieurs des agents de la Police Nationale d'Haïti" (Internal Rules of Employment of the Haitian National Police). Discipline encompasses rigorous implementation of the rules regarding how the service functions, critical exploitation of its results, continuous control, and a system of reward/punishment based on individual performance.

The construction of the Haitian police as a disciplinary institution is a pervasive endeavor, concerning organizational design as well as the behavior of individual police officers. Through the creation of disciplinary machinery, the prototypes of which were classical Europe's military organizations, indistinct masses are made visible and organized into goal-oriented functional elements performing specific tasks, and in defined relation one to another (Foucault 1995, 162). The law constituting the police enumerates its fundamental institutions and organizational units; it spells out in detail the specific functions and tasks of each one; it designs their hierarchical relations and territorial jurisdictions; and it establishes an internal control mechanism (the Inspectorate General), in charge of receiving complaints, conducting inquiries, and establishing sanctions.

Once the machinery's architecture was designed, each of the organizational units was structured internally according to the same methodology: partition, definition of functions, and interaction rules. The "Réglements" defines the different "units" in which police officers perform their duties along functional lines. These are General Services Units, Specialized Units, and Judiciary Police Units. Each unit's functions were spelled out in detail, as were its personnel and ranks. The functions of each rank were defined both through the codification of its internal relations (i.e., to other ranks in the same unit) and of its external ones (i.e., to ranks in other units). Rank definition is indeed a key feature of disciplinary institutions as they emerged in classical Europe. For Foucault, "Discipline is an art of rank, a technique for the transformation of arrangements" (1995, 146). Through "ranks" individuals are situated within a hierarchy and become interchangeable (level and function matter, not the individual); they are situated in a network of relations and defined by their position within it. The distribution of ranks reinforces discipline through mechanisms of reward and punishment such as promotion or demotion, establishes systems of performance assessment and comparison linked to measurable criteria, and fosters normalization (Foucault 1995, 181).

After designing the organizational machinery in a disciplinary manner, the "Réglements" focused on the definition of all routine tasks to be performed by the police and the correct modalities for their execution.

These tasks were divided into two categories: service to be rendered within the police post and service to be rendered in the public domain. The definition of tasks included such details as the frequency by which the facilities of the police headquarters had to be cleaned, the procedures for recording delays, the ways of registering telephone calls, and the prohibition of reading newspapers or drinking on duty. A section titled "discipline" spelled out the means by which control had to be exerted within the police and rewards or punishments ("les recompenses et les punitions") administered. Control was to be exerted in a continuous manner to all cogs of the machine. The first element of control was accurate record keeping with regard to personnel activity. The reporting system had to include comprehensive records of police personnel activities, to include a record of the people dealt with by the police (register of people in prison; register of security chambers; register of people brought to the police station), as well as records of materials and goods (register of vehicles and objects consigned at the police station; register of lost and found objects). Reports had to be rendered in writing, through the hierarchical chain. This correctional character of control as it was exerted within the disciplinary machinery was spelled out as follows: "Control . . . is understood as a continuous action which must be applied to all areas with a view of seeking possible improvements" (Ministry of Justice, Republic of Haiti 1997, 70). Feedback was to be given to individuals with regard to specific actions, in order to achieve behavior transformation and performance improvement.

The section of the "Réglements" dedicated to rights and duties of the personnel outlined the discipline to be exerted on police officers' bodies. It defined rules for proper behavior and physical appearance such as dressing and grooming, appearance of uniforms, rules for food and drink consumption, and rules for addressing the public and superiors. Work schedules, identification documents, and ways of treating weapons were also spelled out. Any alteration to the given pattern of appearance was considered a *faute* subject to disciplinary action.

The modalities of correction and administration of punishment within the police force were described in detail in the Police Disciplinary Code (reprinted in Ministry of Justice, Republic of Haiti 1997, 70–74). MICIVIH considered this code "among the most important measures taken to end the impunity traditionally enjoyed by Haitian security forces." It "defines the sanctions applicable at each level of the command structure; [and] . . . establishes a scale of punishment for a large number of infractions" (MICIVIH 1996b, 28). The code is indeed "disciplinary" in the Foucauldian sense: it identifies those entitled to inflict punishment and prescribes its administration according to the principle of proportionality and modulation of the offense. Institutional design was not the only way through which international disciplinarization of the Haitian police was conducted. Training was also a very important element of this endeavor. Training institutions such as the Académie Nationale de Police and the Ecole Nationale de Police were included as integral parts of the national police force. Disciplinarity regarded not only internal modalities of functioning of the police. It also extended to rules for dealing with citizens. These rules included, among others, the obligation of keeping a record of each and every detainee, to include time and reason for detention, the name of the police officers responsible for arrest and custody, and the transfers and decisions regarding the detainee. Other rules pertained to the detention of minors, conducting arrests, and the requirement for written orders (Ministry of Justice, Republic of Haiti 1997).

In summary, the UN deployed an array of tools to transform the Haitian police into a disciplined and disciplinary institution. Embedded in the UN political rationale is the idea that the HNP had to be transformed from an instrument for preservation of sovereignty and disorderly "vigilante" squads into a disciplined institution in charge of fostering people's well-being. In the UN political imaginary, in order to become democratic, "abnormal" states had to change the way their institutions (in the first place, institutions of punishment) exerted power. Their modality of rule had to be transformed from the unrefined ways of the king, focused on self-preservation and exerted through the theatrical unleashing of violence on the body of the offenders, into codified, predictable, rational, and effective ways of disciplinarity. The blueprint for the UN understanding of its mission in Haiti is the governmental rationality that had accompanied the formation of states in classical Europe, that is, disciplinarity and the "science of police."

PANOPTICISM REVISITED: FROM THE CENTRAL GAZE TO DISPERSED OBSERVATORIES

The analysis conducted so far situated the genealogy of the UN political rationale in the blueprint traced in the reformation of penal institutions in Europe. For Foucault the architectural figure of disciplinary power is

Jeremy Bentham's ideal type of a prison, the Panopticon. The pioneering work of François Debrix (1999) analyzed peacekeeping along this analogy. For Debrix, post–Cold War UN peacekeeping functioned as a surveillance *dispositif* and a simulacrum of centralized power amplified by the media. However, the architectonical figure of the Panopticon cannot easily be taken as a metaphor of the general functioning of security in the international arena. As the analysis of MICAH conducted here shows, UN peacekeeping does not necessarily work as a centralized *dispositif* of surveillance or through the projection of the image of the Leviathan.[17] Long after the media attention has faded, surveillance and transformation devices implemented through peacekeeping continue to operate in dispersed and multifarious ways. In addition, the UN is not necessarily the only "actor" involved in processing the reformation and transformation of local institutions. Programs of reform are inserted at critical junctures of state institutions and carried out in conjunction with programs implemented by other actors, for which the UN provides a legitimizing space but is not necessarily the organizing or even the coordinating center.

The case of the UN peace-building operation in Haiti (MICAH), which was established after the withdrawal of the peacekeeping component in 1999, shows that different bilateral actors deployed independent reform programs in key Haitian state institutions, under a loose "coordination" umbrella provided by the UN. When the UN withdrew from Haiti in the year 2000, the institution-building and human rights–related tasks of both the peacekeeping and the civilian components of its presence in Haiti coalesced in the mandate of the MICAH, which started its operations on 15 March 2000 (UN General Assembly 1999e). In addition to continuing the consolidation of the democratization process through institution building and reforms of the police and the judiciary, MICAH was mandated to perform coordination functions through the representative of the secretary-general and head of the mission. While these "coordination" functions were not at first supposed to be the key task of MICAH, political and financial pressure by donors (against the views expressed by the UN experts) steered the implementation of the mandate in this direction. The Needs Assessment Mission deployed by the UN

17. Foucault defined the term *dispositif* as follows: "What I'm trying to pick out with this term is, firstly, a thoroughly heterogenous ensemble consisting of discourses, institutions, architectural forms, regulatory decisions, laws, administrative measures, scientific statements, philosophical, moral and philanthropic propositions–in short, the said as much as the unsaid" (1980, 194).

secretary-general in October 1999 to explore the grounds for a continuation of the UN presence recommended that MICAH continue to take an active role in carrying out the mandated advisory and institution-building tasks and that the mission be composed of three "pillars" (justice, police, and human rights).[18] Each one of these pillars would include the functions of technical advisors to key officials of the Haitian government. For the Needs Assessment Mission a "critical mass of staff would be necessary to perform the functions of the Mission," and "the positions identified for the three mutually reinforcing and complementary (integrated) pillars of justice, police and human rights . . . [were] considered the minimum necessary for . . . satisfactory performance" (UN General Assembly 1999c, para. 8). While member states in principle supported MICAH's mandate, they did not provide the funds to perform the mandated functions, with the exception of the "coordination" task. Out of a budget of USD 24 million, which the UN needs-assessment mission estimated to be the bare minimum for MICAH to perform its mandate, only 45 percent was to be financed through the UN regular budget (UN General Assembly 1999b, 1999c).[19] This portion of funds was allocated to pay for the positions in the cabinet of the representative of the secretary-general, the heads of pillars, and the administration. The remaining 55 percent, which was to cover the costs of the technical assistance component of the mission, depended on voluntary contributions from member states.[20]

The UN could not exert control over the actual availability of funds pledged by member states as voluntary contributions. As these funds materialized only partially and very late, the three technical pillars remained

18. The mission was deployed in Haiti in October 1999. It was composed of UN staff members from the Department of Political Affairs and the Department of Peacekeeping Operations (DPKO), and of representatives of "Friends of Secretary-General for Haiti." I participated in the mission as the DPKO representative. The Friends of the Secretary-General for Haiti were Argentina, Canada, Chile, France, the United States of America, and Venezuela. Diplomatic representatives of these states closely worked with the secretariat in defining and programming UN activities in Haiti. Representatives of some of these states participated in the needs assessment mission; they contributed to drafting the resolution establishing MICAH; and they lobbied the secretariat concerning allocation of funds.

19. The funds available through the assessed budget are provided by the regular contributions of member states to the United Nations and allocated by the United Nations to specific activities. Their availability is certain. On the other hand, voluntary contributions through trust funds may be pledged but not paid, or withdrawn on short notice.

20. "The Secretary-General . . . indicated that the implementation of the recommendations of the needs assessment mission would require resources estimated at approximately $24 million, of which $10 million would need to be funded from the regular budget and $14 million from voluntary contributions, the latter in respect of technical assistance component of the program" (UN General Assembly 1999b).

mostly empty shells until October, just a few months before the end of the mission mandate.[21] The institutional memory was also seriously jeopardized as staff members who had a consolidated experience in the country were let go. MICAH was constituted as a "head without a body," a framework to facilitate bilateral initiatives in Haiti. Yet, since member states design, finance, and implement bilateral programs independently, the UN has very little knowledge and control over the goals and practices of these programs.[22]

MICAH cannot easily be assimilated to the architectural figure of the Panopticon, which portrays images of total control and surveillance over the points of application of power. Instead, the UN facilitated the opening of multiple visibility points within the institutions of the Haitian state. Surveillance in this context is exerted through the capillary insertion of multiple and decentralized bilateral observation devices at strategic points of the "abnormal" state's institutions. While the "steering" power of the UN with regard to bilateral programs was close to nonexistent, its presence provided a framework for legitimacy within which a multifarious array of independent actors with different constituencies and agendas offered advice, collected information, and steered change according to their preferred strategies. MICAH operated as an assemblage of practices conducted by different actors, connected more by isomorphism of discourses, modalities, and techniques than a coordinating center or even shared political goals.

MORE DISCIPLINE, MORE UNREST: REASONS FOR UN WITHDRAWAL

On 9 November 2000, the UN secretary-general recommended the withdrawal of MICAH, putting to an end the UN peacekeeping and peacebuilding presence in Haiti (UN General Assembly 2000c). The reason for this withdrawal was not the achievement of the mandated goals. On the

21. The final Report of the Secretary-General on MICAH reads as follows: "It is recalled that the recruitment of substantive staff of MICAH was delayed because of financing problems and that the first advisers did not begin to arrive in Haiti until mid-June 2000. Thereafter, staff were progressively recruited and deployed and, by mid-October, the three pillars of MICAH—justice, police and human rights—had a total of 68 advisers assigned to the Ministry of Justice, HNP, the Prison Authority, the Judges School and the Office of the Ombudsman, as well as to MICAH regional offices, a human rights verification unit and units working with civil society partners" (UN General Assembly 2000c).

22. It must be noted that the viability of performing coordination functions was thoroughly discussed during the works of the Needs Assessment Mission and that this task was

contrary, withdrawal was recommended because of the lack of success. Disputes over local elections mismanagement in 1997 had caused the suspension of economic assistance to Haiti. In this regard, the Secretary-General Report on the United Nations Transition Mission in Haiti mentions electoral fraud, "voter's indifference," and "poorly trained poll watchers." The participation of the electorate did not exceed 2 or 3 percent (UN Security Council 1997c). In May 2000, the opposition contested the results of the parliamentary elections (which were held in an orderly manner with 50 percent of popular participation), on the grounds that the provisional electoral council did not calculate the electoral results according to the provisions of the electoral law.[23] As a solution could not be found to this dispute, bilateral donors did not resume funding to the Haitian government, rechanneled aid through NGOs, and withdrew the funding for the upcoming presidential elections. The UN and the OAS chose not to monitor the process, and eventually the UN mission was withdrawn. The reduction of international assistance caused a fall in the Haitian gourde and a subsequent rise in the price of basic commodities, many of which were imported. Climbing fuel prices exacerbated the inflation. Having lost international support, the forthcoming presidential elections (in which Aristide was running again for president and was expected to win) were to be financed by internal resources instead of international aid. The resulting constraints on government spending spurred unrest in the public sector (UN General Assembly 2000c, 3).

Electoral processes are quite a costly endeavor. In Haiti they are usually conducted with internationally produced ballots, and considerable resources must be mobilized for overcoming local logistical difficulties that include the lack of communication and transportation hubs. For instance, rechanneling aid through nongovernmental organizations as a response to the failure of the Haitian government to meet internationally established electoral procedures jeopardized the very programs that the UN had sponsored, such as prison, police, and judiciary reforms. In addition, internationally funded NGOs promoted diverse and disconnected agendas, often reflecting the bilateral interests of sponsoring states. Given the shortage of economic resources in the hands of the Haitian

---

seen by a number of UN representatives as very problematic due to the impossibility of the United Nations exerting any control or influence on bilateral programs.

23. All seventeen of the Senate contests held on 21 May were won on the first round (sixteen of them by Fanmi Lavalas and one by an independent). However, according to the Haitian electoral law, a runoff would have been required for eight of those seats for which no candidate obtained an absolute majority of all votes.

government, police salaries and supplies were extremely minimal and haphazard, and the situation of prisons and the judiciary remained critical. Violent crime climbed as police officers were allegedly involved "in robbery, extortion and abduction as well as drug trafficking" (UN General Assembly 2000c, 13). The situation of prisons and the judiciary was also critical. "Poor record keeping in both prisons and courts compounded the difficulties in tracking cases" and facilitated violations such as illegal or arbitrary detentions. Conditions of detention, such as "inadequate food, medical treatment, sanitary conditions, and recreation time outside cells," continued to constitute serious problems (4).

The rampant economic crisis, combined with the withdrawal of financial resources that were needed to sustain the very institutions established by the UN, led to social discontent, delegitimization of the government, and political turmoil. In February 2000 the UN, unsupported by member states, withdrew in front of the exacerbation of the problems it had meant to solve when it was deployed: lack of democracy, development, and peace. In the words of Secretary-General Annan,

> In the absence of any solution to the crisis, popular discontent seems likely to mount in response to the rising prices and increasing poverty, and may lead to further turmoil. A combination of rampant crime, violent street protests and incidents of violence targeted at the international community could severely limit the ability of MICAH to fulfill its mandate. Its capacity to function effectively has already been adversely affected by the withdrawal or reduction of once-important bilateral programmes of assistance in the areas of justice and public security. At bottom, MICAH support is contingent upon legitimate counterparts who enjoy the esteem of the Haitian people and that of the international community. (UN General Assembly 2000c, 7)

The timing of this withdrawal, shortly before the presidential elections where Aristide was expected to regain power, signaled the unwillingness of the international partners to witness and implicitly legitimize the process. On 29 February 2004, the UN returned to Haiti in the aftermath of a coup d'état that ousted Aristide for the second time.[24] As this book goes to press, Haiti is still facing the same issues. Attempts to build the Haitian

24. On 29 February 2004, the Security Council authorized the deployment of multinational forces in Haiti under chapter 7 on the ground that "the situation in Haiti constitutes

state through rule making, institutional design, disciplinarization, codification, training, and the deployment of observation and conditionality did not succeed. Instead of producing order, peace, and a jump-starting of development as predicted by developmentalist and democratic peace theories, institutional importation in Haiti entailed the depletion of political and economic resources, did not tame social turmoil, and increased dependence on international actors. The catastrophic earthquake that struck Haiti in January 2010 just exacerbated the country's extreme poverty and the weakness of the state institutions that were put in place by international peacekeepers.

SHINING INSTITUTIONS AND GLOOMY POVERTY: REFLECTIONS AND QUESTIONS ON TRANSPLANTING TECHNOLOGIES OF GOVERNMENT

Having used Foucault's historical analysis of the transformation of the modalities of power in Europe and his theoretical formulations of disciplinarity and—to a lesser extent—government to trace the genealogy and explore the modalities of the UN peacekeeping political rationale and practices in Haiti, I will now address the reasons for the ironic outcomes of this endeavor.

The UN project in Haiti revolved around three main trajectories: governmentality, disciplinary, and dispersed visibility. Through these three trajectories the UN aimed at transplanting a governmental reason whose genealogy I have traced in classical Europe. It was a governmental project because the UN privileged institutional reforms over other types of interventions, with the expectation that these reforms would bring about at the same time democracy, development, and peace.[25] It was a disciplinary project because the UN endeavored to design Haitian penal institutions as disciplinary and disciplined machineries. It was a project aimed at bringing about visibility because by measuring, counting,

---

a threat to international peace and security, and to stability in the Caribbean especially through the potential outflow of people to other states in the subregion." See UN Security Council (2004a). On 30 April 2004, by Resolution 1542 the Security Council established the United Nations Stabilization Mission in Haiti (UN Security Council 2004b).

25. For Dean, governmentalization of government designates the process by which the "problematization, scrutiny and reformation" of government becomes central, and is believed to be the instrument for changing societies: "Society can be transformed, according to this view, but this will no longer happen through conscious design based on the rational knowledge of social processes but through the transformation of the mechanisms through which it had previously been governed" (Dean 1999, 193–97).

recording, coding, and defining laws and rules, the UN attempted to make the Haitian state institutions and the life process they govern legible, transparent, and predictable.

Notwithstanding its ambitions, the UN program of reform did not achieve what it promised. Contrary to democratic peace predictions, promoting peace, democracy, and development through processes of state building patterned on Western Europe's political imaginary faced defeat in Haiti. The establishment of costly institutions combined with the lack of international financial support to the government strained the economy, fostered internal disorder and political turmoil, reinforced international conditionality, contributed to the leverage of nonstate actors with economic power (such as drug dealers), created trade-offs with alternative uses of resources, and stifled instead of promoting the creation of a viable local economy.

The UN political rationale in Haiti is rooted in functionalist and developmentalist theoretical frameworks. Functionalism sees institutions as separate spheres of society that can be isolated from context (Robinson 1996), and developmentalism sees Western modalities of government as universally valid benchmarks that can be transplanted with predictable effects.[26] Within these frameworks it is possible to address political and economic problems of "failed states" in technical terms. As Cockayne has argued, neoliberal conceptions of peace that divorce politics from political economy, combined with the narrow frame of reference of the peacekeeping mandate, contributed to producing the unintended consequences of the UN intervention in Haiti (Cockayne 2009).

Foucault's historicism and genealogical method of inquiry provide tools for unsettling universalistic claims and highlighting the situatedness of modalities of government promoted as universal benchmarks. Ideas of individual liberties, human rights, and justice as they are understood from the Enlightenment on are tightly linked with disciplinary and codified modalities of exertion of control and punishment.[27] Human

26. In the 1990s the literature on democracy and democratization proliferated, and a full review of this debate is beyond the scope of this book. It is, however, worthwhile to highlight the main theoretical divides. Liberal theorists (Dahl 1971, 1989; Huntington 1991; Linz and Stepan 1996; Schumpeter) tend to identify democracy with its procedural and institutional aspects. Scholars who draw on the "republican" tradition emphasize aspects of representation, consensus, access, and accountability of government (Gamarra 1994; Habermas 1996; O'Donnell 1992; Tilly 1995). Scholars inspired by Marxist theories emphasize the issue of equality and the indissociability of institutions from society (Gramsci 1997; Held 1989; Robinson 1996).

27. Foucault's position on the relation between discipline and modern notions of liberty and rights is not free of ambiguity. On the one hand, he sees disciplinarity as a counterweight to

rights and discipline are twins. Liberal-democratic regimes operate in conjunction with the bodies of knowledge and power that operate the disciplinarization and domestication of citizenship (Pizzorno 1992). These processes played a key role in establishing the power of the state as the main modality of organization of political life in Europe. However, institutions do not work in isolation from domestic and international politics and the economy, and the effects of transplanting them are not universally predictable but case-specific. Institutions are the expression of rationalities of power and government that emerge in given historical conditions. In attempting to carry out state building through the blueprint traced by the Enlightenment reformers, the UN intervention in Haiti precipitated instead the disintegration of the capacity of local administrations to govern. Policing through surveillance and investigation may be extremely difficult in situations of scarce resources and technological means, even more so when the state is not in the condition of generating wealth to provide and sustain them. Judicial procedures based on instructional rather than inquisitorial modalities require expert personnel, a structured administration, laboratories, computers, and so forth—in summary, a complex apparatus of knowledge and technology. Furthermore, effective policing of tiny infractions is likely to increase the prisons' population and judicial backlog. In a situation like the Haitian one, where the judiciary was already unable to process existing cases and prisons were unsuitable for decently accommodating convicts, the increasing number of inmates resulting from a more capable police force contributed to creating chaos. When international assistance was suspended or rechanneled as a consequence of the Haitian government's failure to meet international standards of electoral processes, the impossibility of providing justice officials and the police with livable salaries made them easy prey for international drug dealers and political manipulation.

Furthermore, investments in costly administrative "democratic" apparatuses siphoned resources from alternative uses. In this light, Colin Granderson, former executive director of MICIVIH, wrote, "Despite the widespread interest in human rights promotion, the ordinary Haitian would have preferred to see the Mission get more deeply involved in addressing his or her basic everyday needs and contributing to socio-economic development, if only at the micro-level" (Granderson 1997, 28).

---

the Enlightenment's juridical discourse of liberation and equality (Foucault 1995, 222); on the other hand, he indicates that carceralization, in addition to legalizing disciplinarity, is also a means for avoiding abuses in punishment (302).

SIX

NORMALIZING DEMOCRACY AND HUMAN RIGHTS
Discipline, Resistance, and Carceralization in Croatia's
Pacification and Euro-Atlantic Integration

Some mingling of history and philosophy can . . . exhibit
how possibilities came into being, creating, as they did so,
new conundrums, confusions, paradoxes, and opportunities
for good and evil.

—Hacking 2002, 7

INTRODUCTION

The analysis of the peacekeeping operation in Haiti demonstrated that
the UN political imaginary was drawn along the lines of a blueprint that
emerged in classical Europe. In light of this blueprint, the previous chapter

Sections of this chapter have been republished with minor modifications from *Journal of*
International Relations and Development 11:222–50. ©2008 Palgrave Macmillan Ltd. 1408-
6980/08. Reproduced with permission of Palgrave Macmillan.

explored the ironic political effects of the encounter between local poverty and an ethnocentric political rationale that prescribed the disciplinarization of government institutions as the means for achieving peace, democracy, and development. This chapter explores the mechanisms of government put in place by international organizations in the process of the pacification and Europeanization of Croatia, and the strategies of resistance undertaken by local administrations.

In Croatia, international organizations deployed disciplinary and governmental methods for monitoring, transforming, and steering the state's behavior toward its populations. These practices also inscribed spaces of resistance that have been used by different local government constituencies to accommodate, contest, or hijack international agendas. This chapter provides insights into how international regimes of practices in the post–Cold War era operate through isomorphic but not centralized normalizing processes, and illustrates the interaction between these regimes and local actors. It also provides an empirically grounded theoretical support for conceptualizations of power as the structure of human interactions and of resistance as strategic transformative action. Critiques of governmentality theories inspired by Agamben (which I call the sovereignty-biopolitics literature) conceptualized power as domination and resistance as total rejection of its inscriptions. The case of Croatia shows that international normalizing regimes of practices do not produce totalizing effects of domination but resisted regimes of carceralization. International power modalities of functioning are far more complex than a real or simulated projection of the might of the Leviathan. In the face of the proliferation of threats, international organizations attempt to tame risk by transforming states perceived as disorderly into normal and responsible actors. The security of liberal states depends internally on the exercise of liberty by normalized subjects (Dean 1999, 116–17). Similarly, international security is seen as the result of the "responsible behavior" of market democracies. International regimes elicit the proliferation and intensification of mechanisms for monitoring, assessing, and steering behavior. However, the effect of these regimes is not the obliteration of political life. Instead, normalization opens spaces for the definition of continuously renovated modalities of resistance. This chapter challenges totalizing representations of power as well as romanticized representations of "resistance" as a path to "liberation." It also questions positions that see "bottom up" solutions as necessarily more benign than internationally imposed models (Richmond 2008). The resistance of Croat governmental agencies to implementing the international agenda of promoting the reintegration of the Serb minority shows that the political effects of power and resistance are ambiguous, never overdetermined, and need to be explored in their contingent interactions.

THE UNITED NATIONS IN CROATIA AND THE LEGACY OF CONFLICT

When Croatia declared its independence in October 1991, Serbs living in its territory started an armed rebellion, especially in areas where they constituted a significant part of the population. The rebels were sustained by the Yugoslav National Army. UN involvement in the conflict started in 1991, when the Security Council imposed an arms embargo on Yugoslavia. In 1992 the Security Council authorized the establishment of the first peacekeeping operation in the former Yugoslavia, the United Nations Protection Force, or UNPROFOR (UN Security Council 1992), to restore peace and security in the region and to create the conditions for the implementation of the strategies developed by the International Conference on the Former Yugoslavia (ICFY).[1] UNPROFOR was at first deployed in the three United Nations Protected Areas (Eastern Slavonia, Western Slavonia, and Krajina). After the population movements that occurred as a consequence of the conflict, these areas were mostly populated by Serbs and governed by Serb authorities (UN 1998). When Bosnia and Herzegovina declared independence—a move supported by Bosnian Croats and Muslims but opposed by Serbs—the conflict escalated to that area. In Croatia, a cease-fire between the Croatian government and the Serb authorities in Krajina was signed in 1994 under the auspices of the ICFY. In order to implement this agreement, to monitor military forces crossing international borders, and to support humanitarian aid delivery, the Security Council established the United Nations Confidence Restoration Operation (UNCRO), which lasted from 31 March 1995 until November the same year (UN Security Council 1995).

In 1995 the Croatian government recovered part of the territory lost to the Krajina Serbs through two military operations: "Flash," which regained Western Slavonia in May, and "Storm," which regained the areas known as UN Sectors North and South in August. In order to prevent an escalation of the conflict to Eastern Slavonia, a group of countries known as the Contact Group (France, Germany, Russia, the United Kingdom,

---

1. The ICFY was established shortly after the beginning of the crisis in the region by the United Nations and the European Community to attempt to find a diplomatic solution to the conflict.

and the United States) brokered talks between the Croatian government and Serb authorities in Eastern Slavonia. These talks led to the establishment of UNTAES, the United Nations Transitional Administration in Eastern Slavonia, which lasted from 15 January 1996 until 15 January 1998 (UN Security Council 1996). The UNTAES mandate was spelled out in the "Basic Agreement on the Region of Eastern Slavonia, Baranja and Western Sirmium" (known as the Erdut Agreement or the Basic Agreement) signed on 12 November 1995 and witnessed by the UN and the United States. After its mandate came to an end, UNTAES was followed by a nine-month operation, the United Nations Police Support Group (UNPSG), to monitor the implementation of the agreements reached under Erdut's umbrella, especially with regard to police reform and the return of displaced persons (UN Security Council 1997g).[2] The war in the region ended with the signing on 14 December 1995 of the peace accord known as the Dayton Agreement.[3]

The Balkan conflict triggered a massive population upheaval, the consequences of which are still felt today. Many people lost their homes to new occupants, and the ethnic composition of entire areas changed. Prewar state institutions, administrative structures, and archives were destroyed or lost. Questions that were irrelevant before secession, such as who was to be considered a "citizen" of the new republics, became of paramount importance. The Yugoslav planned economy, common market, and production area collapsed; industrial facilities closed down, and entire areas were abandoned as a consequence of ethnic violence, landmines, and lack of employment opportunities.[4]

The young and productive parts of the population find the sluggish economy a disincentive to return to many parts of Croatia.[5] Economic stagnation is especially acute in areas that were industrialized before the war, and depopulation reinforced the state of economic depression.

2. The mandate of the Police Support Group was established for a single nine-month period beginning on 16 January 1998 and ending on 15 October 1998 by United Nations Security Council S/RES/1145 (1997).

3. For a full text of this agreement, see United States Institute for Peace Library, Peace Agreements Digital Collection (1995a and 1995b).

4. An in-depth analysis of the causes of the Balkan conflicts and an analysis of state formation in Croatia has been conducted by others and is beyond the scope of this work. See, for instance, Bartlett (2003); Bellamy (2003); Croatian Helsinki Committee for Human Rights (2001); Goldstein (1999); International Commission on the Balkans (1996); Kralic (1997); Suppan (2003, 116–39); Tanner (1997); United Nations (1998).

5. The president of the Joint Council of Municipalities, Jovan Ajdukovic, in a conversation with the author held in Osijek on 9 May 2003, indicated that the lack of economic perspectives is a major deterrent for young people to return.

While in rural areas—such as, for example, the Baranja region—people were somehow able to restart their activities once the land had been cleared of landmines, in industrial areas—such as, for example, the Vukovar region—people still face severe difficulties, as most prewar industries have not reopened.[6]

The population shifts that took place during and in the aftermath of the war entailed the depopulation or changed the ethnic composition of entire areas. While exact data about the number of displaced people are not available (the issue is still politically loaded), the estimates provided below are meant to outline in general terms the dimension of problem. Between 1991 and 1995 more than 500,000 people both of Croat and Serb origins were displaced either within or from Croatia. As of the end of 2002, some 305,000, or 61 percent, of people originally displaced had returned (ICG 2002). Of the total number of returnees, approximately 68 percent are Croatian of Croat origin and 32 percent are Croatian Serbs. Of the about 220,000 Croatian Croats who were displaced between 1991 and 1995 (80,000 of whom fled Eastern Slavonia after the atrocities that occurred in Vukovar), about 207,000 had returned by the end of 2002 (OSCE 2002; Republic of Croatia Ministry of Public Work 2003; Republic of Croatia ODPR 2002). In addition, about 150,000 Croats who were not living in Croatia before the conflict and who resettled there as refugees have now earned Croatian citizenship. However, of the about 300,000 Serbs who were displaced during the conflict, only 98,000 were recorded as returned in the year 2002 (ICG 2002). The Serb population in Croatia dropped from 12 percent of the total in 1991 to 4.5 percent, according to the data of the 2001 census.[7]

Normalizing Croatia by International Peace Agreements and Euro-Atlantic Integration

In Croatia numerous international organizations intervened to carry out the normalization of the country through disciplinary and governmental

6. Before the war about 33,000 inhabitants of the Vukovar region (or more than a third of the population) were employed. This number dropped to 4,223 after the war. Between 1990 and 2000 the number of unemployed persons in Osjek-Baranja County more than doubled (from 14,405 to 33,051), while it tripled in Vukovar-Sirmium County (from 7,318 to 21,624). The trend registered in the Osjek-Baranja area reflects a general trend throughout Croatia (Smoljan 2003).

7. 2001 Croatian Census. All data about population are to be taken with a grain of salt. It must be recalled that some of the people registered as citizens or permanent residents do not actually live in Croatia but across the border, especially in Serbia and Montenegro, and that the data of the census may have been skewed by the fact that many may have chosen not to declare themselves as Serbs.

mechanisms. Here I explore these processes from the establishment of UNTAES until the admission of Croatia as a candidate to the EU. At the onset of UNTAES, the UN brokered the Erdut peace agreement that, along with its annexes, set the framework for international normalizing, disciplinary, and governmental practices. The central organizing concept for the Erdut Agreement's definition of the mandate of UNTAES and of the Croatian government's long-term principles of conduct was "respect for human rights." The territorial integration of Eastern Slavonia was carried out in exchange for respecting the rights of the Serb minority. In addition, the peace agreement, by establishing specific benchmarks to be achieved and administrative arrangements to be undertaken, translated the general principles it stipulated into a governmental mechanism. Erdut established the basis for disciplinary processes of transformation of the Croatian institutions. It elicited the government's active engagement in this transformation and the continuous tutorship, examination, and assistance of international organizations. It also institutionalized international scrutiny by establishing an international diplomatic body for monitoring performance. The pages that follow discuss these processes.

The Erdut Agreement consists of three sections. The first regards short-term provisions for the administration of Eastern Slavonia under UNTAES (articles 1–5 and 12); the second includes provisions of general validity regulating the protection of human and civil rights (articles 6–9); and the third includes provisions regarding the monitoring of the implementation of the agreement after the withdrawal of UNTAES (article 10–11) (Correl 2001).[8] The first set of provisions entrusted UNTAES with the governmental tasks to be carried out during the transitional period. These were restoring public services, training and building professionalism in the police, organizing elections, and facilitating the appointment of a local Serb self-government. The second section of the agreement not only established Croatia's benchmarks regarding human rights but also translated general idioms into specific policy prescriptions. Croatia was to respect the "highest standards of internationally recognized human rights and fundamental freedoms." This meant, specifically, that all those who left the region had the right to return; that all previous permanent residents of the Republic of Croatia who came to the region had the right to stay; that the same standards of human rights should apply to all,

8. Correl's internal document, which was circulated by the UNLO to the Zagreb-based international partners, reconfirmed the continuing validity of the provisions of the Erdut Agreement after the end of peacekeeping.

regardless of ethnicity; and that all those whose property was illegally taken or who were forced to abandon it had the right to repossess it, receive compensation, or gain assistance for reconstruction.

The third section of the agreement established international disciplinarity as an open-ended modality of international governance that would exceed the goals of peacekeeping. It detailed mechanisms for monitoring the implementation of Erdut's provisions after the withdrawal of UNTAES, and for reporting on progress. In this regard, it stipulated that "after the expiration of the transition period and consistent with established practice, the international community should monitor and report on respect of human rights in the Region on a long-term basis"; and it constituted a diplomatic body, known as the Article 11 Commission, in charge of monitoring "the implementation of . . . [the Erdut] Agreement, particularly its human rights and civil rights provisions, to investigate all allegations of violations . . . , and to make appropriate recommendations" (art. 10–11). The Article 11 Commission was steered by the UNLO and was open to major international organizations and bilateral diplomatic representations present in Croatia. The Commission was a loosely institutionalized *dispositif* for monitoring and steering policy. Membership was open but not mandatory.[9] The commission established a forum for sharing ideas and devising specific strategies of political pressure on the government. Meetings were called on an ad hoc basis and held at the UNLO or at bilateral embassies. Most often, preparatory discussions were held informally at diplomatic gatherings or dinner tables. However, the commission was not a unitary agent of domination. While all spoke the idiom of human rights established in Erdut, members of the commission often emphasized different sets of priorities and were divided along the lines of bilateral agendas on which topics should be pushed with the Croatian government. For example, the ambassador from Germany was stricter than the one from Spain on the issue of property repossession, while Italy linked the issue of Serbia's repossession of property to the restitution of Italian property expropriated in Istria after World War II.[10]

---

9. As of July 2001, the Article 11 Commission included, in addition to the head of the UNLO, the ambassadors from Austria, Belgium, Canada, Finland, France, Germany, Great Britain, Greece, Italy, Japan, the Netherlands, Norway, Poland, Portugal, the Russian Federation, Spain, Sweden, Switzerland, and the European Union, as well as the rotating EU ambassador, the OSCE head of mission, the head of the European Union Military Monitor Mission, and the head of the UN High Commissioner for Refugees (UNHCR).

10. I participated in several meetings of the Article 11 Commission. The information provided here has been garnered in this context.

Disciplinarity requires the active engagement of its subjects in the process of their transformation, defines benchmarks and goals, and monitors compliance. In a letter to the president of the Security Council (known as "Letter of Intent"), subsequently attached as an annex to the Erdut Agreement, the Croatian government committed to respect the conditions stipulated there, defined in detail the benchmarks to be achieved, and submitted the process of transformation of its institutional arrangements to continuing international scrutiny (UN Security Council 1997e). The letter stipulated the administrative arrangements for minority representation in bodies of local government and public services in the Danube region. Accordingly, the Serb minority would be entitled to proportional representation (including in senior positions) in the local health services, police, and judiciary; furthermore, the posts of sub-prefect in the counties of Osijek-Baranja and Vukovar-Srijem would be reserved for a Serb. The letter went into such detail as to specify that "for at least the first year following local elections, the number of local police from the Serb and other non-Croat ethnic communities shall be approximately 700 to 800" (UN Security Council 1997e, para. 4). The number of seats to be reserved for national minorities in the House of Representatives and the Parliament would reflect the next census results; the Joint Council of Municipalities was recognized as the representational body of the Serb community; senior posts in the Ministry of Reconstruction and Development, the Office for Displaced Persons and Returnees (ODPR), and those "at a level no lower than Assistant Minister in the Ministry of Interior, Justice, Education and Culture" would be assigned to Serbs (UN Security Council 1997e, para. 7). The Croatian government also recognized the right to educational and cultural autonomy, in line with what was established in other annexes to the Erdut Agreement.[11] It acknowledged that minorities had the right to be educated in their language and script;[12] that existing schools could not be amalgamated before consulting with minority representatives; that a moratorium on teaching the history of former Yugoslavia between 1989 and 1997 was to be in effect for five years; that diplomas earned under the Krajna rule would be valid; and that school principals' ethnic representation would be proportional to demographic

11. Declaration on Educational Certificates (11 March 1997); Agreement on the Distribution of Principals' Positions (4 August 1997); Decision on Curriculum Content (4 August 1997); Declaration on Minority Education Rights (6 August 1997); Letter of Agreement of the Ministry of Education (7 August 1997).

12. Serbian uses the Cyrillic alphabet while Croatian uses Latin letters.

composition. In addition, the Croatian government restated its commitment to defer military service for members of the Serb community.

In his final report on UNTAES, Secretary-General Annan, while recommending the withdrawal of peacekeeping forces, indicated that the process of normalization that started during the UNTAES mission was the first step of a long-term transition that required, in addition to Croatia's commitment, the continuing joint effort of international actors in monitoring the country's performance and assisting its transformation through an array of means. As normalization was not yet accomplished, international disciplinarity should continue. In particular, the UN monitored the performance of the Croatian government in regulating processes designed to foster human life with a view toward bettering them. Biopolitics intensified as a trajectory of international governance. In the secretary-general's words, although "the political and institutional framework for the reintegration of civil administration . . . was finalized" (UN Security Council 1997f, para. 2), the reintegration of public services and enterprises was by and large completed, the principle of proportionality in public employment mostly respected, and demilitarization accomplished, a number of administrative arrangements that had been stipulated in Erdut and its annexes were yet to be implemented. The integration of the education and health care systems was still problematic, as was the reintegration of the social welfare system, in particular with regard to the recognition of years of work under the Republika Srbska Krajna (RSK). The report also underscored that Erdut's stipulations met resistance through administrative obstruction from local political constituencies. In the secretary-general's words, Serb returns and reintegration were inhibited by three factors: "legal and financial obstacles to the recovery of property; unrealistic government deadlines for Serb application for reconstruction assistance and delays in government funding for reconstruction of Serb houses; and the uncertain economic and social situation in the areas of potential return" (UN Security Council 1997f, para. 5). In addition, there were reasons for concern regarding the application of the Amnesty Law and the fairness of trials for human rights violations when the accused were Serbs. The administrative instruments through which the international agencies intended to bring about the normalization of Croatia through disciplinary mechanisms had also become the spaces for exertion of resistance by local political constituencies.

The secretary-general reiterated that international agencies should set the agenda by spelling out which matters needed the Croatian government's most urgent attention: administrative reforms concerning a vast array of aspects of population life, such as social welfare, education, refugee returns, and local government.[13] In order to translate general aspirations into tools for international governance, the secretary-general included in his report a list of annexes to the Erdut Agreement by which Croatia committed to undertake specific administrative reforms, thus establishing specific benchmarks subject to international scrutiny and assessment. The list includes, in addition to the Erdut Agreement and the Letter of Intent, twenty-five agreements covering in fine detail a vast array of aspects of public administration, such as labor rights, the integration of public utilities and communication networks into the Croatian system, the integration of health and education institutions, the integration and issuing of public records, the welfare and pension system, the establishment of minority representation bodies, the integration of the judiciary and the police, and a number of matters related to minority return.[14] By annexing these sub-agreements to the report that established the withdrawal

13. "Immediate priorities of the Government of Croatia for the coming winter must include the extension of national social welfare into the region to avert grave humanitarian difficulties for vulnerable groups; completion of the reintegration of health facilities and personnel; resolution of the substantial difficulties in the education sector as a whole; improvement of the conditions for return of all displaced persons in conditions of safety, economic security and personal dignity; completion of the establishment of fully functioning local government; and cessation of back-tracking on its commitment to defer conscription for two years for Serbs in the region" (UN Security Council 1997f, 34).

14. These are: Affidavit on the Rights of Public Employees (16–18 December 1996); Annex to the Affidavit (14 February 1997); Law on Convalidation (22 September 1997); Letter of Agreement by the Croatian Highway Administration (21 March 1997); Letter of Agreement by Croatian State Radio and Television (2 April 1997); Letter of Agreement by the Croatian Post and Telecommunications Administration (9 May 1997); Letter of Agreement by the Croatian Water Administration (22 May 1997); Agreement by the Croatian Pension Fund on Pension Services (29 May 1997); Letter of Agreement by the Croatian Railways (6 June 1997); Agreement by the Ministry of Health on Regional Health Services (6 June 1997); Letter of Agreement by the Croatian Electricity Company (22 July 1997); Letter of Agreement by the Croatian Forestry Commission (26 June 1997); Declaration on Educational Certificates (11 March 1997); Agreement on the Distribution of Principals' Positions (4 August 1997); Decision on Curriculum Content (4 August 1997); Declaration on Minority Education Rights (6 August 1997); Letter of Agreement by the Ministry of Education (7 August 1997); Joint Statement on the Reintegration of the Tax Department (4 September 1997); Joint Statement on Reintegration of the Employment System (11 September 1997); Joint Statement on Reintegration of the Social Welfare System (11 September 1997); Agreement on Recognition and Handover of Record Books (25 September 1997); Memorandum of Understanding on Restructuring the Transitional Police Force (undated); Agreement on the Joint Working Group on Returns (23 April 1997); Organization of the Joint Council of Municipalities (23 May 1997); Declaration on Conditions for Judicial Reintegration (19 September 1997).

of UNTAES, the secretary-general instituted their continuing validity and reinforced the Erdut Peace Agreement as an enduring governmental instrument in the hands of international organizations. Indeed, by subscribing to these agreements, Croatia accepted international governmental intervention and made itself permanently "internationally accountable": "Taken together with the provisions of the Croatian Constitution, those agreements for which Croatia has made itself internationally accountable, provide a comprehensive political and institutional framework of guarantees, which, if fully implemented, will allow the people of the region to exercise freely their rights and obligations as equal citizens of Croatia" (UN Security Council 1997f, para. 7).

The process of the normalization of Croatia through international disciplinary and governmental mechanisms continued after the withdrawal of the UN's Blue Helmets. While at this stage, the accession to the EU was playing a major role in steering the process of normalization in Croatia, as we will see in the following section, until June 2003, the UN continued to directly monitor the implementation of the Erdut Agreement in Croatia through the liaison office in Zagreb. Issues of minority rights, returns and reintegration, property repossession, and reform of the judiciary were also included in the mandates of the UN High Commissioner for Refugees (UNHCR) and the Office for the High Commissioner for Human Rights, in addition to a number of local and international NGOs. The OSCE reported on compliance with the human rights provisions of the Erdut Agreement. These agencies monitored and promoted normalization of the Croatian state by deploying an array of mechanisms, including advisory activities to the central government with regard to legal reform; diplomatic *démarches* by the Article 11 Commission on specific issues regarding minorities; informal lobbying; advising local administrations and redesigning judiciary systems; and advocacy activities and legal support for minorities.

Legal reforms were among the main instruments in the hands of international organizations for normalizing Croatian governmental processes, that is, making them abide by internationally established benchmarks of minority human rights. In June 2001, at the initiative of the OSCE, a joint legal working group (JLWG) was established to advise the government on reforms pertaining to returns and the reintegration of minorities and to support the diplomatic activities of the Article 11 Commission. The JLWG (which included representatives of the Croatian government and experts of the UNLO, the OSCE, the EU, and the UNHCR) met periodically to discuss these matters.[15] Its international component provided verbal advice and detailed working papers on laws concerning issues such as the establishment of a comprehensive regime for the repossession of the housing property taken from the Serb minority during the 1991–95 conflict; the establishment of guarantees with regard to transparent and efficient administrative procedures for the return and legalization of former habitual residents of Croatia; the promotion of proceedings to compensate for damage caused by Croatian armed forces during the war; the nondiscriminatory implementation of the law on reconstruction; and the clarification and transparent implementation of the convalidation of years of work under the RSK for retirement purposes.

The closure in June 2003 of the UNLO (the symbolic custodian of the Erdut Agreement and the last vestige of UN peacekeeping) marked, in international eyes, the conclusion of the process of pacification of the country. However, international organizations, including the OSCE, the EU, and NATO, continued to monitor Erdut's implementation and to deploy a combination of disciplinary and governmental means to monitor, tutor, and steer Croatia's normalization. In addition, the Community for Reconstruction, Development, and Stabilization (CARDS) program, guided by the Council of Europe, provides financial and technical assistance, and legal reforms regarding minority rights are coached by the European Commission for Democracy through Law (the Venice Commission).[16] Reports are prepared, statistical information collected, funds invested, advice provided, and assistance given in order to make Croatia a democratic and "normal" country by European standards. Assimilation is promoted through scrutiny, standardization, examinations, and reward/punishment mechanisms. "Government by community," a modality of liberal government relying on processes of inclusion/exclusion (Rose 1999), is a key tool in the hands of international Euro-Atlantic

15. I represented the UNLO at this JLWG.

16. Croatia has been a member of the Council of Europe since 1996. On its accession to the council, Croatia committed to carry out the Venice Commission's recommendations regarding amendments to the 1991 Constitutional Law on Human Rights and Rights of Minorities. In addition, in accordance with these commitments, international advisers appointed by the Council of Europe participate in cases before the Constitutional Court of Croatia regarding minority rights.

organizations. In order to be included, states must become normally functioning elements of the "international community," which would mean that they are considered capable of active self-management, have performing market economies, are liberal democracies, are led by predictable administrations, and are responsible protectors of the health and wealth of their citizens.

Discipline is standardizing and individualizing. For Foucault, in disciplinary institutions diverse individuals are assisted by tailored programs designed to accompany their personal transformation from deviance (or disease) into normality or health. To achieve these results, an array of *savoirs* and techniques (for instance, criminal psychology, penitentiary literature, clinical medical science, and military training) emerge that, on the one hand, treat individuals as unique entities with their specific characteristics and path of "development," and on the other hand, include them in fields of comparison and standardization. The pages that follow discuss how similar techniques were adopted and adapted in the process of Europeanization of Croatia.

Croatia signed the Stabilization and Association Agreement on 29 October 2001 and submitted its application for membership to the EU on 21 February 2003. In April 2004 the European Commission issued a positive opinion on Croatia's application (Commission of the European Communities 2004). In December 2004 the European Council endorsed the commission's opinion, and Croatia became a full candidate to the EU in October 2005. The conditions for the association of Croatia with the EU stipulated in the Stabilization and Association Process (SAP) continued and intensified the processes of normalization set in place in UNTAES (Commission of the European Communities 2002). The SAP implemented the international governmental tools in the hands of international actors through the definition of multiple benchmarks and modalities for assessing progress in respect of human rights, democracy, and liberalization of the economy. It also emphasized continuity between procedures of pacification and procedures of normalization: "[The SAP] underpin[s] the implementation of the Dayton/Paris and Erdut agreements and bring[s] basic stability and prosperity to the region" (Commission of the European Communities 2002).

The process of accession of southeastern European countries to the EU established in the SAP is set out as a disciplinary project that combines elements of reward and punishment, surveillance and training, examination and assistance, standardization and individualization.[17] Southeastern European countries are provided with incentives for reform by offering a "credible prospect for membership once the relevant conditions have been met." In order to be admitted, each "potential candidate" has to undergo periodic examinations: "Effective implementation of the Stabilization and Association Agreements is a prerequisite for any further assessment by the EU of the country's prospects of accession" (European Union 2009). The SAP aims to obtain standardized results through individualized methods. The transformation from abnormality into normality and from "deviancy" to "responsibility" is at the same time an individualizing and standardizing process, in which one's performance is compared with that of others and assessed according to benchmarks that are the same for all. On the one hand, each country must "achieve the adoption of European standards." In this regard, "the destination for all countries is expected to be the same: the full realization of association after a transitional period through implementation of the same core obligations" (European Union 2009). On the other hand, each Stabilization and Association Agreement is signed individually and "tailored to the circumstance of each country." The EU plays a role similar to a tutor, a trainer, or a psychologist to guide each individual country to normality: "The EU will work with each country to bring them closer to the standards which apply to the EU." As with any personalized training or program, the "Stabilization and Association process is . . . designed to be a flexible and dynamic process, evolving in line with changes in the region, the EU and the world" (European Union 2009).

Characteristics of democracy and respect for minorities are, along with economic criteria and adherence to European political, economic, monetary, and administrative standards, the benchmarks to be achieved to meet the conditionality for Croatia's admission into Europe.[18] In expressing its positive opinion on Croatia's accession to EU candidacy, the commission emphasized that Croatia's democratic institutions are "stable," that

17. The agreement to the Stabilization and Association Process by the countries in the region was sealed at the Zagreb Summit, held on 24 November 2000. The countries concerned were Croatia, Bosnia and Herzegovina, Serbia and Montenegro, the Former Yugoslav Republic of Macedonia, and Albania.

18. "Specifically, these criteria are: —Stability of institutions guaranteeing democracy, the rule of law, human rights and respect for and protection of minorities; —the existence of a functioning market economy, as well as the ability to cope with competitive pressures and market forces within the Union; —the ability to take on the obligations of membership, including adherence to the aims of political, economic and monetary union" (Commission of the European Communities 2004).

they "function properly," and that the 2002 and 2003 elections were "free and fair." While acknowledging that fundamental rights are by and large respected, the commission underscored that more must be done with regard to the Serb minority rights and judicial reform and for the implementation of laws improving the functioning of institutions.

With regard to the economic criteria, the commission indicated that Croatia is a functioning market economy. However, it recommended reforms aimed at extending mechanisms of standardization, visibility, and simplification to an array of issue areas still affected by legal and administrative confusion. In this regard, establishing a comprehensive property record system, clarifying administrative functions, unifying systems for taxation, and improving the performance of the judicial sector are considered the main priorities. The extension of consistent, clear, and continuous mechanisms of government is not only the main foundation for the "good governance" of each single state but also the precondition for the accession to supranational structures. Normalized states need stable legal processes and unified administrative mechanisms in order to become legible, visible, and governable for international institutions. Issues of "good governance," or governability through standardized administrative processes and unified systems, are considered key elements of Croatia's capacity to carry out the EU requirements.

Processes of visibility and simplification are matched by the intensification of mechanisms of international surveillance, necessary to accompany Croatia in its process of normalization. The commission emphasized that "to assist Croatia in the preparation of accession negotiations, a comprehensive screening exercise would need to be undertaken. . . . This Opinion is accompanied by a draft European Partnership for Croatia which identifies the priorities which it needs to address in preparing for accession. The Commission will report regularly to the Council on the progress made by Croatia on its preparation for EU membership" (Commission of the European Communities 2004, 20). The international commitment to make Croatia visible, legible, and governable is exemplified by the UNDP engagement in developing a system of statistical data collection in line with the EU's Nomenclature Territory of Statistics (NUTS) (UNDP 2003). Statistics, as Foucault has shown, were a central *savoir* in the construction of government practices based on knowledge and administration of territory of a population. Statistics made an array of local processes legible and governable to central administrations. In the post–Cold War international regime, these processes became the subject of scrutiny and betterment by international agencies, a new point of application of international government. For the UNDP, the implementation of a statistical system compatible with European standards would not only facilitate Croatia's administrative capacity and ability to carry out its commitments to the EU but also ease the implementation of international governmental mechanisms through the EU regional development policy.[19] The criteria for the collection of information had to be standardized, and Croatia had to be included in a field of comparable elements. "Croatian counties, municipalities and towns" would have to be classified "according to the model used by the bearers of the EU's structural policy and of Member States' regional policies" (UNDP 2003, 20). This process was not unproblematic. The introduction of the NUTS system in Croatia required that decisions be made with regard to the administrative organization of the territory, and that this organization be clarified and stabilized.[20] However, the UNDP report underscored that the numerous changes to the territorial organization of Croatia that had taken place in the last fifty years made collecting consistent and standardized information particularly difficult.[21] Some of the territorial arrangements required by the EU statistical system antagonized local political interests and were actively obstructed by local constituencies. This was the case, for instance, when the redefinition of territorial units to accommodate European standards would affect the calculation of the presence of refugees in certain regions and therefore the continuation of international subsidies to those areas.

19. "For the harmonization of the European Union regional policy, the establishment of the degree of regional development of a specific country, as well as for the formulation, implementation and monitoring of regional policy, there is a need to develop a harmonious system of statistical regions, which will allow the collection and processing of comparable data. . . . By introducing the NUTS, Croatia would be a step closer to Europe but also to the formulation, implementation and monitoring of regional policy" (UNDP 2003, 20).

20. "Croatia lacks systematic regional statistics. By dividing the territory of the Republic of Croatia into statistical regions it will be possible to establish regional statistics, as well as to harmonize regional data and assure their comparability as a basis for formulation of regional policy. The regions of comparable size (in terms of population size) belong to the same NUTS level, and it is therefore possible to make comparisons and various conclusions regarding different aspects of development of the regions. Only by analyzing the data collected using a common methodology in regions of the same level is it possible to compare counties, groups of counties, municipalities and cities, calculate certain indicators and monitor effects of regional development measures" (UNDP 2003, 135).

21. "In the last fifty or so years administrative organization of the territory of the Republic of Croatia has been rather unstable. The division of state territory into regions is questionable still today and the regional policy is becoming barely discernable. There is no system of monitoring statistical data needed for the implementation, control and evaluation of regional policy measures" (UNDP 2003, 133).

The process of association with NATO was carried out through idioms and techniques very similar to the ones adopted by the EU. These are standardization and individualization, advice and counseling, periodic examination, and mechanisms of reward or punishment. The NATO Membership Action Plan (MAP) "is a NATO program of advice, assistance and practical support tailored to the individual needs of countries wishing to join the Alliance" (NATO n.d.). It includes a broad range of activities of the aspiring members who must voluntarily subject themselves to continuous scrutiny, counseling, examination, and rehabilitation with regard to political and technical matters:

> The MAP's main features are the submission by aspiring members of individual annual national programmes on their preparations for possible future membership, covering political, economic, defence, resource, security and legal aspects; a focused and candid feedback mechanism on aspirant countries' progress on their programmes that includes both political and technical advice, as well as annual meetings between all NATO members and individual aspirants at the level of the North Atlantic Council to assess progress; and a defence planning approach for aspirants which includes elaboration and review of agreed planning targets. (NATO n.d.)

Progress toward internationally established benchmarks is assessed in the yearly meetings of the North Atlantic Council with individual aspirants. Nevertheless, counseling and training are continuous: "Throughout the year, meetings and workshops with NATO civilian and military experts in various fields allow for discussion of the progress report on activities under the MAP" (NATO n.d.).

The idioms and the techniques for steering and modifying behavior used by the UN, the EU, the UNDP, and NATO are isomorphic but not centralized. While these institutions share the same language discourses and instruments, they are not a unitary agent of power that can be patterned on the metaphor of the Leviathan. Representations of international organizations as a singular source of power carrying out dominating goals fail to grasp the innovative and specific modalities through which regimes of practices of international government are deployed. In contrast with notions of power as domination, patterned on the unitary and "deductive" power of the king, post–Cold War international regimes of practices work by deploying multiple but isomorphic instruments and by mobilizing the cooperation and active engagement of their targets in the process of their own transformation (Brigg 2002).

RESISTING INTERNATIONAL NORMALIZATION

The international deployment of multifarious means of normalization and disciplinarization was matched by the local constituencies' differentiated strategies of resistance. Resistance was not carried out through simple acts of rejection of all inscriptions of international power. On the contrary, resistance was often coupled with accommodation and was exerted in complex ways, all through the very administrative instruments set in place by international actors.

The JLWG became not only an instrument for internationals to foster legislation amendments but also a locus where the Croatian government deployed strategies of partial accommodation and/or hijacked the international agenda. The latter included deferring discussion of key issues, providing the JLWG meetings with statistics and data that were virtually incomprehensible, sending officials with no decision-making power to meetings, deferring discussion of key topics of the agenda by focusing on marginal issues, and passing legislation that was part of the JLWG agenda without consulting the group. For instance, in January 2003 the Croatian government forwarded to the parliament three laws on compensation for damage caused by the Croatian armed forces without consulting with the international partners. The international members suspended the JLWG until further notice in protest of the Croatian government's lack of commitment to its work.[22]

In some other cases, international organizations and diplomatic bilateral representatives were able to regulate Croatian administrative arrangements and to force compliance with the benchmarks established in the Erdut Agreement. For instance, when in 2001 the Croatian government started a police-restructuring program in Eastern Slavonia, the

22. On 23 January the principals of the international organization members of the JLWG addressed a letter to the prime minister in this regard. The motivations for suspension of the activities of the working group were given as follows: "We regret the failure of the Croatian side to take advantage of the possibilities offered by the JLWG. Pending renewal of a clear Government commitment to the JLWG along the lines that we have suggested, we therefore do not find it useful to convene other meetings of the JLWG" (Letter from the Joint Legal Working Group 2003).

Article 11 Commission took an official *démarche*[23] with the Ministry of Interior to request compliance with the principle of ethnic proportionality established in the Memorandum of Understanding (MOU) on the Restructuring of the Transitional Police Force in the UNTAES region.[24] In its *démarche,* the Article 11 Commission requested respect for proportionality in all police command positions in Eastern Slavonia and went into such detail as to indicate that, in line with Croatia's international commitments, 15.78 percent of uniformed police personnel in Eastern Slavonia should be Serbs. In practical terms, that meant adding a further 101 Serbs to the ones who were already planned for by the Ministry of Interior. However, the international "success" remained limited in scope. As of November 2005, the Eastern Slavonian police force remained the only multiethnic one in Croatia.[25] At that time, national minorities were still underrepresented in the police workforce, where only 2 percent were from minority groups (as compared to 7.5 percent in the population) (OSCE 2005).

In most cases international governmental and disciplinary efforts were met with a mixture of formal accommodation and practical sabotage. On 13 December 2002, under pressure from international counterparts, the Croatian Parliament adopted the Constitutional Law on the Rights of National Minorities (CLNM). This law provided that multiethnicity should be observed in administrative and judicial bodies, including the police, in all Croatian territories. A step in the implementation of the CLNM was

---

23. *Démarche* of 27 July 2001 with the Deputy Minister of Interior, undertaken jointly by the UNLO and the OSCE.

24. The MOU is listed among the twenty-seven agreements of continuing validity annexed to the secretary-general's report of 4 December 1997 (UN Security Council 1997f). Diverging interpretations between the Croatian government and the international partners (the OSCE and the Article 11 Commission in particular) regarding the meaning of proportionality delayed the full implementation of proportional ethnic representation. While the position of the bilateral partners of Croatia and the Zagreb-based international organizations was that only officers in uniform should be included in calculations, the government counted civilian personnel dealing with administration, cleaning, and other types of services.

25. Notwithstanding international pressure, the Ministry of Interior did not make proportionality of representation in the police force throughout the Croatian territory its first priority. For example, the public competition for the retraining of 250 attendants for the occupation of police officers published in 2003 does not include any provision regarding ethnic proportionality. Upon inquiry by the OSCE Police Adviser, the Ministry of Interior indicated that out of these 250 posts, 50 are reserved for women and minorities. However, this information could not be confirmed in any public document (interview with David Hancock, OSCE Police Adviser, OSCE Zagreb, conducted at OSCE Headquarters on 10 June 2003).

the adoption in March 2003 of the Electoral Legislation for Local and Regional Bodies.[26] In line with the provisions of this legislation, elections for minority councils were held on 18 May. However, the timing chosen by the government for these elections, called at short notice and held in the immediate aftermath of a long period of vacation connected with the Catholic and Orthodox Easter, was not designed to favor widespread participation. Voter turnout was rather low throughout the territory. Serbs and Roma were among the minorities with the lowest participation rates. The Law on Terrorist Acts, regarding compensation for property destroyed during the conflict by the Croatian army, is another instance of accommodation and sabotage. Under international pressure, in July 2003 the Croatian government passed the Law on Terrorist Acts. However, at the same time, the government declared many premises not eligible for compensation and very few owners were able to receive reconstruction assistance.

While the central government, concerned with scoring political points internationally in view of Croatia's accession to the EU, made efforts to accommodate international demands, local administrations, especially in the areas where the conflict was fierce and ethnic resentment high, tended to obstruct the implementation of all legislation that went against the interests of their constituencies. The issue of restitution of the housing properties expropriated from Serbs during the conflict was high on the agenda of international normalization of Croatia, and a very touchy political problem, especially for Croatian local administrations. During the Flash and Storm operations, by which Croatia regained the Serb-controlled areas, more than 170,000 people of Serb ethnicity were displaced into Bosnia and Herzegovina and into Serbia and Montenegro. Immediately after Flash and Storm, the Croatian government passed the Law on Temporary Take-Over and Administration of Specified Property (LTTP), which provided that those who had fled and did not return within ninety days would lose the right to reoccupy their residences. By means of this legislation, the government took over about 18,500 houses once occupied mostly by Croatian Serbs who had fled the area, and reallocated them to Bosnian and domestic Croats, including internally displaced persons (IDPs) and settlers (Republic of Croatia Ministry of Public Work 2003). As of the end of 2007, the government

26. Republic of Croatia "Amendments to the Law on the Election of Members of Representative Bodies of Local and Regional Self-Government Units," adopted by the parliament on 11 March 2003.

and its international partners had reconstructed some 188,000 houses out of 196,000 that were destroyed during the conflict. However, until 2003 some 142,000 houses reconstructed by the government were allocated almost exclusively to Croats. Discriminatory provisions included in the 1996 Law on Reconstruction with regard to allocation of funds made this possible (ICG 2002).

Throughout the process, local administrations resisted the implementation of legislation that could harm their political constituency. Court decisions were made at a very slow pace, and evictions of Croats were rarely executed unless alternative accommodations were available. An example of court delay is the case of a seventy-nine-year-old Serb, Nikola Kljajic, who had been waiting for housing repossession for eight years. Despite the fact that the court ruled in his favor in 1999 and 2004, as of April 2006 Kljajic was not able to repossess his home due to lack of enforcement of the court's decision (OSCE 2006). In addition, even when houses have been repossessed, owners have often found them looted and have had no recourse to recover damages other than by starting a costly private lawsuit with little chance of success. The policy of local administrations concerning access to utilities when the applicants were Serb families is another instance of obstruction: in many cases returnees had not been able to get utilities reconnected unless they paid the former occupants' outstanding bills. Some areas inhabited by minorities were not provided with basic services such as road maintenance or snow plowing during the winter.

In 2002, in response to complaints about the ineffective and discriminatory practices of the local housing commission, the government centralized the housing repossession process at the ministerial level. Since 2003 Croatian Serbs have represented 95 percent of the beneficiaries of government reconstruction programs (OSCE 2008). With the exception of about two hundred cases still pending, the property repossession process was completed in 2005 (OSCE 2005). However, administrative obstruction from local constituencies has made repossession difficult to sustain. As of 2006 only 25 percent of the property returned was inhabited by the prewar owners (OSCE 2006). Property rights are part of commonly accepted liberal legal language. However, in Croatia, socially owned flats further complicated the housing repossession issue. In urban areas under the former Yugoslavian regime, families were entitled to live in socially owned flats as part of their work benefits. Serbs who fled their homes during the war were deprived of these rights, either on the basis of an absence of more than six months (as established in prewar legislation) or on the basis of the ninety-day deadline for return set in the LTTP. In a war situation, these deadlines were difficult to meet. The Croatian government had for years resisted addressing this category of apartments, and international actors, without a consolidated legal ground on which to base their claims, were less vocal in advocating restitution than in the case of private property. Notwithstanding the government's progress in taking the necessary administrative steps, as of January 2008 a housing solution still had to be found for more than half of the Croatian Serbs who lived in former socially owned apartments and who had applied for housing care (OSCE 2008).[27]

Unintended consequences are also at play. The territorial limitation of the provisions of the Erdut Agreement produced ironic effects. Because occupancy rights in the UNTAES region were not canceled, the mostly Croat returnees were able to regain their houses. The same was not true for those Serbs who were displaced into the UNTAES region during the war and attempted to return to their homes in other areas of Croatia. Returns to the Danube region were mostly "majority returns." By stating the right of all to their residences, Erdut protected the rights of the Croat majority whose homes were occupied by minority Serbs. However, as its provisions were territorially limited to Eastern Slavonia, the Erdut Agreement offered no remedy for Serbs who were evicted from the Danube region but were not able to repossess property in other parts of Croatia. Attempts to deal with the issue of returns in a comprehensive manner were reflected in the implementation in 2005 of the "Sarajevo Process" by which Croatia, Serbia, and Montenegro indicated their commitment to find a regionally integrated solution to the problem of displaced people. The implementation has, however, been undertaken at a very slow pace.

The use of administrative means to resist minority reintegration is not limited to the housing issue. Under the Yugoslav state, citizens who were not born within the administrative borders of what later became independent states, but who were working and living there, were considered habitual residents and had full right to stay. After secession, this right was often refused to Serbs attempting to return to Croatia. Furthermore, as Croatian citizenship legislation discriminates on the basis of

27. As of 2007, out of the 30,000 former Occupancy and Tenancy Rights holders displaced during the war, some 13,000 applied for housing care programs. By the end of 2007, 4,500 of these cases had been positively resolved, 2,000 were denied, 2,800 were awaiting resolution, and 3,900 that had received positive consideration were still awaiting implementation (OSCE 2008).

ethnicity, ethnic Croats who had never resided in Croatia before the conflict easily obtained citizenship, while Serbs and other minorities who used to be permanent residents continue to face obstacles. These obstacles are aggravated by the slow response of local administrations to minority applications for personal records and identification documents, which are necessary to exert rights in a modern state bureaucracy.

Notwithstanding the conditions stipulated in the annexes to the Erdut Agreement, the Croatian social welfare system continued to delay the full implementation of the Law on Convalidation passed by the parliament in October 1997. This law provides for the recognition of the years worked under the RSK for retirement purposes. The lack of recognition of those years of service makes unavailable the only source of basic income for thousands of Serb former employees who would otherwise be eligible for pensions. International agencies assessed Croatia's progress toward normalization as sufficient to be admitted as a candidate into the EU. While ethnically motivated physical confrontations or threats to life are rare, in areas where the process of returns is still underway, Serbs still face verbal harassment and arrests for alleged war crimes that remain often unsubstantiated. In areas heavily affected by conflict, such as Eastern Slavonia, Serbs and Croats still carry on separate lives and send their children to different schools. While the war of guns is over, the war of looks and words is still ongoing.[28] The nationalistic agenda remains an appealing one to many who were involved with or have been affected by the war. The street protests that followed the December 2005 capture of Croatian general Ante Gotovina, indicted as a war criminal by the International Criminal Tribunal for Yugoslavia yet a hero to many, may signal that the various techniques of administrative and legal normalization deployed by international actors are not matched by normalization of the internal political process.

As William Connolly has argued, legal language does not determine court decisions, while culture, ethos, and social acceptance resist normalization and escape totalizing processes (Connolly 2004). In Croatia, international normalization is enacted through the continuous refinement and redeployment of international mechanisms to scrutinize, assess, and transform the state. These mechanisms in turn foster the opening of new spaces for resistance and agonic political endeavors. However, as the analysis of the interaction among international power,

28. A writing contest I organized and managed in high schools in Eastern Slavonia in 2003 highlighted that youths of Croat and Serb ethnicity still lived separate lives and blamed each other for the war.

the practices of the Croatian government, and local authorities has demonstrated, processes of local resistance are not necessarily conducive to the liberation of subjugated minorities.

TRANSPARENT REGULATIONS, OPAQUE POLITICS: REFLECTIONS ON POWER, RESISTANCE, AND LIBERATION

The internationally sponsored peace agreements and activities of various international agencies in Croatia illustrate the migration to the international arena of governmental techniques that were previously adopted within states. For Foucault, the disciplinarization of penal institutions produces a particular type of population, the "delinquent." Delinquency is a form of subjectification connected with the practices and expertise that emerged contextually with the invention of the prison and the shift of modalities of punishment from haphazard violence to disciplinarization. While the offender's body was the point of application of the revenge of the king, the delinquent is the subject of multifarious *dispositifs* of surveillance and techniques of correction of the soul deployed in the context of the carceral system (Foucault 1995). Carceral institutions do produce an intensification of the techniques aimed at the delinquent's normalization, but they are not successful in totally obliterating resistance. While power relations are uneven, complete domination—that is, "when the determining factor saturates the whole" (Foucault 1982b, 221)—is not the normal outcome of relations of power. Freedom does not disappear in the process. On the contrary, it is a precondition for power to be exerted (Foucault 1982b, 221). For Foucault, carceralization not only describes the modality of the prison but can also be read as a more general way of ruling societies based on surveillance, knowledge, and discipline. The case of Croatia explored here shows that carceralization is a key trajectory of post–Cold War international regimes. International order is sought through the proliferation of instruments of international knowledge, surveillance, control, and disciplinarization of elements of the international arena that are subjectified as "delinquents." However, while intensifying these governmental mechanisms, international organizations' political rationales and techniques of government do not completely succeed in normalizing delinquent states but are met with diverse strategies of resistance.

In Croatia, international agreements signed in the context of peacekeeping constitute the starting point of a normalizing process that continues beyond the withdrawal of the UN's Blue Helmets under the umbrella of regional organizations, such as the EU, NATO, and the OSCE. These organizations rely on Erdut's peace agreement idioms, stipulations, and prescriptions to set in place and expand benchmarks, rules, regulations, monitoring, assistance, assessment, and reward/punishment mechanisms. International organizations attempt to regulate and normalize the conduct of state institutions and local administrations through the multiplication of disciplinary techniques. These processes have been accommodated and resisted by Croatian governmental agencies through the very instruments deployed by the international bodies. The strategies are multifarious, the outcomes mixed, and the political effects uneven. The tactics of the central government for sidestepping the advice of the JLWG, the local administrations' lack of implementation of evictions when illegal occupants were Croats, the slow recognition of pension rights for Serbs, and the difficulties Serbs encounter in obtaining citizenship and identification documents constitute examples of this resistance. When international demands with regard to minority rights could not be satisfied without hurting the interests of ethnic Croats, they were hijacked by local administrations. International normalization has been resisted in Croatia by local governmental agencies. Resistance has been exerted through the very spaces opened by international disciplinary endeavors in a variety of ways, spanning from accommodation to overt administrative obstruction.

In his analysis of discourses of power in Western political thought, Barry Hindess argued that Foucault's most relevant theoretical contribution is a distinctive understanding of power that distances itself both from theoretical traditions that conceive of it as capability (Hobbes) and traditions that see it as rooted in legitimacy and consent (Locke). In both of these traditions, power is understood "as enhancing the capacity of those who possess it, and consequently, insofar as it impinges on other persons, as an imposition on the freedom of those persons" (Hindess 1996, 96). In these frameworks, power is a "quantity" exerted on autonomous agents, and the research agenda focuses on analyzing its effects on ontologically free, rational, and moral individuals. Its effects are assessed in terms of the *difference* between the real and a postulated ideal (Hindess 1996, 149). Dwelling on these conceptualizations of power, critical theories (in particular the Frankfurt school) articulate the problematic of emancipation as part of the problematic of legitimacy: illegitimate power is the main obstacle to the achievement of individual autonomy. The critical referents of Hindess in this regard are Marcuse and Habermas. Regardless of their differences, both Marcuse's and Habermas's conceptualizations of power and resistance rely on "an image of the autonomous individual which provides an ideal against which the present can be measured; . . . [and] the claim that such an ideal could be realized in a realm of social existence that is not structured by the illegitimate effects of power" (Hindess 1996, 95). In this context, the subject (ontologically autonomous) and power (conceptualized along the lines of oppressive sovereignty) are defined by a relation of externality, where each is endowed with attributes and qualities that precede their relationship. "Emancipation" is then presented as an ideal condition of individual autonomy against the oppressive effects of social forces. Foucault moves away from this fixation with sovereignty and legitimacy and provides an elaboration of power as the ubiquitous feature of human interactions (Hindess 1996, 96–101). While for Habermas and Marcuse "emancipation" presupposes a relation of externality between the subject and power, for Foucault the subject and power are imbricated with each other.[29] Exploring power is indeed a way of exploring "the different modes by which, in our culture, human beings are made subjects" (Foucault 1982b, 208). Resistance does not relate to power in an oppositional but rather in a transformative manner. For Foucault, freedom is a practice in agonic relation with power, not a natural condition of human life. Liberty and power stand in a relation of "complicated interplay" (Foucault 1982b, 221). In Foucault's own words, "At the very heart of the power relationship, and constantly provoking it, are the recalcitrance of the will and the intransigence of freedom. Rather than speaking of an essential freedom it would be better to speak of an 'agonism' of a relationship which is at the same time reciprocal incitation and struggle; less of a face-to-face confrontation which paralyzes both sides than a permanent provocation" (Foucault 1982b, 221–22).

29. In his exploration of the uses of the notion of emancipation, Ernesto Laclau argues that both secular and religious emancipatory discourses rely on dichotomous understandings that posit a total externality between the oppressor and the oppressed. For Laclau the relation between the oppressor and the oppressed is one of undecidability: "To be oppressed is part of my identity as a subject struggling for emancipation; without the presence of the oppressor my identity would be different" (Laclau 1996, 17). Thus, for Laclau, contemporary social struggles put us face to face with the very possibilities that are opened by our finitude. To reflect this conceptualization, Laclau chooses to the word "freedom" instead of "emancipation." A debate on the semantics of emancipation, freedom, and liberation are beyond the scope of this study. I have chose to use mostly the term "liberation" because this is the term of choice of the literature I am critically addressing.

In summary, as the structure of relations brought to bear, power is unstable, ambiguous, and reversible. Its does not entail eliminating liberty, and domination is only its extreme manifestation. In this framework very little can be said about power in general. Here power must be studied in its contingent modalities and strategic interactions with resistance. Biopolitics-sovereignty scholars, relying on Giorgio Agamben's reading of Foucault (Agamben 1998), move away from understandings of power as an agonic, contingent, and reversible structure of human interactions. Power is patterned along the metaphor of sovereignty, and the focus shifts from strategic interaction to domination (Edkins, Pin-Fat, and Shapiro 2004; Prozorov 2004, 2007).[30] Agamben sees the Nazi concentration camp as the paradigm of modern power, where the coupling of sovereignty and biopolitics produces violent and totalizing effects (Agamben 1998). Here the subject is stripped of political life, to be reduced to "bare life," that is, life excluded from juridical order. Building on Agamben, Prozorov argues that modern power is a totalizing project that *abducts* human existence in all its aspects: "When sovereign and biopolitical powers are combined, we . . . deal with . . . a genuinely absolute abduction of human existence that mends all separations and no longer excludes anything from its operations" (Prozorov 2007, 107). For Prozorov freedom is ontologically "anterior and exterior to any form of positive order" (Prozorov 2007, 10) and essentially antagonistic to it. All discourses of power "sacrifice the experience of freedom by turning human existence into a project" (Prozorov 2007, 9). Prozorov envisages two ways out of the totalizing inscriptions of liberal power. On the one hand, building on Carl Schmitt, Prozorov situates the exit point in the sovereign act of decision on exceptions through which the foundation of political order is established (Prozorov 2004).[31] On the other hand, he identifies resistance as "bottom up" individual acts of total rejection of the inscriptions of biopolitics (Prozorov 2007). For Prozorov, the most

---

30. For a critique of Agamben's discussion of sovereignty and power, see also Neal (2004). For Neal, Agamben poses the problem of sovereignty in rather apolitical and juridico-philosophical terms, and creates caricatured extremes. On the contrary, Foucault engages in a historical critique of sovereignty, in particular of sovereignty in its Hobbesian form, as the emanation from a single center of power.

31. Here Prozorov differs from Agamben. While for Agamben the sovereign's decision on exception is the basis for the reduction of political life to bare life, for Prozorov the sovereign's decision on exception constitutes a pristine constitutional moment of political life and the "way out" from the totalizing inscriptions of liberal power.

radical aspect of Foucault's elaboration of resistance is recasting "freedom in terms of dispossession," that is, weakening power by refusing its care. From this perspective, which is shared by other scholars such as Edkins and Pin-Fat, resistance is articulated as absolute rejection of the diagram of power, its "drawing lines." As Edkins and Pin-Fat would have it, "since sovereign power relies on two things—first, the drawing of lines between forms of life and, second, the production thereby of a generalized bare life—there are two ways in which the demand for a return to politics can be articulated: first the refusal of sovereign distinctions and the acceptance of bare life" (Edkins, Pin-Fat, and Shapiro 2004, 12–13).

Here resistance is conceptualized as the sovereign's act of foundational creation or as the individual's total rejection of power rather than an agonic game of contestation where both power and resistance are continuously reformulated. Political life consists of escaping power through acts of "dispossession" by which humanity will achieve "the end of the exodus of the subject of freedom from the diagram, the recovery of one's potentiality for being from its biopolitical confinement" (Prozorov 2007, 146). Liberated from all constraints, diagrams, and inscriptions, a freed humanity will live in a world of pure possibilities: "Elated by the infinite expanse of possibilities now available to him, he breaks into a run, eager to return to a life he never had" (Prozorov 2007, 152). The subject, constituted for Foucault within contingent relations of power and resistance, comes back here in full force as an ontological a priori endowed with freedom. As a new end of history is envisaged, both power (conceptualized along the lines of sovereignty) and the autonomous rational individual become the referents for grand narratives of oppression and liberation and universal prescriptions for reaching a "freer freedom" (Rose 1992). Not surprisingly, for Prozorov, governmentality studies are a mere redescription of liberal discourses of governance: "Because they do not foresee an opening onto the exterior of the diagram [of power] they do not have much to say about the problematic of resistance" (Prozorov 2004). Prozorov's conceptualizations of resistance and liberation remain trapped in understandings of power as capacity and legitimacy in a relation of externality with the subject. The research agenda that emerges here is concerned with asking "why the postulated ideal conditions do not exist" (Hindess 1996, 149). Instead, research agendas generated in the context of governmentality theories focus on "what happens" and explore practical questions of the modalities of deployment of power. Here the problematic of freedom is studied as an articulation of the problematic of liberal governance, rather than as the measure of the gaps between a real and an ideal condition of humanity. As Nikolas Rose would have it,

> Freedom . . . is no "natural" property of political subjects, awaiting only the removal of constraints for it to flower forth in forms that will ensure the maximization of economic and social well-being. The practices of modern freedom have been constructed out of an arduous, haphazard and contingent concatenation of problematizations, strategies of government and techniques of regulation. This is not to say that our freedom is a sham. It is to say that the agonistic relation between liberty and government is an intrinsic part of what we have come to know as freedom. (Rose 1996, 61–62)

Unlike Agamben-inspired readings of liberalism, political agency in this framework is not seen as the quest for a pristine freedom by a subject that is ontologically independent from and inevitably crushed by power, but as constituted within a series of uneven and agonic situated responses to contingent conditions that in turn it transforms.

Bhabha's elaboration of postcolonial relations as hybridization instead of binary opposition between fixed and distinct identities offers interesting tools for exploring the effects of governmental rationalities. As Ilan Kapoor has shown, for Bhabha agency and subjection are intimately related (Kapoor 2008, 12). Bhabha defines hybridization as follows: "Colonial hybridity is not a problem of genealogy or identity between two different cultures which can then be resolved as an issue of cultural relativism. Hybridity is a problematic of colonial representation and individuation that reverses the effects of the colonialist disavowal, so that other 'denied' knowledges enter upon the dominant discourse and estrange the basis of its authority—its rules of recognition" (Bhabha 1985, 156). Resistance, in this framework, is not portrayed as binary opposition to or total rejection of a unified totalizing assemblage of power. The political challenge is played instead at the level of meaning, through moves that, because they recognize and question discourses of power that at the same time unsettle their universality claim, erode their unity, and appropriate and transform them. For Bhabha,

> The display of hybridity—its peculiar "replication"—terrorizes authority with the *ruse* of recognition, its mimicry, its mockery.

Such a reading of colonial authority profoundly unsettles the demand that figures at the centre of the originary myth of colonialist power. It is the demand that *the space it occupies be unbounded,* its reality *coincident* with the emergence of an imperialist narrative and history, its discourse *nondialogic,* its enunciation *unitary,* unmarked by the trace of difference—a demand that is recognizable in a range of justificatory Western "civil" discourses." (Bhabha 1985, 158; emphasis in original)

In Kapoor's view, Bhabha sends a note of caution to those whose response to subjection is direct opposition, a warning that "overcoming domination, far from getting rid of it, often occasions its mere reversal" (Bhabha 1985, 55, cited in Kapoor 2008, 123). Agency, in this framework, is seen as negotiation more than as dispossession or "opposition": "The agent must play with the cards s/he is dealt, and the hegemon, despite the appearance of absolute strength, needs or desires the subaltern" (Kapoor 2008, 124).

Jacqueline Best has shown that one should not be seduced by contemporary political rationales' own promise of infallibility. The management of ambiguity in the name of a "technocratic ideal of reason" is one of the aspirations of liberal governmentality. Indeed, representing social events as totally calculable is part of high modernist attempts to "depoliticize the term, ignoring its social constitution and denying the power of its act of naming and defining" (Best 2008, 363). For Best, ambiguity should be included in current analyses of governmental tactics and relates to government at three levels. Ambiguity, like uncertainty and risk, can simultaneously be "an object of governance—that one seeks to contain—a strategic asset in governance—that is exploited to achieve a certain end—and a limit to governance—as that which exceeds efforts to control" (Best 2008, 363). More specifically,

the slipperiness of communication and its openness to multiple and even subversive interpretations can pose a significant problem for government and lead to strategies for *governing ambiguity.* At the same time, . . . ambiguity can itself be a strategic asset for those who seek to *govern through ambiguity.* Yet, even in such cases the ambiguity will always exceed efforts to control and exploit it, generating unintended meanings and effects and acting as a *limit to governance.* Such practices and problems thus do not simply parallel those for managing risk and uncertainty, but also complicate those efforts in interesting ways. (Best 2008, 356; emphasis in original)

To conclude, the goal of the analysis proposed here is not to explore the conditions of a freer freedom, or to construct a romanticized rhetoric of rejection as ways of escaping or subverting domination. I employ a governmentality framework to interrogate tactics and practices of power. This interrogation does not propose apocalyptic or totalizing views, cast an entirely negative judgment on all international power manifestations (Larner and Walters 2004a, 2004b), or, for that matter, attach an unqualified liberation power to resistance. In a governmentality framework, the exercise of freedom (intended as agonic political struggle) is not reached mainly through acts of total rejection, be they rooted in the sovereign's foundational decision on exception or in the layperson's total refusal of power's inscriptions. More modestly, the struggle for freedom is sought through activities and modalities of inquiry that "unsettle the obvious" aspects of idioms and practices of power. If (contingent) possibilities of unsettling the inscription of the diagram are possible, they result from inquiries that explore the formation of idioms of government (and resistance), question their universal normative claim, and denaturalize their accepted practices. As Nikolas Rose puts it, "The destabilization of our ethical repertoire is an ethical work upon ourselves" (Rose 1999, 10). Instead of prescribing paths for liberation, governmentality provides "tools of inquiry in the hands of those who question the universal validity of our current practices" (Rose 1999, 19). It is this methodological concern that makes governmentality studies very different from the biopolitics-sovereignty literature, from liberal accounts that take prevailing discourses and idioms for granted, and from sociologies of rule that focus on identifying established patterns and regularities.[32] As I have written in chapter 2, a governmentality approach to the analysis of international security questions both "a social ontology that converts boundaries and standards central to modern life into precepts of rationality, morality or self realization" (Connolly 1987, 9) and romanticized conceptualizations that unreflectively attach liberation or "emancipatory" qualities to resistance. It brings to light the normalizing effects that international political rationalities produce, the contestation they elicit, and the ambiguous outcomes of the interplay between power and resistance. One of the implications of conceptualizing resistance as an agonic activity imbricated with power is that no uncontested ethical value can be unreflexively

---

32. For a more extensive discussion of the epistemological differences between governmentality studies and sociologies of rule, see Rose (1999, 19).

SEVEN

CONCLUSIONS

> *My point is not that everything is bad, but that every-*
> *thing is dangerous, which is not exactly the same as bad. If*
> *everything is dangerous, then we always have something to*
> *do. So my position leads not to apathy but to hyper- and*
> *pessimistic activism.*
>
> —Foucault 1982a, 231–32

In recent years governmentality theories have been recognized as a distinctive theoretical approach to the study of international relations (Merlingen 2006). This body of literature focuses on the analysis of regimes of practices, such as the *how* of power, its idioms, its technologies, its multiple and contingent configurations, and local interaction and effects. For Foucault, "to analyze 'regimes of practices' means to analyze programmes of conduct which have both prescriptive effects regarding what is to be done (effects of 'jurisdiction') and codifying effects regarding what is to be known" (Foucault 1991b, 75). Relevant questions in this regard are how specific idioms and rationalities have come to exist, how they are translated into practices of government, what forms of subjectification emerge, what spaces of resistance are opened, how these openings are strategically used by different actors, and what political effects are produced in the process. Inquiries do not examine the legitimacy of power, but the modalities of its legitimization and continuous transformation. This book has mapped the idioms and governmental mechanisms deployed by international organizations for maintaining order in the post–Cold War era. Through the analysis of UN policy documents and of the idioms and modalities of government deployed in the peacekeeping operation in Haiti and in the process of pacification and Europeanization of Croatia, I have shown that in the post–Cold War era, international security regimes of practices operate through the proliferation and intensification of mechanisms for monitoring, steering, and disciplining potentially disorderly states and through biopolitical means for monitoring and protecting populations. Contextually with the reformulation of the problematic of security in terms of risk, international organizations attempt to bring about security by transforming states perceived as disorderly into normal and responsible actors. Beginning in the 1990s, idioms of democracy converged with idioms of security. Normality is identified with liberal democracy, and various degrees of international threats with nondemocratic regimes. The establishment of democracy, a market economy, and human rights are seen as instruments for the pacification of disorderly states in the context of UN peacekeeping operations, as well as criteria for these states' inclusion into international political associations and military alliances.

Idioms of democracy, market economy, and human rights subjectify states that lack these qualities as *abnormal* and make them the referents for practices of disciplinarization and the potential target of forcible intervention. The figure of the abnormal in the classical era was connected to the "social monster," someone who deviated from normal behavior or appearance, or who stood outside the law. The emergence of the social figure of the abnormal was matched by an intensification of emphasis on norms as well as with the implementation of extreme measures against those who would not abide by these norms. In the post–Cold War era, governmental and disciplinary techniques for monitoring and transforming states are coupled with biopolitical idioms that subjectify nondemocratic states as political and moral monsters. Thus, while force by itself is less and less considered an effective way of governing disorder, the subjectification of nondemocratic states as monsters and the reframing of intervention in ethical terms reinforce the legitimization of international use of force. International use of force for restoring democracy or fostering human security and protecting populations is coupled with the application to state institutions of techniques that liberal governments experimented with on individuals. The production of responsible states is pursued through international disciplinary and governmental initiatives, such as the prescription of administrative procedures, advice on an array of legal matters, scrutiny and assessment of results, financial aid, normalization of knowledge so as to make governmental procedures and populations visible and transparent to international agencies, and inclusion/exclusion mechanisms.

International government entails the proliferation of auditing and assessment mechanisms that include states in a field of international comparison concerning an array of issue areas.[1] The intensified use of conditionality (for instance, for accession to the EU and NATO in the case of Croatia, or for obtaining international funding in the case of Haiti) is an international modality of "governing by community" (Rose 1999) that, based on standardized data collection, reporting, and periodic examinations, establishes inclusion or exclusion from supranational structures or aid networks. In the last decades of the twentieth century, inclusion into or exclusion from particular communities and the conditionality attached to public assistance became a means for normalizing abnormal individuals and transforming them into functioning elements of society. In order to be admitted into the community of citizens and receive the full benefits that derive from this status, "abject" individuals must undergo moral reformation and behave responsibly and rationally (Rose 1999). Similarly, full admission of states into the "international community" is linked to their "responsible behavior." By means of these processes of inclusion or exclusion, the international community of democracies deploys normalization techniques designed to continue beyond peacekeeping and purports to constitute itself as a regulated, transparent, and predictable moral space in opposition to obscure, undemocratic, and morally deviant borderlands. In the post–Cold War era, normalizing international regimes work through assemblages that bring together apparently "illiberal" trajectories of government, such as forcible intervention, with more modern modalities of rule such as disciplinarity, surveillance, regulation, and responsibility as a way of taming

1. On the relevance of auditing as a technology of liberal government, see Rose (1996 and 1999) and Power (1994).

international disorder and promoting security. As Nikolas Rose put it, "Those mechanisms and devices operating according to a disciplinary logic . . . seek to produce the subjective conditions, the forms of self mastery, self-regulation and self control, necessary to govern a nation now made up of civilized citizens" (quoted in Burchell, Gordon, and Miller 1996, 44). If we substitute "nation" with "international space" and "citizens" with "states," we see that the modalities of post–Cold War international government are isomorphic to internal mechanisms of rule that emerged within nation states as modalities for conducting populations' conduct.

This book has shown that the post–Cold War era normalizing regime functions along three main trajectories: institutional disciplinarity (the capillary transformation of the institutions of potentially disorderly states and the implementation of dispersed and capillary observation *dispositifs*); governmentalization (the establishment of standardized and detailed rules of behavior for national governments, the deployment of mechanisms of control, reward, and punishment, and inclusion in or exclusion from international political structures); and biopolitics (the increasing focus of international organizations on populations both as a subject of government and knowledge, and as a referent for direct intervention). However, notwithstanding the intensification of these mechanisms of control and transformation and the expanded legitimization of intervention, the post–Cold War international security regime does not achieve its stated goals, nor does it produce overarching effects of "domination," but rather of carceralization. Resistance and unintended consequences are at stake. Democratization in Haiti is imagined as the result of a process of social engineering aimed at the reconstruction of penal institutions as disciplinary machines. This reconstruction is carried out through processes of institutional design, codification, training, visibility, and simplification. Local, noncodified practices had to be standardized and punishment consistently and continuously dispensed according to established rules. However, these forms of institutionalization are unsustainable in a situation of extreme poverty. They reinforce dependence on international assistance and, as a result, they undermine instead of building what they purport to construct, that is, the Haitian state.

The insights provided by the exploration of the case of Haiti open the way for a few reflections on democracy and for a critique of functionalist theoretical frameworks that see institutions as a separate sphere of society. The case of Haiti indicates that, in the peacekeeping imaginary, the construction of modern states and the respect for liberties are strictly intertwined with the engineering of disciplinary and surveillance mechanisms. Peacekeepers and human rights workers enacted processes aimed at building predictable penal institutions. In their imaginary, these institutions had to be reformed so as to constitute a continuous system; punishment had to be made certain and regulated by law; modalities of punishment had to be codified and proportionate to the offense; and determination of guilt had to be extricated from the ordeal of torture and included in the field of common reason. Indeed, the case of Haiti suggests that the techniques of power that govern through control and surveillance are the same ones that guarantee citizens' rights as we understand them from the Enlightenment on. The case of Haiti also shows that institutions do not work as a separate sphere of society that can be transplanted with predictable effects. In situations of extreme poverty and lack of internally generated wealth, the prescriptions of "good governance" may foster further disaggregation of the state. Democratic governments rely on relatively sophisticated techniques and costly processes. They are based on the availability of instruments for the collection of capillary information about population, such as census, citizenship, birth and death records, identity cards, electoral certificates, social security numbers, and the like. These processes require material and human resources. In cases of extreme poverty, electoral processes may siphon resources from alternative uses. Compliance with internationally set high standards and technologically rich procedures for elections may become an additional element of dependence resulting in the instability of local governments; similarly, technologically rich judicial and policing procedures that presuppose extensive institutionalization of the juridical system may end up making justice impracticable. Instead of "building the state," UN-promoted institutional reforms foster internal disorder, dependence on international aid, and the blurring of national and international spaces of government. Prodemocracy peacekeeping interventions aim at implementing programs that, at least on paper, are egalitarian: they apply the same rules to all, codify and regulate state institutions, and subject them to scrutiny both from the inside and from the outside. Nevertheless, these practices adopt the political imaginary elaborated in Europe during the Enlightenment as a universal ideal that can be exported regardless of its conditions of implementation. Processes of formal institutionalization are thicker than their anodyne stated programmatic goals. They are, often, the means for implementing bilateral agendas and political preferences,[2] and produce consequences that escape the control of international organizations.

In the context of Croatia, international biopolitical and governmental endeavors for protecting minorities are continuously challenged by the central government's lukewarm cooperation and the local administrations' obstruction. During the UNTAES and the process of admission into the EU, a plurality of internal processes of government were regulated by peace agreements and international law.[3] The biopolitical concern with the well-being of populations, or, in Pasquino's words, "cura promovendi salutem," was included in supranational conditionality and became a dimension of international security. International agreements purported to regulate the way the Croatian government administers populations. However, these efforts were continuously resisted through multifarious strategic moves by local governmental agencies. While the pacification and Europeanization of Croatia are sought through an assemblage of techniques that include knowledge, surveillance, control, and disciplinarization, international organizations' political rationales and governmental practices do not succeed in normalizing the "delinquent" state, but are met with multifarious strategies of resistance. They do not produce totalizing effects of domination but resisted regimes of carceralization. The effect of these regimes is not the obliteration of political life, but the opening of new spaces for the exertion of multifarious strategies of resistance. While power relations are uneven, freedom does not disappear, but it remains as a "recalcitrance of the will," a transformative force, and the precondition for power to be exerted (Foucault 1982b, 221–22). The case of Croatia also questions romanticized images of resistance that see it as a process of "liberation" against the oppressive nature of power. Resistance, in this case, does not produce liberatory effects for the Serb minority. The political effects of power and resistance are ambiguous and not overdetermined by normalizing powers. Their "benign" or "malignant" effects need to be explored in the light of their contingent manifestation and not romanticized through grand narratives of oppression and liberation.

The outcomes of the analysis conducted in this book open the way for a few considerations regarding the role of the UN in the international security

2. For the notion of "thick descriptions," see Geertz (1983).

3. It will be recalled that Foucault argued that as government took shape as a way of rule distinct from sovereignty, law became an instrument to "arrange things" in order to achieve a plurality of ends. See Foucault (1991a, 95).

system. François Debrix has argued that the UN is facing marginalization due to its failure to credibly represent simulacra of world order (Debrix 1999). However, Debrix's analysis relies on a conceptualization of international power in peacekeeping as a projection through the media of the (simulated) might of the Leviathan. Because the simulated Leviathan's credibility was challenged by failures, Debrix argues, the UN has become increasingly irrelevant. The study of UN discourses of security as well as of the peacekeeping operations in Haiti and in Croatia conducted in this book show that the UN still performs important functions in sustaining global regimes for governing disorder. The United Nations' role in maintaining international order is carried out through processes of social engineering that are much more capillary, decentralized, and multifarious than the image of the Leviathan would suggest. At the beginning of the twenty-first century, the UN continues to mobilize ideology and resources regardless of its failures to deliver what it promised. It provides the forum for elaborating, communicating, and legitimizing the political rationale of the new global order. It continues to create consensus around themes and issues; it provides the political umbrella for an array of bilateral surveillance and policy agendas; it pulls together bilateral military, civilian, and economic resources for carrying out the post–Cold War governmental and disciplinary security regime; and it provides the professional personnel and expertise for biopolitical interventions to protect populations and for moralizing state institutions.

The assessment of peacekeeping conducted here denaturalizes its political rationale and explores the uneven effects of the interactions of this practice with the complexities of local situations and in the context of broader techniques of international government of risk, such as the process of accession to the EU. This analysis is rooted in a conceptualization of power as the structure of human interactions. It contributes an empirically grounded investigation of modalities of exertion of power and cautions against adopting universalizing praise or condemnation of international intervention. Evaluations of international power exerted through peacekeeping can only be carried out through a case-by-case diagnostic of its outcomes.[4]

As Friedrich Kratochwil, in commenting about methodologies for social sciences, has put it,

4. For a discussion of an "outcome-oriented," politically engaged approach to international policy making, see Kennedy (2001).

> We have to reflect critically on the links between . . . practices and their conceptualizations, without privileging either process, i.e., viewing one as essentially determined by the other. Admittedly, this might not make for an analysis that satisfies or comes close to the ideal of a social "science" concerned with the discovery of universal laws or constant causal mechanisms. It nevertheless might be all we can do for capturing the open-ended nature [of] mankind's "history" and for providing a diagnostic for appraisal. (Kratochwil 2004, 11)

While social theory based on conceptualizations of power as the structure of human interaction unsettles the notion (so rooted in the Western philosophical tradition) of an autonomous rational and moral subject prior to any contingent social relation, it does not lead to deterministic visions of political life. There are no overarching effects of oppression in power inscriptions, or, for that matter, warranted outcomes of liberation in strategies of resistance. Instead, actors (be they individuals, groups, or states) are the result of processes of subjectification whose effects are never overdetermined, but always open-ended and negotiated in the continuous—and uneven—struggles between modalities of power and strategic acts of resistance. Research agendas that question totalizing discourses of any kind play a role in opening the way for modest agonic political activities that are not funded on total rejection or utopian idealization, but on practical inquiries about "what happens." As Barry, Osborne, and Rose aptly put it, "The present is less an epoch than an array of questions; and the coherence with which the present presents itself to us . . . is something to be *acted upon* by historical investigation, to be cut up and decomposed so that it can be seen as put together contingently out of heterogeneous elements each having their own conditions of possibility" (Barry, Osborne, and Rose 1996, 5).

International political rationales and security practices entail transformations and acts of resistance that, for good or for bad, do not always follow the trajectories envisaged by planners, and produce different political and social consequences under different circumstances. While critically addressing, through empirical cases, the modalities and effects of a liberal political rationality of government in the context of peacekeeping, this book does not cast an overarching condemnation of these means. To use Graham Burchell's words, "it is by no means obvious that in every case they are clearly better or worse than the methods they have replaced" (Burchell, Osborne, and Rose 1996, 35). In other words, while exploring modalities of government, this inquiry does not provide an overarching "political evaluation of governmental techniques" (Burchell, Osborne, and Rose 1996, 35). While not having the ambition of devising suggestions for better policy, this work, however, invites "informed prudence," a methodological and ethical attitude in policy making that recognizes the difference among particular situations and takes these differences into consideration in order to make judgments and take action.[5]

5. For a discussion of "informed prudence" as a way of moral reasoning, see Jonsen and Toulmin (1988). Aristotle made a distinction between *episteme* (or science), based on abstract and universal understanding, and *phronesis*, a practical wisdom that takes into account the diversity of concrete situations. Jonsen and Toulmin describe two different approaches to ethical issues: "One of these frames these issues in terms of principles, rules and other general ideas; the other focuses on the specific features of particular kinds of moral cases. In the first way general ethical rules relate to specific moral cases in a *theoretical* manner, with universal rules serving as 'axioms' from which particular moral judgments are deducted as theorems. In the second, this relation is frankly *practical,* with general moral rules serving as 'maxims,' which can be fully understood only in terms of the paradigmatic cases that define their meaning and force" (Jonsen and Toulmin 1988, 23).

PRIMARY SOURCES

General

Commission on Human Security. 2003. *Human Security Now*. Available at http://www.humansecurity-chs.org/finalreport/Outlines/outline.pdf (accessed 22 April 2010).

European Commission Enlargement. 2006. "Accession Criteria." Available at http://ec.europa.eu/enlargement/enlargement_process/accession_process/criteria/index_en.htm (accessed 29 April 2010).

European Security Strategy. 2003. "A Secure Europe is a Better World." Approved by the European Council held in Brussels on 12 December 2003. Available at http://www.consilium.europa.eu/uedocs/cmsUpload/78367.pdf (accessed 29 April 2010).

International Commission on Intervention and State Sovereignty (ICISS). 2001. "The Responsibility to Protect: Report of the International Commission on Intervention and State Sovereignty." Available at http://www.iciss-ciise.gc.ca/report2-en.asp (accessed 22 April 2010).

International Commission on the Balkans. 1996. *Unfinished Peace*. Report. Washington, D.C.: Carnegie Endowment for Peace.

United Nations (UN). 1994. *Yokohama Strategy and Plan of Action for a Safer World: Guidelines for Natural Disaster Prevention, Preparedness, and Mitigation*. World Conference for Natural Disaster Reduction, Yokohama, Japan, 23–27 May. Available at http://www.undp.org/cpr/disred/documents/miscellanous/yokohamastrategy.pdf (accessed 29 April 2010).

———. 1996. *See under* Primary Sources, Haiti.

———. 1998. *See under* Primary Sources, Croatia.

———. 2002. *Report of the International Conference on Financing for Development*. Monterrey, Mexico, 18–22 March. New York: United Nations Publications.

———. 2005. The 2005 World Summit Web site. Available at http://www.un.org/summit2005/ (accessed 29 April 2010).

United Nations Conference on Environment and Development (UNCED). 1992. Rio de Janeiro, Brazil, 3–14 June.

United Nations Department of Peacekeeping Operations Web site. 2010. Available at http://www.un.org/Depts/dpko/dpko/bnote.htm (accessed 29 April 2010).

United Nations Development Program (UNDP). 1994. *Human Development Report 1994: New Dimensions of Human Security*. Oxford: Oxford University Press.

———. 1997. *Governance for Sustainable Growth and Equity*. Report of International Conference, New York, 28–30 July. New York: United Nations Publications.

———. 1998. *See under* Primary Sources, Haiti.

———. 1999. *See under* Primary Sources, Haiti.

———. 2003. *See under* Primary Sources, Croatia.

———. 2004. *Reducing Disaster Risk: A Challenge for Development*. United Nations Development Programme, Bureau for Crisis Prevention and Recovery. Available at http://www.undp.org/cpr/whats_new/rdr_english.pdf (accessed 29 April 2010).

———. n.d. *Governance and Democratic Development in Latin America and the Caribbean*. New York: United Nations Publications.

United Nations Economic and Social Council. 1999. *Report of the Secretary-General. Development in Africa: Implementation of the Recommendations in the Report of the Secretary-General to the Security Council and the General Assembly, Specifically the Implementation and Coordinated Follow-up by the United Nations System of Initiatives in Africa*. E/1999/79 of 14 June.

United Nations Economic Commission for Latin American and the Caribbean (ECLAC). 2001. "Rio de Janeiro Platform for Action on the Road to Johannesburg 2002." PLEN/1/Rev.1 of 9 November. Available at http://www.eclac.cl/dmaah/noticias/paginas/5/8435/platform1.pdf (accessed 13 June 2010).

United Nations Economic Commission for Latin America and the Caribbean (ECLAC) and United Nations Environment Program (UNEP). 2001. Regional Preparatory Conference of Latin America and the Caribbean for the World Conference on Sustainable Development (Johannesburg, South Africa, 2002).

United Nations General Assembly. 1993a. *See under* Primary Sources, Haiti.

———. 1993b. *See under* Primary Sources, Haiti.

———. 1993c. *See under* Primary Sources, Haiti.

———. 1993d. *See under* Primary Sources, Haiti.

———. 1994a. *Support by the United Nations System of the Efforts of Governments to Promote and Consolidate New or Restored Democracies*. Letter from the Permanent Representative of Nicaragua to the United Nations addressed to the Secretary-General. A/49/713 of 23 November.

———. 1994b. *See under* Primary Sources, Haiti.

———. 1994c. *See under* Primary Sources, Haiti.

———. 1995a. Beijing Declaration. A/CONF.177/20.

———. 1995b. *Support by the United Nations System of the Efforts of Governments to Promote and Consolidate New or Restored Democracies*. Report of the Secretary-General. A/50/332 of 7 August.

———. 1995c. *Support by the United Nations System of the Efforts of Governments to Promote and Consolidate New or Restored Democracies*. Resolution. A/RES/50/133 of 20 December.

———. 1996a. *Public Administration and Development*. Resolution. A/50/225 of 19 April.

———. 1996b. *Support by the United Nations System of the Efforts of Governments to Promote and Consolidate New or Restored Democracies*. Letter dated 17 December 1996 from the Secretary-General addressed to the President of the General Assembly. A/51/761 of 20 December. Reprinted under the title "Agenda for Democratization DPI1867(97.I.3)."

———. 1996c. *Support by the United Nations System of the Efforts of Governments to Promote and Consolidate New or Restored Democracies*. Report of the Secretary-General. A/51/512 of 18 October.

———. 1996d. *See under* Primary Sources, Haiti.

———. 1996e. *See under* Primary Sources, Haiti.

———. 1996f. *See under* Primary Sources, Haiti.

———. 1996g. *See under* Primary Sources, Haiti.

———. 1997a. *Renewing the United Nations: A Programme for Reform*. Report of the Secretary-General. A/51/950 of 14 July.

———. 1997b. *Support by the United Nations System of the Efforts of Governments to Promote and Consolidate New or Restored Democracies*. Note Verbale dated 10 September 1997 from the Permanent Representative of Romania to the United Nations addressed to the Secretary-General. A/52/334 of 11 September.

———. 1997c. *Support by the United Nations System of the Efforts of Governments to Promote and Consolidate New or Restored Democracies*. Report of the Secretary-General. A/52/513 of 21 October.

———. 1998. *Support by the United Nations System of the Efforts of Governments to Promote and Consolidate New or Restored Democracies*. Report of the Secretary-General. A/53/554 of 29 October.

———. 1999a. *Support by the United Nations System of the Efforts of Governments to Promote and Consolidate New or Restored Democracies*. Report of the Secretary-General. A/54/492 of 22 October.

———. 1999b. *See under* Primary Sources, Haiti.

———. 1999c. *See under* Primary Sources, Haiti.

———. 1999d. *See under* Primary Sources, Haiti.

———. 1999e. *See under* Primary Sources, Haiti.

———. 2000a. *Support by the United Nations System of the Efforts of Governments to Promote and Consolidate New or Restored Democracies*. Report of the Secretary-General. A/55/489 of 13 October.

———. 2000b. *United Nations Millennium Declaration*. Resolution. A/RES/55/2 of 8 September. Available at http://www.un.org/millennium/declaration/ares552e.htm (accessed 29 April 2010).

———. 2000c. *See under* Primary Sources, Haiti.

———. 2001a. *Road Map Towards the Implementation of the United Nations Millennium Declaration*. Report of the Secretary-General. A/56/326 of 6 September.

———. 2001b. *Support by the United Nations System of the Efforts of Governments to Promote and Consolidate New or Restored Democracies*. Report of the Secretary-General. A/56/499 of 23 October.

———. 2001c. *Support by the United Nations System of the Efforts of Governments to Promote and Consolidate New or Restored Democracies. Letter from the Permanent Representative of Benin to the United Nations Addressed to the Secretary-General. Cotonou Declaration*. Fourth International Conference on New and Restored Democracies. Cotonou, 4 to 6 December 2000. A/55/489 of 5 April.

———. 2002a. Report of the World Summit on Sustainable Development. Johannesburg, South Africa. A/CONF.199/20 of 26 August–6 September.

———. 2002b. *Support by the United Nations System of the Efforts of Governments to Promote and Consolidate New or Restored Democracies*. Resolution. A/RES/56/96 of 30 January.

———. 2003a. *Implementation of the United Nations Millennium Declaration*. Report of the Secretary-General. A/58/323 of 2 September.

—. 2003b. *Support by the United Nations System of the Efforts of Governments to Promote and Consolidate New or Restored Democracies.* Letter from the Permanent Representative of Mongolia to the United Nations addressed to the Secretary-General. A/58/387 of 18 September.

—. 2004. *A More Secure World: Our Shared Responsibility.* Report of the High Level Panel on Threats, Challenges, and Change. UN Doc. A/59/565 (2004).

—. 2005a. "Draft Resolution Referred to the High-Plenary Meeting of the General Assembly at Its Fifty-ninth Session: 2005 World Summit Outcome." A/60/L.1 of 15 September. Available at http://www.who.int/hiv/universalaccess2010/worldsummit.pdf (accessed 29 April 2010).

—. 2005b. *In Larger Freedom: Towards Development, Security, and Human Rights for All.* A/59/2005 of 21 March. Available at http://www.un.org/largerfreedom/contents.htm (accessed 29 April 2010).

United Nations General Assembly and Economic and Social Council. 2002. *Report of the Secretary-General. The Role of Public Administration in the Implementation of the United Nations Millennium Declaration.* A/57/762-E/2002/82 of 16 August.

United Nations Security Council. 1992. *See under* Primary Sources, Croatia.

—. 1993a. *See under* Primary Sources, Haiti.

—. 1993b. *See under* Primary Sources, Haiti.

—. 1993c. *See under* Primary Sources, Haiti.

—. 1994a. *See under* Primary Sources, Haiti.

—. 1994b. *See under* Primary Sources, Haiti.

—. 1994c. *See under* Primary Sources, Haiti.

—. 1995. *See under* Primary Sources, Croatia.

—. 1996a. *See under* Primary Sources, Haiti.

—. 1996b. *See under* Primary Sources, Haiti.

—. 1996c. *See under* Primary Sources, Croatia.

—. 1997a. *See under* Primary Sources, Haiti.

—. 1997b. *See under* Primary Sources, Haiti.

—. 1997c. *See under* Primary Sources, Haiti.

—. 1997d. *See under* Primary Sources, Haiti.

—. 1997e. *See under* Primary Sources, Croatia.

—. 1997f. *See under* Primary Sources, Croatia.

—. 1997g. *See under* Primary Sources, Croatia.

—. 2000. Resolution on Women, Peace and Security. S/Res/1325 (2000) of 31 October.

—. 2004a. *See under* Primary Sources, Haiti.

—. 2004b. *See under* Primary Sources, Haiti.

—. 2006. *Report of the Secretary-General on Women, Peace, and Security.* S/2006/770 of 27 September.

World Bank. 1992. *Governance and Development.* Washington, D.C.: International Bank for Reconstruction and Development.

—. 1994. *Governance, the World Bank Experience.* Washington, D.C.: International Bank for Reconstruction and Development.

—. 2000. Public Sector Group. Poverty Reduction and Economic Management (PREM) Network. *Reforming Public Institutions and Strengthening Governance.* Washington, D.C.: International Bank for Reconstruction and Development.

—. 2009. "Governance Matters 2009: Worldwide Governance Indicators, 1996–2008." Available at http://info.worldbank.org/governance/wgi/index.asp (accessed 13 June 2010).

BIBLIOGRAPHY

152

Aristide, Jean Bertrand. 1996. "Turn Formal Democracies into Living Ones." *Novib Network* 2, no. 5 (October). Address given at Novib conference in Oegstgeest on 19 September. Available at The Ethical Spectacle Web site, http://www.spectacle.org/397/aristide/html (accessed 29 April 2010).

MICIVIH. 1995. *MICIVIH News* 1, no. 1 (August). Available at http://www.un.org/rights/micivih/rapports/news1.htm (accessed 24 April 2010).

———. 1996a. *Le système judiciaire en Haïti: Analyse des aspects pénaux et de procédure pénale.* May. Available at http://www.un.org/rights/micivih/renforen.htm (accessed 29 April 2010).

———. 1996b. *The Haitian National Police and Human Rights.* Report. July. Available at http://www.un.org/rights/micivih/renforen.htm (accessed 29 April 2010).

———. 1997. *Les prisons en Haïti.* Report. July. Available at http://www.un.org/rights/micivih/renforen.htm (accessed 29 April 2010).

Ministry of Justice, Republic of Haiti. 1995. *Décret du 29 Juin 1995 portant à la création de l'Administration Pénitentiaire Nationale (APENA).* Moniteur no. 50. 29 June.

———. 1997. *Protéger et servir: Recueil de textes et des réglementations applicables à la police nationale. Compilé avec l'aimable concours de la Mission Civile Internationale en Haïti, OAS/ONU (MICIVIH).* 2nd ed.

Ministry of Justice, Republic of Haiti. Direction of the Haitian National Police. 1996. *Code de discipline générale de la PNH.*

"Text of President Clinton's Address on Haiti." 1994. *Washington Post,* 16 September.

United Nations (UN). 1996. *Les Nations Unies et Haïti, 1990–1996.* Introduction by Boutros Boutros-Ghali. United Nations Blue Books 11. New York: Department of Public Information.

United Nations Development Program (UNDP). 1998. "Rapport de la mission d'evaluation. Assistance technique au développement institutionnel de la Police Nationale d'Haïti." Unpublished. 5 September.

———. 1999. *Premiers eléments de evaluation de la mission de justice PNUD. Préambule: La justice en Haïti. Le système des Nations Unies—Analyse des actions et recommandations.* Draft.

United Nations General Assembly. 1993a. *Human Rights Questions: Human Rights Situations and Reports of Special Rapporteurs and Representatives.* Report of the Special Rapporteur, Mr. Nigel S. Rodley, Submitted Pursuant to the Commission on Human Rights. Resolution 1992/32. A/48/561 of 10 November.

———. 1993b. *The Situation of Democracy and Human Rights in Haiti.* Note of the Secretary-General transmitting to the General Assembly the Special Rapporteur's provisional Report on the Situation of Human Rights in Haiti. A/48/561 of 10 November.

———. 1993c. *The Situation of Democracy and Human Rights in Haiti.* Resolution. A/RES/47/20B of 20 April.

———. 1993d. *The Situation of Democracy and Human Rights in Haiti.* Resolution. A/RES/48/27 of 6 December.

———. 1994b. *Human Rights Questions: Human Rights Situations and Reports of Special Rapporteurs and Representatives. Situation of Human Rights in Haiti.* Note by the Secretary-General transmitting the Interim Report on the Situation of Human Rights in Haiti submitted by the Special Rapportuer of the Commission of Human Rights pursuant to Commission Resolution

1994/80 and Economic and Social Council Decision 1994/266. A/ /49/513 of 14 October.

——. 1994c. *The Situation of Democracy and Human Rights in Haiti*. Resolution. A/RES/49/27A of 5 December.

——. 1996d. *The Situation of Democracy and Human Rights in Haiti*. Resolution. A/RES/50/86B of 12 April.

——. 1996e. *The Situation of Democracy and Human Rights in Haiti*. Resolution. A/RES/50/86B of 6 Febuary.

——. 1996f. *The Situation of Democracy and Human Rights in Haiti*. Resolution. A/RES/50/86B of 12 April.

——. 1996g. *The Situation of Democracy and Human Rights in Haiti*. Resolution. A/RES/50/86C of 9 September.

——. 1999b. *International Civilian Support Mission in Haiti*. Programme Budget Replications of Draft Resolution A/54/L.36. Report of the Advisory Committee on Administrative Budgetary Questions of 9 December.

——. 1999c. *The Situation of Democracy and Human Rights in Haiti*. Programme Budget Replications of Draft Resolution A/54/L.36. Statement Submitted by the Secretary-General in Accordance with Rule 153 of the Rules and Procedures of the General Assembly of 29 November.

——. 1999d. *International Civilian Support Mission in Haiti*. Resolution. A/RES/54/193 of 17 December.

——. 1999e. *The Situation of Democracy and Human Rights in Haiti*. A/54/629 of 22 November. Letter of the Secretary-General addressed to the President of the General Assembly transmitting the Report of the Needs Assessment Mission.

——. 2000c. *The Situation of Democracy and Human Rights in Haiti. International Civilian Support Mission in Haiti (MICAH)*. Report of the Secretary-General. A/55/618 of 9 November.

United Nations Security Council. 1993a. *Resolution* [on the question concerning Haiti]. S/RES/841 (1993) of 16 June.

——. 1993b. *Resolution* [on the question concerning Haiti]. S/RES/867/1993 (1993) of 23 September.

——. 1993c. *Resolution* [on the question concerning Haiti]. S/RES/875/1993 (1993) of 16 October.

——. 1994a. *Report of the Secretary-General on the United Nations Mission in Haiti (UNMIH)*. S/1994/828 of 15 July.

——. 1994b. *Resolution* [on the question concerning Haiti]. S/RES/905 (1994) of 23 March.

——. 1994c. *Resolution* [on the question concerning Haiti]. S/RES/917 (1994) of 6 May.

——. 1996a. *Resolution* [on the question concerning Haiti]. S/RES/1063 (1996) of 28 June.

——. 1996b. *Resolution* [on the question concerning Haiti]. S/RES/940 (1994) of 31 July 1994.

——. 1997a. *Report of the Secretary-General on the United Nations Support Mission in Haiti (UNSMIH)*. S/1997/244 (1997) of 24 March.

——. 1997b. *Report of the Secretary-General on the United Nations Transition Mission in Haiti (UNTMIH)*. S/1997/832 of 31 October.

——. 1997c. *Resolution* [on the question concerning Haiti]. S/RES/1141 (1997) of 28 November.

———. 1997d. *Resolution* [on the question concerning Haiti]. S/RES/1997/564 (1997) of 19 July.

———. 2004a. *Resolution* [on the question concerning Haiti]. S/RES/1529 (2004) of 29 February.

———. 2004b. *Resolution* [on the question concerning Haiti]. S/RES/1542 of 30 April.

Croatia

Commission of the European Communities. 2002. *Croatia: The Stabilization and Association Process (SAP), First Annual Report.* Report from the Commission. Brussels, 4 April, COM (2002), 163 final.

———. 2004. *Croatia: Opinion on the Application of Croatia for Membership of the European Union.* Brussels, 20 April, COM (2004), 257 final.

Correl, Hans. 2001. Note to Mr. Guehenno. Croatia: Status of "Erdut Agreement." UN internal document. 21 June.

Croatian Helsinki Committee for Human Rights. 2001. *Military Operation Storm and Its Aftermath.* Report. Zagreb: HHO.

European Union. 2009. European Commission Enlargement. "The Western Balkan Countries on the Road to the European Union." Available at http://ec.europa.eu/enlargement/enlargement_process/accession_process/how_does_a_country_join_the_eu/sap/history_en.htm (accessed 13 June 2010).

International Crisis Group (ICG). 2002. *A Half-Hearted Welcome: Refugee Returns to Croatia.* Balkans Report No. 138.

Letter from the Joint Legal Working Group Addressed to the Prime Minister of Croatia. 2003. Internal document. 23 January.

North Atlantic Treaty Organization (NATO). n.d. *Membership Action Plan (MAP).* Available at http://www.nato.int/issues/map/ (accessed 29 April 2010).

Organization for Security and Cooperation in Europe (OSCE). 2002. *Statistical Background Paper: Displacement, Return, and Settlement Since the Beginning of the Armed Conflict in Croatia.* Internal document, unpublished, 3 May.

———. 2003. *Status Report No. 13 of December 2003.* 7 March. Available at http://www.osce.org/zagreb/documents.html?lsi=true&limit=10&grp=253 (accessed 20 May 2010).

———. 2004. *Status Report No. 15 on Croatia's Progress in Meeting International Committments Since July 2004.* 21 November. Available at http://www.osce.org/documents/mc/2004/11/3828_en.pdf (accessed 28 April 2010).

———. 2005. *Status Report No. 17: On Croatia's Progress in Meeting International Commitments Since July 2004.* 10 November. Available at http://www.osce.org/documents/mc/2005/11/17011_en.pdf (accessed 28 April 2010).

———. 2006. *Report on Property Repossession.* 9 June. Available at http://www.osce.org/documents/mc/2006/06/19522_en.pdf (accessed 28 April 2010).

———. 2008. *Report of the Head of the OSCE Office in Zagreb, Ambassador Jorge Fuentes to the OSCE Permanent Council.* 6 March. Available at http://www.osce.org/documents/mc/2008/03/30456_en.pdf (accessed 28 April 2010).

———. n.d. *Housing Care.* Available at http://www.osce.org/zagreb/29544.html (accessed 29 April 2010).

Republic of Croatia. 2003. *Amendments to the Law on the Election of Members of Representative Bodies of Local and Regional Self-Government Units.* Adopted by Parliament on 11 March.

Republic of Croatia. Ministry of Public Works, Reconstruction, and Construction. 2003. *Return of Displaced Persons and Refugees: Repossession of Property.* Zagreb, January. Paper distributed at the Briefing on the Progress in the Process of Returns of Refugees 2000–2003. Sheraton Hotel, Zagreb, 3 February.

Republic of Croatia. Office of Displaced Persons and Returnees (ODPR). Governmental Commission on Returns. 2002. *Report on Return Program.* April.

United Nations (UN). 1998. Department of Peacekeeping Operations, Lessons Learned Unit. *United Nations Transitional Administration in Eastern Slavonia (UNTAES). January 1996–January 1998.* New York. July.

United Nations Development Program (UNDP). 2003. *Human Development Report: Croatia 2002.* Zagreb: UNDP Croatia.

United Nations Security Council. 1992. *Resolution* [on the question concerning Croatia]. S/RES/743 (1992) of 21 February.

———. 1995. *Resolution* [on the question concerning Croatia]. S/RES/981 (1995) of 31 March.

———. 1996c. *Resolution* [on the question concerning Croatia]. S/RES/1037 (1996) of 15 January.

———. 1997e. *Letter Dated 13 January 1997 from the Government of Croatia Addressed to the President of the Security Council.* S/1997/27 of 13 January, annex.

———. 1997f. *Report of the Secretary-General on the United Nations Transitional Administration in Eastern Slavonia, Baranja, and Western Sirmium.* S/1997/953 of 4 December, annex 1.

———. 1997g. *Resolution* [on the question concerning Croatia]. S/RES/1145 (1997) of 19 December.

United States Institute for Peace Library. Peace Agreements Digital Collection. 1995a. Bosnia and Herzegovina: The General Framework Agreement for Peace in Bosnia and Herzegovina. Available at http://www.usip.org/files/file/resources/collections/peace_agreements/dayton.pdf (accessed 26 April 2010).

———. 1995b. Croatia: Basic Agreement on the Region of Eastern Slavonia, Baranja and Western Sirmium. Available at http://www.usip.org/files/file/resources/collections/peace_agreements/croatia_erdut_11121995.pdf (accessed 26 April 2010).

SECONDARY SOURCES

Adas, Michael. 1989. *Machines as the Measure of Men: Science, Technology, and Ideologies of Western Dominance.* Ithaca: Cornell University Press.

Agamben, Giorgio. 1998. *Homo Sacer: Sovereign Power and Bare Life.* Stanford: Stanford University Press.

Americas Watch and National Coalition for Haitian Refugees. 1993. *Silencing a People: The Destruction of Civil Society in Haiti.* New York: Human Rights Watch.

Ammitzboell, Katarina. 2007. "Unintended Consequences of Peace Operations on the Host Economy from a People's Perspective." In *The Unintended Consequences of Peacekeeping Operations,* edited by Chiyuki Aoi, Cedric de Coning, and Ramesh Thakur, 69–90. Tokyo: United Nations University Press.

Andersen, Louise, Bjørn Møller, and Finn Stepputat. 2007. *Fragile States and Insecure People? Violence, Security, and Statehood in the Twenty-first Century.* New York: Palgrave Macmillan.

Aoi, Chiyuki, Cedric de Coning, and Ramesh Thakur. 2007. *The Unintended Consequences of Peacekeeping Operations.* Tokyo: United Nations University Press.

Archibugi, Daniele. 1993. "The Reform of the United Nations and Cosmopolitan Democracy." *Journal of Peace Research* 30, no. 3: 301–15.

———. 2004. "Cosmopolitan Democracy and Its Critics: A Review." *European Journal of International Relations* 10, no. 3: 437–73.

Archibugi, Daniele, and David Held. 1995. *Cosmopolitan Democracy: An Agenda for a New World Order.* Cambridge: Polity Press.

Arendt, Hannah. 1977. "What Is Freedom?" In *Between Past and Future,* 143–72. Harmondsworth: Penguin.

Auguste, Yves L. 1987. *Haïti et les Etats-Unis: 1862–1900.* Port-au-Prince: Imprimerie Henry Deschamps.

Badie, Bertrand. 2000. *The Imported State: The Westernization of the Political Order.* Stanford: Stanford University Press.

Barber, Benjamin R. 1998. "More Democracy! More Revolution!" *The Nation,* 26 October, 11–15.

Barnett, Michael. 1995. "The New United Nations Politics of Peace: From Juridical Sovereignty to Empirical Sovereignty." *Global Governance* 1, no. 3: 79–97.

Barry, Andrew, Thomas Osborne, and Nicholas Rose, eds. 1996. *Foucault and Political Reason: Liberalism, Neo-liberalism, and Rationalities of Government.* Chicago: University of Chicago Press.

Bartlett, William. 2003. *Croatia: Between Europe and the Balkans.* London: Routledge.

Bayart, Jean-François. 1996. "L'historicité de l'Etat importé." In *La Greffe de l'État,* edited by Jean-François Bayart, 11–39. Paris: Editions Karthala.

Bayart, Jean-François, Stephen Ellis, and Beatrice Hibou, eds. 1999. *The Criminalization of the State in Africa.* Bloomington: Indiana University Press.

Beck, Ulrich. 1992. *Risk Society: Towards a New Modernity.* Translated by Mark Ritter. London: Sage Publications.

———. 2000. *What Is Globalization?* Cambridge: Polity Press.

Bellamy, Alex. 2003. *The Formation of Croatian National Identity: A Centuries-Old Dream.* Manchester: Manchester University Press.

———. 2004. "The Next Stage in Peace Operations Theory." *International Peacekeeping* 11, no. 1: 17–38.

Bellamy, Alex, and Paul Williams. 2004. "Introduction: Thinking Anew About Peace Operations." *International Peacekeeping* 11, no. 1: 1–15.

———, eds. 2005. *Peace Operations and Global Order.* London: Routledge.

Bellamy, Alex, Paul Williams, and Stuart Griffin. 2004. *Understanding Peacekeeping.* Cambridge: Polity Press.

Bellegarde-Smith, Patrick. 1990. *Haiti: The Breached Citadel.* Boulder, Colo.: Westview Press.

Besson, Jean. 1992. "Freedom and Community: The British West Indies." In *The Meaning of Freedom: Economics, Politics, and Culture After Slavery,* edited by Frank McGlynn and Seymour Drescher, 183–222. Pittsburgh: University of Pittsburgh Press.

Besson, Jean, and J. Momsen. *Land and Development in the Caribbean.* London: Macmillan, 1987.

Best, Jacqueline. 2008. "Ambiguity, Uncertainty, and Risk: Rethinking Indeterminacy." *International Political Sociology* 2, no. 4: 355–74.

Bhabha, Homi K. 1985. "Signs Taken for Wonders: Questions of Ambivalence and Authority Under a Tree Outside Delhi, May 1817." *Critical Inquiry* 12, no. 1: 144–65.

———. 1992. "Freedom's Basis in the Indeterminate." *October* 61 (Summer): 46–57.

Bickerton, Christopher J. 2007. "State Building: Exporting State Failure." In *Politics Without Sovereignty: A Critique of Contemporary International Relations,* edited by Christopher Bickerton, Philip Cunliffe, and Alexander Gourevitch, 93–111. London: UCL Press.

Bickerton, Christopher J., Philip Cunliffe, and Alexander Gourevitch, eds. 2007. *Politics Without Sovereignty: A Critique of Contemporary International Relations.* London: UCL Press.

Bigo, Didier. 2000. "When Two Become One: Internal and External Securitization in Europe." In *International Relations Theory and the Politics of European Integration,* edited by Morten Kelstrup and Michael C. Williams, 171–204. London: Routledge.

Brigg, Morgan. 2002. "Post Development, Foucault, and the Colonization Metaphor." *Third World Quarterly* 23, no. 3: 421–36.

Brinkerhoff, Derick W, and Jean-Claude Garcia-Zamor, eds. 1986. *Politics, Projects, and People: Institutional Development in Haiti.* New York: Praeger.

Burchell, Graham, Colin Gordon, and Peter Miller, eds. 1991. *The Foucault Effect: Studies in Governmentality.* Chicago: University of Chicago Press.

Burnell, Peter. 2000. "Democracy Assistance: Origins and Organizations." In *Democracy Assistance: International Co-operation for Democratization,* edited by Peter Burnell, 34–66. London: Frank Cass.

Buzan, Barry. 1983. *People, States, and Fear: The National Security Problem in International Relations.* Chapel Hill: University of North Carolina Press.

Buzan, Barry, and Ole Wæver. 2003. *Regions and Powers: The Structure of International Security.* Cambridge: Cambridge University Press.

Buzan, Barry, Ole Wæver, and Jaap de Wilde. 1998. *Security: A New Framework for Analysis.* Boulder, Colo.: Lynne Rienner.

Castor, Suzy. 1988. *L'occupation Américaine d'Haïti.* Port-au-Prince: Imprimerie Henry Deschamps.

———. 1991. "L'expérience démocratique haïtienne." In *Haïti à l'aube du changement,* edited by Suzy Castor et al. Port-au-Prince: Centre de Recherche et de Formation Économique et Sociale pour le Développement.

Chandler, David. 2001. "International Justice." *New Left Review* 2, no. 6: 55–66.

———. 2004. *Constructing Global Civil Society: Morality and Power in International Relations.* Basingstoke: Palgrave Macmillan.

———. 2006. *Empire in Denial.* London: Pluto Press.

———. 2008. "Human Security: The Dog That Didn't Bark." *Security Dialogue* 39, no. 4: 427–38.

Chesterman, Simon. 2003. *You, the People: The United Nations Transitional Administrations and State-building.* Oxford: Oxford University Press.

Chomsky, Noam. 1987a. "Objectivity and Liberal Scholarship." In *The Chomsky Reader,* edited by J. Peck, 83–120. New York: Pantheon.

———. 1987b. *Turning the Tide: U.S. Intervention in Central America and the Struggle for Peace.* Boston: South End Press.

Cockayne, James. 2009. "Winning Haiti's Protection Competitions: Organized Crime and Peace Operations Past, Present, and Future." *International Peacekeeping* 16, no. 1: 77–99.

Colin, Leys. 1996. *The Rise and Fall of Development Theory.* Bloomington: Indiana University Press.

Connolly, William E. 1987. *Politics and Ambiguity.* Madison: University of Wisconsin Press.

———. 2004. "The Complexity of Sovereignty." In Edkins, Pin-Fat, and Shapiro 2004, 23–40.

Cooper, Neil. 2005. "Picking Out the Pieces of Liberal Peace: Representations of Conflict Economies and the Implications for Policy." *Security Dialogue* 36, no. 4: 463–78.

———. 2006. "Peaceful Warriors and Warring Peacemakers." *Economics of Peace and Security Journal* 1, no. 1: 20–24.

Cox, Ronald. 1994. *Power and Profits: U.S. Policy in Central America.* Lexington: University Press of Kentucky.

———. 1997. "Private Interests and U.S. Foreign Policy in Haiti and the Caribbean Basin." In *Contested Social Orders and International Politics,* edited by David Skidmore, 187–207. Nashville: Vanderbilt University Press.

Crawford, Gordon. 2001. *Foreign Aid and Political Reform: A Comparative Analysis of Democracy Assistance and Political Conditionality.* Basingstoke: Palgrave.

Dahl, Robert A. 1971. *Polyarchy: Participation and Opposition.* New Haven: Yale University Press.

———. 1989. *Democracy and Its Critics.* New Haven: Yale University Press.

Dean, Mitchell. 1999. *Governmentality: Power and Rule in Modern Society.* London: SAGE.

Dean, Mitchell, and Barry Hindess, eds. 1998. *Governing Australia: Studies in Contemporary Rationalities of Government.* Cambridge: Cambridge University Press.

Debrix, François. 1996. "Deploying Vision, Simulating Action: The United Nations and Its Visualization Strategies in a New World Order." *Alternatives: Social Transformation and Humane Governance* 21, no. 1: 67–92.

———. 1999. *Re-envisioning Peacekeeping: The United Nations and the Mobilization of Ideology.* Minneapolis: University of Minnesota Press.

DeWind, Josh. 1989. "Economic Assistance and Democratization in Haiti." Conference Paper 20. Columbia University: New York University Consortium.

———. 1990. "Elections Without Democracy? The Impact of the United States Economic Assistance on Politics in Haiti." *Cimarron: New Perspectives on the Caribbean* 2, no. 3: 64–83.

DeWind, Josh, and David H. Kinley III. 1988. *Aiding Migration: The Impact of International Development Assistance on Haiti.* Boulder, Colo.: Westview Press.

Dia, Mamadou. 1996. *Africa's Management in the 1990s and Beyond: Reconciling Indigenous and Transplanted Institutions.* Washington, D.C.: World Bank.

Diehl, Paul F. 1993. *International Peacekeeping.* Baltimore: Johns Hopkins University Press.

———, ed. 1989. *The Politics of International Organizations: Patterns and Insights.* Chicago: Dorsey Press.

Dillon, Michael, and Julian Reid. 2001. "Global Liberal Governance: Biopolitics, Security, and War." *Millennium Journal of International Studies* 30, no. 1: 41–66.

———. 2009. *The Liberal Way of War: Killing to Make Life Live.* London: Routledge.

Doyle, Michael W., and Nicholas Sambanis. 2006. *Making War and Building Peace: United Nations Peace Operations.* Princeton: Princeton University Press.

Dreyfus, Hubert L., and Paul Rabinow. 1982. *Michel Foucault: Beyond Structuralism and Hermeneutics.* Chicago: University of Chicago Press.

Duffield, Mark. 2002a. *Global Governance and the New Wars: The Merging of Development and Security.* London: Zed Books.

———. 2002b. "Reprising Durable Disorder: Network War and Securitization of Aid." In *Global Governance in the Twenty-first Century: Alternative Perspectives on World Order,* edited by Björn Hettne and Bertil Odén, 74–101. Stockholm: Expert Group on Development Issues.

———. 2007. *Development, Security, and Unending War: Governing the World of Peoples.* Cambridge: Polity Press.

Duffield, Mark, and Nicholas Waddell. 2006. "Securing Humans in a Dangerous World." *International Politics* 43, no. 1: 1–23.

Dunn, Thomas L. 1996. *Michel Foucault and the Politics of Freedom.* Lanham, Md.: Rowman and Littlefield.

Dupuy, Alex. 1989. *Haiti in the World Economy: Class, Race, and Underdevelopment Since 1700.* Boulder, Colo.: Westview Press.

———. 1997. *Haiti in the New World Order: The Limits of Democratic Revolution.* Boulder, Colo.: Westview Press.

Durch, William, ed. 1993. *The Evolution of Peace Keeping.* New York: St. Martin's Press.

Easterly, William. 2007. "The Ideology of Development." *Foreign Policy,* no. 161 (July–August): 31–35.

Edkins, Jenny, Veronique Pin-Fat, and Michael Shapiro, eds. 2004. *Sovereign Lives: Power in Global Politics.* New York: Routledge.

Elman, Miriam F., ed. 1997. *Paths to Peace: Is Democracy the Answer?* Cambridge: MIT Press.

Engelbert, Pierre, 1997. "Review: The Contemporary African State: Neither African nor State." *Third World Quarterly* 18, no. 4: 767–75.

Escobar, Arturo. 1988. "Power and Visibility: Development and the Invention and Management of the Third World." *Cultural Anthropology* 3, no 4: 428–43.

———. 1995. *Encountering Development: The Making and Unmaking of the Third World.* Princeton: Princeton University Press.

Esteva, G. 1992. "Development." In *The Development Dictionary: A Guide to Knowledge as Power,* edited by W. Sachs, 6–25. London: Zed Books.

Falk, Richard. 1999. *Predatory Globalization: A Critique.* Cambridge: Polity Press.

———, ed. 1991. *The United Nations and a Just World Order.* Boulder, Colo.: Westview Press.

Farmer, Paul. 1991. *AIDS and Accusation: Haiti and the Geography of Blame.* Berkeley and Los Angeles: University of California Press.

———. 1994. *The Uses of Haiti.* Monroe, Maine: Common Courage Press.

Fass, Simon M. 1988. *Political Economy in Haiti: The Drama of Survival.* New Brunswick, N.J.: Transaction Books.

Fauriol, Georges A., and James L. Oberstar, eds. 1993. *The Haitian Challenge: U.S. Policy Considerations.* Washington, D.C.: Center for Strategic and International Studies.

Ferguson, James. 1987. *Papa Doc, Baby Doc: Haiti and the Duvaliers.* Oxford: Basil Blackwell.

———. 1994. *The Anti-Politics Machine: Development, Depoliticization, and Bureaucratic Power in Lesotho.* Minneapolis: University of Minnesota Press.

Finnemore, Martha. 1996. *National Interests in International Society*. Ithaca: Cornell University Press.

———. 2003. *The Purpose of Intervention: Changing Beliefs About the Use of Force.* Ithaca: Cornell University Press.

Finnemore, Martha, and Kathryn Sikkink. 1998. "International Norm Dynamics and Political Change." *International Organization* 52, no. 4: 887–917.

Foucault, Michel. 1965. *Madness and Civilization*. Translated by Richard Howard. New York: Pantheon.

———. 1972a. *The Archeology of Knowledge*. New York: Pantheon.

———. 1972b. *Microphysique du Pouvoir*. Paris: L'Arc.

———. 1973. *The Birth of the Clinic: An Archaeology of Medical Perception*. Translated by Alan Sheridan Smith. New York: Pantheon.

———. 1980. *Power/Knowledge: Selected Interviews and Other Writings, 1972–1977.* Edited by Colin Gordon. New York: Pantheon.

———. 1982a. "On the Genealogy of Ethics: An Overview of Work in Progress." In Dreyfus and Rabinow 1982, 229–52.

———. 1982b. "The Subject and Power." In Dreyfus and Rabinow 1982, 208–26.

———. 1990. *The History of Sexuality*. Vol. 1, *An Introduction*. New York: Vintage Books.

———. 1991a. "Governmentality." In Burchell, Gordon, and Miller 1991, 84–104.

———. 1991b. "Questions of Method." In Burchell, Gordon, and Miller 1991, 73–86.

———. 1994. *The Order of Things: An Archaeology of Human Sciences*. New York: Vintage Books.

———. 1995. *Discipline and Punish: The Birth of the Prison*. 2nd ed. New York: Vintage Books.

———. 1997. *The Essential Works of Michel Foucault, 1954–1984*. Vol. 1, *Ethics: Subjectivity and Truth*. Edited by Paul Rabinow. Translated by Robert Hurley et al. New York: New Press.

———. 2003a. *Abnormal: Lectures at the Collège de France, 1974–1975*. Edited by Valerio Marchetti and Antonella Salomoni. Translated by Graham Burchell. London: Verso.

———. 2003b. *Society Must Be Defended: Lectures at the Collège de France, 1975–76.* Edited by Mauro Bertani and Alessandro Fontana. Translated by David Macey. New York: Picador.

———. 2007. *Security, Territory, Population: Lectures at the Collège de France, 1977–78.* Edited by Michel Senellart. Translated by Graham Burchell. Basingstoke: Palgrave.

Foucault, Michel, and Michel Senellart. 2008. *The Birth of Biopolitics: Lectures at the Collège de France, 1978–79*. Basingstoke: Palgrave.

Franke, Volker, and Andrea Warnecke. 2009. "Building Peace: An Inventory of UN Peace Missions Since the End of the Cold War." *International Peacekeeping* 16, no. 3: 407–36.

Gamarra, Eduardo. 1994. "Market-Oriented Reforms and Democratization in Latin America: Challenges of the 1990s." In *Latin American Political Economy in the Age of Reforms: Theoretical and Comparative Perspectives for the 1990s*, edited by William C. Smith, Carlos H. Acuna, and Eduardo A. Gamarra, 1–14. Miami: North-South Center.

Geertz, Clifford. 1983. *Local Knowledge*. New York: Basic Books.

Gélins-Adams, Marlye, and David Malone. 2003. "Haiti: A Case of Endemic Weakness." In *State Failure and State Weakness in a Time of Terror,* edited by Robert I. Rotberg, 287–304. Washington, D.C.: Brookings Institution Press.

Gills, Stephen. 1995. "Globalization, Market Civilization, and Disciplinary Neo-Liberalism." *Millennium: Journal of International Studies* 24, no. 3: 399–423.

Goldstein, Ivo. 1999. *Croatia: A History.* London: Hurst.

Görg, Christoph, and Joachim Hirsch. 1998: "Is International Democracy Possible?" *Review of International Political Economy* 5, no. 4: 585–615.

Gourevitch, Philip. 1978a. "The International System and Regime Formation: A Critical Review of Anderson and Wallerstein." *Comparative Politics* 10, no. 3: 419–38.

———. 1978b. "The Second Image Reversed: The International Sources of Domestic Politics." *Organizations International* 32, no. 4: 881–912.

Gower, Peter. 2001. "The New Liberal Cosmopolitanism." *New Left Review* 2, no. 11: 1–14.

Gramsci, Antonio. 1997. *Selections from the Prison Notebooks.* Edited by Quintin Hoare and Geoffrey N. Smith. New York: International Publishers.

Granderson, Colin. 1997. "Institutionalizing Peace: The Haiti Experience." Paper presented at the Aspen Institute Conference, "Honoring Human Rights: From Peace to Justice." Mohonk Mountain House, New Paltz, N.Y., 12–14 September.

Griffin, Keith. 2003. "Economic Globalization and Institutions of Global Governance." *Development and Change* 34, no. 5: 789–807.

Guehenno, Jean-Marie. 2001. "The Impact of Globalization on Strategy." In *Turbulent Peace: The Challenges of Managing International Conflict,* edited by Chester A. Crocker, Fen Osler Hampson, and Pamela Hall, 83–95. Washington, D.C.: United States Institute for Peace.

Gunder, Frank, A. 1967. *Capitalism and Underdevelopment in Latin America.* New York: Monthly Review Press.

Habermas, Jürgen. 1984. *The Theory of Communicative Action.* Vol. 1. Boston: Beacon Press.

———. 1996. *The Philosophical Discourse of Modernity: Twelve Lectures.* Cambridge: MIT Press.

Hacking, Ian. 1985. "Styles of Scientific Reasoning." In *Post-Analytic Philosophy,* edited by John Rajchman and Cornel West, 145–65. New York: Columbia University Press.

———. 1990. *The Taming of Chance.* Cambridge: Cambridge University Press.

———. 2002. *Historical Ontology.* Cambridge: Harvard University Press.

Hallward, Peter. 2007. *Damming the Flood: Haiti, Aristide, and the Politics of Containment.* London: Verso.

Hannah, Matthew G. 2000. *Governmentality and the Mastery of Territory in Nineteenth-Century America.* Cambridge: Cambridge University Press.

Hardt, Michael, and Antonio Negri. 2000. *Empire.* Cambridge: Harvard University Press.

Held, David. 1989. *Political Theory and the Modern State: Essays on State, Power, and Democracy.* Stanford: Stanford University Press.

———. 1993. *Prospects for Democracy: North, South, East, West.* Stanford: Stanford University Press.

———. 1995. *Democracy and the Global Order: From the Modern State to Cosmopolitan Governance.* Stanford: Stanford University Press.

———. 1996. *Models of Democracy.* 2nd ed. Stanford: Stanford University Press. (Orig. pub. 1987.)

Held, David, and Anthony Giddens, eds. 1982. *Classes, Power, and Conflict: Classical and Contemporary Debates.* Berkeley and Los Angeles: University of California Press.

Higate, Paul, and Marsha Henry. 2009. *Insecure Spaces: Peacekeeping, Power, and Performance in Haiti, Kosovo, and Liberia.* London: Zed Books.

Hindess, Barry. 1996. *Discourses of Power: From Hobbes to Foucault.* Cambridge: Blackwell.

———. 1998. "Neo-liberalism and the National Economy." In *Governing Australia: Studies in Contemporary Rationalities of Government,* edited by Mitchell Dean and Barry Hindess, 210–26. Cambridge: Cambridge University Press.

Holt, Thomas C. 1992. *The Problem of Freedom: Race, Labor, and Politics in Jamaica and Britain, 1832–1938.* Baltimore: Johns Hopkins University Press.

Huizinga, Johan. 1955. *Homo Ludens: A Study of the Play Element in Culture.* Boston: Beacon Press.

Huntington, Samuel P. 1991. *The Third Wave: Democratization in the Late Twentieth Century.* Norman: University of Oklahoma Press.

Huysmans, Jef. 2004. "A Foucauldian View on Spill-over: Freedom and Security in the EU." *Journal of International Relations and Development* 7, no. 3: 294–318.

Ignatieff, Michael. 1978. *A Just Measure of Pain: The Penitentiary in the Industrial Revolution, 1750–1850.* London: Macmillan.

International Crisis Group (ICG). 2002. *A Half-Hearted Welcome: Refugee Returns to Croatia.* Balkan Report n. 138. 13 December.

Ives, Kim. 1994. "The Unmaking of a President." In Ridgeway 1994, 87–103.

Jabri, Vivienne. 2007. *War and the Transformation of Global Politics: Rethinking Peace and Conflict Studies.* Basingstoke: Palgrave.

Jackson, Patrick Thaddeus, and Daniel Nexon. 1999. "Relations Before States: Substance, Process, and the Study of World Politics." *European Journal of International Relations* 5, no. 3: 291–332.

Jackson, Robert H. 1990. *Quasi-states: Sovereignty, International Relations, and the Third World.* Cambridge: Cambridge University Press.

Jonsen, Albert R., and Stephen Toulmin. 1988. *The Abuse of Casuistry: A History of Moral Reasoning.* Berkeley and Los Angeles: University of California Press.

Kant, Immanuel. 1949. "Perpetual Peace." In *The Philosophy of Kant,* edited by C. J. Friedrich, 430–76. New York: Modern Library. (Orig. pub. 1795.)

Kapoor, Ilan. 2008. *The Post-Colonial Politics of Development.* London: Routledge.

Katzenstein, Peter J. 1996. *The Culture of National Security: Norms and Identity in World Politics (New Directions in World Politics).* New York: Columbia University Press.

Kennedy, Paul. 2001. "The Politics of the Invisible College: International Governance and the Politics of Expertise." *European Human Rights Law Review* 5: 463–98.

Kralic, Josip. 1997. *Storia della Yugoslavia: Dal 1945 ai nostri giorni.* Milano: Bompiani.

Kratochwil, Friedrich. 1982. "On the Notion of 'Interest' in International Relations." *International Organization* 36, no. 1: 1–30.

———. 2004. "Global Governance and the Emergence of World Society: International Relations Meets Sociology." Working paper, European University Institute.

Kratochwil, Friedrich, and John Ruggie. 1986. "International Organization: State of the Art or an Art of the State." *International Organization* 40, no. 4: 753–75.

Laclau, Ernesto. 1996. *Emancipation(s)*. London: Verso.

Laguerre, Michel S. 1989. *Voodoo and Politics in Haiti*. New York: St. Martin Press.

———. 1993. *The Military and Society in Haiti*. Knoxville: University of Tennessee Press.

Larner, Wendy, and William Walters, eds. 2004a. *Global Governmentality: Governing International Spaces*. London: Routledge.

———. 2004b. "Globalization as Governmentality." *Alternatives: Global, Local, Political* 29, no. 5: 495–514.

Latouche, Serge. 1996. *The Westernization of the World*. Oxford: Polity Press.

Lavin, Chad. 2008. *The Politics of Responsibility*. Chicago: University of Illinois Press.

Lawless, Robert. 1992. *Haiti's Bad Press*. Rochester, Vt.: Schenkman Books.

Levine, Andrew. 1981. *Liberal Democracy: A Critique of Its Theory*. New York: Columbia University Press.

Linz, Juan, and Alfred Stepan. 1996. *Problems of Democratic Consolidation: Southern Europe, South America, and Post-Communist Europe*. Baltimore: Johns Hopkins University Press.

Lipschutz, Ronnie D., ed. 1995. *On Security*. New York: Columbia University Press.

Lipschutz, Ronnie D., and James K. Rowe. 2005. *Globalization, Governmentality, and Global Politics: Regulation for the Rest of Us?* London: Routledge.

Löwenheim, Oded. 2007. "The Responsibility to Responsibilize: Foreign Offices and the Issuing of Travel Warnings." *International Political Sociology* 1, no 3: 203–21.

Luke, Timothy, and Gearóid Ó Tuathail. 1997. "On Videocameralists: The Geopolitics of Failed States, the CNN International and (UN)governmentality." *Review of International Political Economy* 4, no. 4: 709–33.

Mac Ginty, Roger. 2008. "Indigenous Peace-Making Versus the Liberal Peace." *Cooperation and Conflict* 43, no. 2: 139–63.

MacLean, Sandra J., David Black, and Timothy M. Shaw, eds. 2006. *A Decade of Human Security: Global Governance and New Multilateralism*. Burlington, Vt.: Ashgate.

Maguire, Robert, et al. 1997. *Haïti prise en otage: Les responses internationales à la recherche d'une identité nationale*. Occasional paper 23. Providence: Thomas J. Watson Institute for International Studies.

Mainwaring, Scott, and Timothy R. Scully, eds. 1995. *Building Democratic Institutions: Party Systems in Latin America*. Stanford: Stanford University Press.

Malone, David. 1997. "Haiti in the International Community: A Case Study." *Survival* 39, no. 2: 126–46.

Mamdani, Mahmood. 1996. *Citizen and Subject: Contemporary Africa and the Legacy of Late Colonialism*. Princeton: Princeton University Press.

Marcuse, Herbert, 1972. *One-Dimensional Man*. London: Abacus.

Maurer, Bill, and Richard Warren Perry, eds. 2003. *Globalization, Law, and Identity*. Minneapolis: University of Minnesota Press.

Mayall, James, ed. 1996. *The New Interventionism, 1991–1994: United Nations Experience in Cambodia, Yugoslavia, and Somalia*. Cambridge: Cambridge University Press.

McFayden, Deidre, Pierre Laramee, Mark Fried, Fred Rosen, and North American Congress on Latin America, eds. 1995. *Haiti: Dangerous Crossroads*. Boston: South End Press.

Merlingen, Michael. 2006. "Foucault and World Politics: Promises and Challenges of Extending Governmentality Theory to the European and Beyond." *Millennium: Journal of International Studies* 35, no. 1: 181–96.

Merlingen, Michael, and Rasa Ostrauskaite. 2007. *European Union Peacebuilding and Policing: Governance and the European Security and Defence Policy.* London: Routledge.

Mintz, Sidney W. 1960. "Le système du marché rural dans l'economie haïtienne." *Bulletin du Bureau d'Ethnologie*, 3rd ser., 23-24-25: 3–14.

———. 1974. *Caribbean Transformations.* Baltimore: Johns Hopkins University Press.

———. 1979. "Slavery and the Rise of Peasantries." *Historical Reflections/Reflexions Historiques* 6, no. 1: 213–42.

———. 1985. *Sweetness and Power: The Place of Sugar in Modern History.* New York: Penguin Books.

———. 1995. "Can Haiti Change?" *Foreign Affairs* 74, no. 1: 73–86.

Mitchell, Timothy. 1990: "Everyday Metaphors of Power." *Theory and Society* 19, no. 5: 545–77.

Moore, Barrington. 1996. *Social Origins of Dictatorship and Democracy: Lord and Peasant in the Making of the Modern World.* Boston: Beacon Press.

Moran, Michael. 2003. *The British Regulatory State: High Modernism and Hyper-Innovation.* Oxford: Oxford University Press.

Moss, Jeremy, ed. 1998. *The Later Foucault: Politics and Philosophy.* London: Sage.

Murray, G. F. 1978a. *Hillside Units, Wage Labor, and Haitian Peasant Land Tenure: A Strategy for the Organization of Erosion Control.* Port-au-Prince: U.S. Agency for International Development.

———. 1978b. *Informal Subdivisions and Land Insecurity: An Analysis of Haitian Peasant Land Tenure.* Port-au-Prince: U.S. Agency for International Development.

———. 1979. *Terraces, Trees, and the Haitian Peasant: An Assessment of Twenty-Five Years of Erosion Control in Rural Haiti.* Port-au-Prince: U.S. Agency for International Development.

———. 1981. *Peasant Tree Planting in Haiti: A Social Soundness Analysis.* Port-au-Prince: U.S. Agency for International Development.

———. 1987. "The Domestication of Wood in Haiti: A Case Study in Applied Evolution." In *Anthropological Praxis: Translating Knowledge into Action,* edited by R. Wulff and S. Fiske, 223–40. Boulder, Colo.: Westview Press.

———. 1996. "A Haitian Peasant Tree Chronicle: Adaptive Evolution and Institutional Intrusion." In *Reasons for Hope,* edited by Anirudh Krishna, Norman Uphoff, and Milton J. Essman, 241–54. West Hartford, Conn.: Kumarian Press.

Nairn, Alain. 1996a. "Haiti Under Cloak." *The Nation,* 26 February, 4–5.

———. 1996b. "Haiti Under the Gun: How U.S. Intelligence Has Been Exercising Crowd Control." *The Nation,* 8 January, 11–15.

Nambiar, Satish. 2004. *A Current Perspective of United Nations Peacekeeping Operations.* November. Available at http://www.peacekeepingbestpractices.unlb.org/PBPS/Library/Current%20Perspective%20revised.pdf (accessed 28 April 2010).

Neal, Andrew. 2004. "Cutting Off the King's Head: Foucault's *Society Must Be Defended* and the Problem of Sovereignty." *Alternatives: Global, Local, Political* 29, no. 4: 373–98.

Nicholls, David. 1985. *Haiti in Caribbean Context: Ethnicity, Economy, and Revolt.* New York: St. Martin's Press.

North American Congress on Latin America (NACLA). 1996. *Report on the Americas* 29, no. 6 (May–June); 30, no. 1 (July–August).

O'Donnell, Guillermo. 1992. "Transitions, Continuities, and Paradoxes." In *Issues in Democratic Consolidation: The New South American Democracies in Comparative Perspective*, edited by Scott Mainwaring, Guillermo O'Donnell, and J. Samuel Valenzuela, 17–56. Notre Dame: University of Notre Dame Press.

Onuf, Nicholas G. 1989. *World of Our Making: Rules and Rule in Social Theory and International Relations.* Columbia: University of South Carolina Press.

———. 1998. *The Republican Legacy in International Thought.* Cambridge Studies in International Relations 59. Cambridge: Cambridge University Press.

Orenstein, Catherine. 1994. "Haiti in the Mainstream Press: Excesses and Omissions." In Ridgeway 1994, 121–22.

Owen, Taylor. 2008. "The Critique That Doesn't Bite: A Response to David Chandler's 'Human Security: The Dog That Didn't Bark.'" *Security Dialogue* 39, no. 4: 445–53.

Paris, Roland. 2000. "Broadening the Study of Peace Operations." *International Studies Review* 2, no. 3: 27.

———. 2001. "Human Security: Paradigm Shift or Hot Air?" *International Security* 26, no. 2: 87–102.

———. 2004. *At War's End: Building Peace After Civil Conflict.* Cambridge: Cambridge University Press.

Pasquino, Pasquale. 1991. "Theatrum politicum: The Genealogy of Capital—Police and the State of Prosperity." In Burchell, Gordon, and Miller 1991, 105–18.

Pender, John. 2007. "Country Ownership: The Evasion of Donor Accountability." In *Politics Without Sovereignty: A Critique of Contemporary International Relations,* edited by Christopher Bickerton, Philip Cunliffe, and Alexander Gourevitch, 112–30. New York: UCL Press.

Perry, Richard Warren, and Bill Maurer, eds. 2003. *Globalization Under Construction: Governmentality, Law, and Identity.* Minneapolis: University of Minnesota Press.

Pizzorno, Alessandro. 1992. "Foucault and the Liberal View of the Individual." In *Michel Foucault, Philosopher,* edited by Timothy Armstrong, 204–11. New York: Routledge.

Porter, Theodore M. 1995. *Trust in Numbers: The Pursuit of Objectivity in Science and Public Life.* Princeton: Princeton University Press.

Pouligny, Beatrice. 2006. *Peace Operations Seen from Below.* West Hartford, Conn.: Kumarian Press.

Power, Michael. 1997. *The Audit Society: Rituals in Verification.* Oxford: Oxford University Press.

Prozorov, Sergei. 2004. "Three Theses on 'Governance' and the Political." *Journal of International Relations and Development* 7, no. 3: 267–93.

———. 2007. *Foucault, Freedom, and Sovereignty.* Burlington, Vt.: Ashgate.

Pugh, Michael. 2003. "Peacekeeping and International Relations Theory: Phantom of the Opera?" *International Peacekeeping* 10, no. 4: 104–12.

———. 2004. "Peacekeeping and Critical Theory." *International Peacekeeping* 11, no. 1: 39–58.

Pugh, Michael, and Neil Cooper. 2004. *War Economies in a Regional Context: Challenges and Transformations.* With Jonathan Goodhand. Boulder, Colo.: Lynne Rienner.

Pugh, Michael, Neil Cooper, and Mandy Turner. 2009. *Whose Peace? Critical Perspectives on the Political Economy of Peacebuilding.* New York: Palgrave Macmillan.

Pupavac, Vanessa. 2005. "Human Security and the Rise of Global Therapeutic Governance." *Conflict, Security, and Development* 5, no. 2: 161–81.

Reid, Julian. 2007. *The Biopolitics of the War on Terror: Life Struggles, Liberal Modernity, and the Defence of Logistical Societies*. Manchester: Manchester University Press.

Reno, William. 1995. *Corruption and State Politics in Sierra Leone*. Cambridge: Cambridge University Press.

Rhodes, R. A. W. 1996. "The New Governance: Governing Without Government." *Political Studies* 44, no. 4: 652–67.

Richmond, Oliver. 2005. *The Transformation of Peace*. Basingstoke: Palgrave Macmillan.

———. 2008. *Peace in International Relations*. London: Routledge.

Ridgeway, James, ed. 1994. *The Haiti Files: Decoding the Crisis*. Washington, D.C.: Essential Books.

Robinson, William I. 1996. *Promoting Polyarchy: Globalization, U.S. Intervention, and Hegemony*. Cambridge: Cambridge University Press.

Rose, Nikolas. 1996. "Governing Advanced Liberal Democracies." In *Foucault and Political Reason: Liberalism, Neo-liberalism, and Rationalities of Government*, edited by Andrew Barry, Thomas Osborne, and Nikolas Rose, 37–64. Chicago: University of Chicago Press.

———. 1999. *Powers of Freedom: Reframing Political Thought*. Cambridge: Cambridge University Press.

Rose, Nikolas, and Peter Miller. 1992. "Political Power Beyond the State: Problematics of Government." *British Journal of Sociology* 43, no. 2: 173–205.

Rosenau, James N. 1995. "Governance in the Twenty-first Century." *Global Governance* 1, no. 1: 13–43.

Rosow, Stephen J. 2000. "Globalization as Democratic Theory." *Millennium: Journal of International Studies* 29, no. 1: 27–45.

Sachs, Wolfgang, ed. 1992. *The Development Dictionary: A Guide to Knowledge as Power*. London: Zed Books.

Schmidt, Hans. 1995. *The United States Occupation of Haiti, 1915–1934*. New Brunswick: Rutgers University Press.

Schmitter, Philippe C. 1997. "Defining, Explaining, and Using the Concept of 'Governance.'" With the assistance of Nicholas Guilhot and Imco Brower. Working paper, European University Institute and Stanford University.

Schwartz, Timoty T. *Travesty in Haiti: A True Account of Christian Missions, Orphanages, Fraud, Food Aid, and Drug Trafficking*. Charleston, S.C.: BookSurge, 2008.

Scott, James. 1998. *Seeing Like a State: How Certain Schemes to Improve the Human Condition Have Failed*. New Haven: Yale University Press.

Schumpeter, Joesph A. 1947. *Capitalism, Socialism, and Democracy*. 2nd ed. New York: Harper and Row.

Simons, Jon. 1995. *Foucault and the Political*. London: Routledge.

Slater, David. 2006. "Imperial Powers and Democratic Imaginations." *Third World Quarterly* 27, no. 8: 1369–86.

Smoljan, Jelena. 2003. "Socio-Economic Aspects of Peace Building: UNTAES and the Organization of Employment in Eastern Slavonia." *International Peacekeeping* 10, no. 2: 27–50.

Snow, Donald M. 1994. *Puzzles, Palaces, and Foggy Bottom: U.S. Foreign and Defense Policy-Making in the 1990s*. New York: St. Martin's Press.

Stephenson, Max, and Laura Zanotti. 2008. "Taming Risk, Making Peace from Below: Community-Based Foundations in Peacekeeping and Peace Building; A Pilot Project." Paper presented at the ARNOVA conference, Philadelphia, 19–21 November.

Sterling-Folker, Jennifer. 2000. "Competing Paradigms or Birds of a Feather? Constructivism and Neoliberal Institutionalism Compared." *International Studies Quarterly* 44, no. 1: 97–119.

Suppan, Arnold. 2003. "Yugoslavism Versus Serbian, Croatian, and Slovene Nationalism: Political, Ideological, and Cultural Causes of the Rise and Fall of Yugoslavia." In *Yugoslavia and Its Historians: Understanding the Balkan Wars of the 1990s,* edited by Normann M. Naimark and Holly Case, 116–59. Stanford: Stanford University Press.

Tadjbakhsh, Shahrbanou, and Anuradha M. Chenoy. 2007. *Human Security: Concepts and Implications.* Routledge Advances in International Relations and Global Politics 51. London: Routledge.

Tanner, Marcus. 1997. *Croatia: A Nation Forced into War.* New Haven: Yale University Press.

Thomas, Carolyne. 2001. "Global Governance, Development, and Human Security: Exploring the Links." *Third World Quarterly* 22, no. 2: 159–75.

Tilly, Charles. 1995. "Globalization Threatens Labor's Rights." *International Labor and Working Class History* 41: 1–23.

Touraine, Alain. 1973. *Production de la société.* Paris: Editions du Seuil.

———. 1978. *La voix et le regarde.* Paris: Editions du Seuil.

Trouillot, Michel Rolf. 1988. *Peasants and Capital: Dominica in the World Economy.* Baltimore: Johns Hopkins University Press.

———. 1990. *Haiti: State Against Nation: Origins and Legacy of Duvalierism.* New York: Monthly Review Press.

———. 1995. *Silencing the Past: Power and the Production of History.* Boston: Beacon Press.

Tully, James. 1999. "The Agonic Freedom of Citizens." *Economy and Society* 28, no. 2: 161–82.

Walters, William, and Jens Henrik Haar. 2005a. *Governing Europe: Discourse, Governmentality, and European Integration.* London: Routledge.

———. 2005b. "Governmentality and Political Studies." *European Political Science* 4, no. 3: 291.

Weir, Erin A. 2006. *Conflict and Compromise: UN Integrated Missions and the Humanitarian Imperative.* Kofi Annan International Peacekeeping Training Center. Available at www.trainingforpeace.org (accessed 17 November 2008).

Weiss, Thomas G., D. P. Forsythe, and R. A. Coate. 2001. *The United Nations and Changing World Politics.* Boulder, Colo.: Westview Press.

Weiss, Thomas G., and Leon Gordenker, eds. 1996. *NGOs, the UN, and Global Governance.* Boulder, Colo.: Lynne Rienner.

White, Nigel D. 2000. "The United Nations and Democracy Assistance: Developing Practice Within a Constitutional Framework." In *Democracy Assistance: International Co-operation for Democratization,* edited by Peter Burnell 67–89. Portland, Ore.: Frank Cass.

Wronka, Joseph. 1998. *Human Rights and Social Policy in the Twenty-first Century.* Lanham, Md.: University Press of America.

Young, James P. 1996. *Reconsidering Liberalism: The Troubled Odyssey of the Liberal Idea.* Boulder, Colo.: Westview Press.

Zanotti, Laura. 2005. "Governmentalizing the Post–Cold War International Regime: The UN Debate on Democratization and Good Governance." *Alternatives: Global, Local, Political* 30, no. 4: 461–87.

———. 2006. "Taming Chaos: A Foucauldian View on UN Peacekeeping, Democracy, and Normalization." *International Peacekeeping* 13, no. 2: 150–67.

———. 2008a. "Imagining Democracy, Building Unsustainable Institutions: The UN Peacekeeping Operation in Haiti." *Security Dialogue* 39, no. 5: 539–61.

———. 2008b. "Normalizing Democracy and Human Rights: Discipline, Resistance, and Carceralization in Croatia's Euro-Atlantic Integration." *Journal of International Relations and Development* 11, no. 3: 222–50.

———. 2009. "Managing Risk, Protecting Populations, Blurring Spaces of Governance: Kofi Annan's Vision for a UN-Led Collective Security System in the New Millennium." In *The United Nations: Past, Present, and Future,* edited by Scott Kaufman and Alisa Warters, 1–13. New York: Nova Science.

———. 2010a. "Failed State Building and Community-Based Foundations: Success Stories in the Cacophony of International Interventions in Haiti." Paper presented at the International Studies Association annual meeting, 17–20 February 2010, New Orleans.

———. 2010b. "UN Integrated Peacekeeping Operations and NGOs: Reflections on Governmental Rationalities and Contestation in the Age of Risk." *International Peacekeeping* 17, no. 1: 17–31.

Zielonka, Jan. 2006. *Europe as Empire: The Nature of the Enlarged European Union.* Oxford: Oxford University Press.

Zolo, Danilo. 2001. *Invoking Humanity: War, Law, and Global Order.* London: Continuum.

INDEX

Boutros-Ghali, Boutros, 43–44, 84 n. 9
Brigg, Morgan, 76
Burchell, Graham, 146
Bush, George H. W., policy in Haiti, 83

calculated spaces of government, 22–23, 29,
    32, 56
capacity building, 48, 77, 84, 131, 134
carceralization, 20, 35–37, 108, 130, 142,
    144. *See also* disciplinarity; penal
    institutions; punishment
    international, 8, 22, 61, 72
Cédras, Raoul, 83, 85
centralization, governmental, 78, 81, 91
Chandler, David, 77
children, 50, 67–68
citizens/citizenship, 42, 105, 129. *See also*
    populations; well-being, promotion of
Civilian Police Mission in Haiti
    (MIPONUH), 85–86
civilized states, 18, 57, 58, 62
civil society, 10, 26, 46–47, 51, 55, 56
classification, principle of, 67, 92–93
Clinton, Bill, policy in Haiti, 83
Cockayne, James, 104
codification, 22, 29, 36, 38, 40, 45, 72, 94, 103,
    104, 106, 110, 111, 119, 158
coercion, 36, 37, 47, 72. *See also* force, use of
    correction and, 61, 62
collective security, 33 n. 16, 36, 49–50, 59–60,
    66, 69–70. *See also* security; security,
    human; security, international
colonialism, 76, 135–36
common good, 27, 34, 40, 42, 51, 56. *See also*
    well-being, promotion of
common truth, rule of, 88, 90
community, international. *See also*
    government by community
    as modality of liberal government, 17–18,
    118–19
    rogue states becoming members of, 20,
    22, 24, 61
    violence against, 102
community, local. *See* resistance, local;
    society, local
Community for Reconstruction,
    Development and Stabilization
    (CARDS), 118
concentration camps, 133
conduct of conduct
    government as, 7, 21, 29, 76
    international, 33, 56
    of populations, 69, 142
confinement, 20, 35 n. 20, 86, 91–92, 93
Connolly, William E., 129

Conseil Superieur de la Magistrature
    (Superior Council of Judges, Haiti), 90
Constitutional Law on the Rights of
    National Minorities (CLNM, Croatia),
    125–26
constructivist theories, 4, 5
Contact Group (Eastern Slavonia), 109–10
container theories of society, 4, 32, 64
control, 22, 25 n. 9, 96, 104, 144
    governing through, 21, 27, 28 n. 3, 143
    mechanisms of, 24, 36, 37
    of populations, 20, 35, 88, 130
Copenhagen criteria (EU), 16 n. 4, 43
correction, 21–22, 36, 56–57, 72, 88, 96
    coercion and, 61, 62
    confinement transformed into, 20, 35 n.
    20, 86, 91–92, 93
    of souls, 7, 24, 35, 88, 130
corruption, 51, 52, 58
Cotonou Declaration, 50
Council of Europe, 118, 119
crimes
    by Haitian police, 102, 105
    prevention of, 86–88, 89, 93
Croatia. *See also* Erdut Peace Agreement,
    administrative reforms, 116–17
    candidacy for EU, 32, 43, 112, 117, 122,
    129, 141, 144
    on Council of Europe, 118 n. 16, 119
    institution building in, 25, 38
    legal reforms 117–18
    local resistance in, 73, 124–30, 138, 144
    normalization of, 111–12, 115–19, 121,
    129
    pacification and Europeanization of,
    10–11, 18, 19, 23, 30, 38, 108, 118–24, 140,
    144
    peacekeeping operations in, 11, 31,
    130–31
    repossession of property in, 129, 171
    statistical regions in, 122 n. 20, 122 n. 21
    UN involvement in, 9, 37, 109–24, 145
Croats, ethnic, 100, 109, 111, 126–27, 129,
    131
culture, 33 n. 17, 88–89

dangers. *See* risks
Dayton Agreement, 110, 119
Dean, Mitchell, 2 n. 2, 7 n. 6, 18, 30 n. 14,
    103 n. 25
Debrix, François, 5, 36 n. 22, 98, 145
delinquents, 35, 62, 72, 93, 130, 144. *See also*
    rogue states
democracy, 34 n. 18, 108. *See also* liberal
    theories, of democracy; Marxist

institutional reforms for, 30, 45–46, 55–56, 78 n. 2
socialist traditions of democracy, 42, 44, 50, 55
social welfare systems, 42, 115–16, 129. *See also* well-being, promotion of
society. *See also* resistance, local
  carceralization of, 35–37
  civil, 10, 26, 46–47, 51, 55, 56
  container theories of, 4, 32, 64
  Haitian structure of, 79–80
  local, 9, 77
  transformation of, 40, 103 n. 25, 104
solidarity, 10, 11, 73 n. 8
souls, correction of, 7, 24, 35, 88, 130
Southeastern Europe, 119–20
sovereignty, 2, 10, 35, 36, 87 n. 12, 108, 133–39. *See also* kings
  Foucault on, 16, 27, 57, 132, 133–34, 144 n. 3
  governmentality and, 19, 25 n. 9, 27, 34
  redefinition of, 62–73
  traditional understandings of, 61, 97
Stabilization and Association Process (SAP, Croatia), 25, 119–20
Stabilization Mission in Haiti (MINUSTAH), 86
standardization, 49, 121
state, the, 4–5. *See also* abnormal states; civilized states; disorderly states; failed states; nondemocratic states; rogue states
  disciplinarity in, 19, 72
  government of, 7, 29, 65
  jurisdiction of, 19, 29, 56, 63, 71, 87, 139
  normalization of, 55–58, 131
  reforms of, 8, 45, 47–48, 51, 129
  responsibilities of, 36, 46 n. 11, 141
  security role of, 61, 63, 68, 70
state building, 22–23, 77
  in classical Europe, 97
  in Haiti, 78, 79–84, 86–93, 104, 105, 106
  weaknesses of, 103, 143
statist doctrines of governance, 55
statistics, 28, 30–32, 49, 68, 121–22
Storm (military operation, Croatia), 109, 126
subjectification, 12, 146
  of dangers, 32–33
  of disorderly elements, 35, 130
  of nondemocratic states, 19–20, 140–41
sufficient ideality, rule of, 88, 89
supranational organizations. *See* international organizations
surveillance, 35, 89, 91, 105, 130. *See also* monitoring; panopticism; scrutiny

governing through, 47, 72, 141–42, 143
international, 8, 121
peacekeeping as, 98, 100, 144

taxation, 53, 82 n. 5
Taylorism, 57 n. 20
territory
  administration of, 77, 78, 121, 122
  control over, 34, 54, 55, 66, 91, 93
  significance of, 25 n. 9, 27
  urbanization of, 87
Third International Conference on New or Restored Democracies and Development (UN, Bucharest, 1997), 44
Third World. *See* developing countries
threats, 29, 140–42. *See also* risks
Toulmin, Stephen, 147 n. 5
training, 24, 29
transformation, 35, 142, 146. *See also* normalization
  of rogue states, 18, 24, 37, 41
  state, 8, 45, 47–48, 51, 129
Transition Mission in Haiti (UNTMIH), 85
Trouillot, Rolf, 81

underdevelopment, 1–2, 45. *See also* developing countries
United Nations (UN), 31, 84. *See also* Agenda for Democratization; Agenda 21; Croatia; Haiti; interventions, international; Millennium Declaration
  Annan's proposals for reform, 19, 34, 50, 62–63, 64, 66, 70, 71
  Charter of, 2, 34, 53, 62–63, 86, 102 n. 24
  in Croatia, 109–24
  democratization efforts, 15, 23, 31, 41–58
  development role of, 55, 64–65
  General Assembly, 84, 86
  good governance as goal of, 15, 16 n. 5, 21, 29, 48, 55
  in Haiti, 37, 78, 83, 84–106, 107–8
  peacekeeping operations, 2, 21–22, 69, 109, 140, 145
  political imaginary of, 2–3, 23, 25, 107–8
  political rationale of, 33–34, 60, 68, 75, 97–98, 103, 145
  Resolution 1325, 67–68
  Security Council, 66, 84, 85, 86, 109
  security role of, 36, 55, 64–65, 144–46
United Nations Commission on Human Security, 67
United Nations Conference on Trade and Development, 48–49